Just The facts101
Textbook Key Facts

Canada Biotechnology Business Opportunities Handbook

by Cram101
Textbook NOT Included

Table of Contents

Title Page

Copyright

Foundations of Business

Management

Business law

Finance

Human resource management

Information systems

Marketing

Manufacturing

Commerce

Business ethics

Accounting

Index: Answers

Just The Facts101

Exam Prep for

Canada Biotechnology Business Opportunities Handbook

Just The Facts101 Exam Prep is your link from
the textbook and lecture to your exams.

**Just The Facts101 Exam Preps are unauthorized and comprehensive reviews
of your textbooks.**

All material provided by CTI Publications (c) 2019

Textbook publishers and textbook authors do not participate in or contribute to these reviews.

Just The Facts101 Exam Prep

Copyright © 2019 by CTI Publications. All rights reserved.

eAIN 444378

Foundations of Business

A business, also known as an enterprise, agency or a firm, is an entity involved in the provision of goods and/or services to consumers. Businesses are prevalent in capitalist economies, where most of them are privately owned and provide goods and services to customers in exchange for other goods, services, or money.

:: Decision theory ::

A _____ is a deliberate system of principles to guide decisions and achieve rational outcomes. A _____ is a statement of intent, and is implemented as a procedure or protocol. Policies are generally adopted by a governance body within an organization. Policies can assist in both subjective and objective decision making. Policies to assist in subjective decision making usually assist senior management with decisions that must be based on the relative merits of a number of factors, and as a result are often hard to test objectively, e.g. work-life balance _____. In contrast policies to assist in objective decision making are usually operational in nature and can be objectively tested, e.g. password _____.

Exam Probability: **High**

1. *Answer choices:*

(see index for correct answer)

- a. Negotiation theory
- b. Decision fatigue
- c. Option grid
- d. Policy

Guidance: level 1

:: Summary statistics ::

_____ is the number of occurrences of a repeating event per unit of time. It is also referred to as temporal _____, which emphasizes the contrast to spatial _____ and angular _____. The period is the duration of time of one cycle in a repeating event, so the period is the reciprocal of the _____. For example: if a newborn baby's heart beats at a _____ of 120 times a minute, its period—the time interval between beats—is half a second. _____ is an important parameter used in science and engineering to specify the rate of oscillatory and vibratory phenomena, such as mechanical vibrations, audio signals, radio waves, and light.

Exam Probability: **Medium**

2. *Answer choices:*

(see index for correct answer)

- a. Percentile
- b. L-moment
- c. weighted mean
- d. Frequency

Guidance: level 1

:: Systems theory ::

A _____ is a set of policies, processes and procedures used by an organization to ensure that it can fulfill the tasks required to achieve its objectives. These objectives cover many aspects of the organization's operations. For instance, an environmental _____ enables organizations to improve their environmental performance and an occupational health and safety _____ enables an organization to control its occupational health and safety risks, etc.

Exam Probability: **High**

3. *Answer choices:*

(see index for correct answer)

- a. decentralized system
- b. equifinality
- c. transient state
- d. process system

Guidance: level 1

:: Foreign direct investment ::

A _____ is an investment in the form of a controlling ownership in a business in one country by an entity based in another country. It is thus distinguished from a foreign portfolio investment by a notion of direct control.

Exam Probability: **Low**

4. *Answer choices:*

(see index for correct answer)

- a. Foreign ownership
- b. Foreign direct investment
- c. EB-5 visa
- d. Oligopolistic reaction

Guidance: level 1

:: Competition (economics) ::

_____ arises whenever at least two parties strive for a goal which cannot be shared: where one's gain is the other's loss.

Exam Probability: **Medium**

5. *Answer choices:*

(see index for correct answer)

- a. Transfer pricing
- b. Competition
- c. Regulatory competition
- d. Economic forces

Guidance: level 1

:: Association of Southeast Asian Nations ::

The Association of Southeast Asian Nations is a regional intergovernmental organization comprising ten countries in Southeast Asia, which promotes intergovernmental cooperation and facilitates economic, political, security, military, educational, and sociocultural integration among its members and other countries in Asia. It also regularly engages other countries in the Asia-Pacific region and beyond. A major partner of Shanghai Cooperation Organisation, _____ maintains a global network of alliances and dialogue partners and is considered by many as a global powerhouse, the central union for cooperation in Asia-Pacific, and a prominent and influential organization. It is involved in numerous international affairs, and hosts diplomatic missions throughout the world.

Exam Probability: **Low**

6. *Answer choices:*

(see index for correct answer)

- a. 2013 IMT-GT Cup
- b. ASEAN
- c. Emblem of the Association of Southeast Asian Nations
- d. ASEAN Human Rights Declaration

Guidance: level 1

:: Free trade agreements ::

A _____ is a wide-ranging taxes, tariff and trade treaty that often includes investment guarantees. It exists when two or more countries agree on terms that helps them trade with each other. The most common _____s are of the preferential and free trade types are concluded in order to reduce tariffs, quotas and other trade restrictions on items traded between the signatories.

Exam Probability: **Medium**

7. *Answer choices:*

(see index for correct answer)

- a. Central Asian Union
- b. CISFTA
- c. European Union Central American Association Agreement
- d. South Asian Free Trade Area

Guidance: level 1

:: Classification systems ::

_____ is the practice of comparing business processes and performance metrics to industry bests and best practices from other companies. Dimensions typically measured are quality, time and cost.

Exam Probability: **Medium**

8. *Answer choices:*

(see index for correct answer)

- a. Mini-international neuropsychiatric interview
- b. Bordeaux Wine Official Classification of 1855
- c. Physiographic regions of the world
- d. Benchmarking

Guidance: level 1

:: Human resource management ::

_____ encompasses values and behaviors that contribute to the unique social and psychological environment of a business. The _____ influences the way people interact, the context within which knowledge is created, the resistance they will have towards certain changes, and ultimately the way they share knowledge. _____ represents the collective values, beliefs and principles of organizational members and is a product of factors such as history, product, market, technology, strategy, type of employees, management style, and national culture; culture includes the organization's vision, values, norms, systems, symbols, language, assumptions, environment, location, beliefs and habits.

Exam Probability: **Low**

9. *Answer choices:*

(see index for correct answer)

- a. Job description management

- b. Work activity management
- c. Organizational culture
- d. Behavioral Competencies

Guidance: level 1

:: Decision theory ::

Within economics the concept of _____ is used to model worth or value, but its usage has evolved significantly over time. The term was introduced initially as a measure of pleasure or satisfaction within the theory of utilitarianism by moral philosophers such as Jeremy Bentham and John Stuart Mill. But the term has been adapted and reapplied within neoclassical economics, which dominates modern economic theory, as a _____ function that represents a consumer's preference ordering over a choice set. As such, it is devoid of its original interpretation as a measurement of the pleasure or satisfaction obtained by the consumer from that choice.

Exam Probability: **Low**

10. *Answer choices:*

(see index for correct answer)

- a. ERulemaking
- b. Option grid
- c. Utility
- d. Decision analysis cycle

Guidance: level 1

:: ::

_____ is the collection of mechanisms, processes and relations by which corporations are controlled and operated. Governance structures and principles identify the distribution of rights and responsibilities among different participants in the corporation and include the rules and procedures for making decisions in corporate affairs. _____ is necessary because of the possibility of conflicts of interests between stakeholders, primarily between shareholders and upper management or among shareholders.

Exam Probability: **Medium**

11. *Answer choices:*

(see index for correct answer)

- a. co-culture
- b. empathy
- c. Corporate governance
- d. imperative

Guidance: level 1

:: Management ::

A _____ is an idea of the future or desired result that a person or a group of people envisions, plans and commits to achieve. People endeavor to reach _____ s within a finite time by setting deadlines.

Exam Probability: **High**

12. *Answer choices:*

(see index for correct answer)

- a. Goal
- b. Hierarchical organization
- c. Best practice
- d. Decentralized decision-making

Guidance: level 1

:: Strategic alliances ::

A _____ is an agreement between two or more parties to pursue a set of agreed upon objectives needed while remaining independent organizations. A _____ will usually fall short of a legal partnership entity, agency, or corporate affiliate relationship. Typically, two companies form a _____ when each possesses one or more business assets or have expertise that will help the other by enhancing their businesses. _____ s can develop in outsourcing relationships where the parties desire to achieve long-term win-win benefits and innovation based on mutually desired outcomes.

Exam Probability: **High**

13. *Answer choices:*

(see index for correct answer)

- a. International joint venture
- b. Bridge Alliance
- c. Defensive termination
- d. Cross-licensing

Guidance: level 1

:: Production and manufacturing ::

_____ is a set of techniques and tools for process improvement. Though as a shortened form it may be found written as 6S, it should not be confused with the methodology known as 6S.

Exam Probability: **Medium**

14. *Answer choices:*

(see index for correct answer)

- a. Critical to quality
- b. Resource Breakdown
- c. Positive recall
- d. Six Sigma

Guidance: level 1

:: Public relations ::

_____ is the public visibility or awareness for any product, service or company. It may also refer to the movement of information from its source to the general public, often but not always via the media. The subjects of _____ include people, goods and services, organizations, and works of art or entertainment.

Exam Probability: **Medium**

15. *Answer choices:*

(see index for correct answer)

- a. Corporate Representatives for Ethical Wikipedia Engagement
- b. Upstate California
- c. Publicity
- d. Aneta Avramova

Guidance: level 1

:: Costs ::

In microeconomic theory, the _____ , or alternative cost, of making a particular choice is the value of the most valuable choice out of those that were not taken. In other words, opportunity that will require sacrifices.

Exam Probability: **Low**

16. *Answer choices:*

(see index for correct answer)

- a. Average cost
- b. Repugnancy costs
- c. Opportunity cost
- d. Flyaway cost

Guidance: level 1

:: Infographics ::

A _____ is a symbolic representation of information according to visualization technique. _____ s have been used since ancient times, but became more prevalent during the Enlightenment. Sometimes, the technique uses a three-dimensional visualization which is then projected onto a two-dimensional surface. The word graph is sometimes used as a synonym for _____ .

Exam Probability: **Low**

17. *Answer choices:*

(see index for correct answer)

- a. Funnel chart
- b. VisAD

- c. Diagram
- d. Webdings

Guidance: level 1

:: ::

_____ refers to a business or organization attempting to acquire goods or services to accomplish its goals. Although there are several organizations that attempt to set standards in the _____ process, processes can vary greatly between organizations. Typically the word " _____ " is not used interchangeably with the word "procurement", since procurement typically includes expediting, supplier quality, and transportation and logistics in addition to _____ .

Exam Probability: **High**

18. *Answer choices:*

(see index for correct answer)

- a. Purchasing
- b. Sarbanes-Oxley act of 2002
- c. deep-level diversity
- d. open system

Guidance: level 1

:: Debt ::

_____, in finance and economics, is payment from a borrower or deposit-taking financial institution to a lender or depositor of an amount above repayment of the principal sum, at a particular rate. It is distinct from a fee which the borrower may pay the lender or some third party. It is also distinct from dividend which is paid by a company to its shareholders from its profit or reserve, but not at a particular rate decided beforehand, rather on a pro rata basis as a share in the reward gained by risk taking entrepreneurs when the revenue earned exceeds the total costs.

Exam Probability: **Medium**

19. *Answer choices:*

(see index for correct answer)

- a. Cessio bonorum
- b. Vulture fund
- c. Debt relief
- d. Money disorders

Guidance: level 1

:: Shareholders ::

A _____ is a payment made by a corporation to its shareholders, usually as a distribution of profits. When a corporation earns a profit or surplus, the corporation is able to re-invest the profit in the business and pay a proportion of the profit as a _____ to shareholders. Distribution to shareholders may be in cash or, if the corporation has a _____ reinvestment plan, the amount can be paid by the issue of further shares or share repurchase. When _____ s are paid, shareholders typically must pay income taxes, and the corporation does not receive a corporate income tax deduction for the _____ payments.

Exam Probability: **Low**

20. *Answer choices:*

(see index for correct answer)

- a. Shotgun clause
- b. Dividend
- c. Australian Shareholders Association
- d. Proxy fight

Guidance: level 1

:: Project management ::

_____ is the right to exercise power, which can be formalized by a state and exercised by way of judges, appointed executives of government, or the ecclesiastical or priestly appointed representatives of a God or other deities.

Exam Probability: **Medium**

21. *Answer choices:*

(see index for correct answer)

- a. Authority
- b. Stages of project finance
- c. Project manufacturing
- d. Social project management

Guidance: level 1

:: Management ::

The _____ is a strategy performance management tool – a semi-standard structured report, that can be used by managers to keep track of the execution of activities by the staff within their control and to monitor the consequences arising from these actions.

Exam Probability: **Low**

22. *Answer choices:*

(see index for correct answer)

- a. Balanced scorecard
- b. Submission management
- c. Success-oriented management

- d. Innovation leadership

Guidance: level 1

:: Financial crises ::

A _____ is any of a broad variety of situations in which some financial assets suddenly lose a large part of their nominal value. In the 19th and early 20th centuries, many financial crises were associated with banking panics, and many recessions coincided with these panics. Other situations that are often called financial crises include stock market crashes and the bursting of other financial bubbles, currency crises, and sovereign defaults. Financial crises directly result in a loss of paper wealth but do not necessarily result in significant changes in the real economy.

Exam Probability: **Medium**

23. *Answer choices:*

(see index for correct answer)

- a. Boom and bust
- b. Mexican peso crisis
- c. Financial crisis
- d. Bull trap

Guidance: level 1

:: Euthenics ::

_____ is an ethical framework and suggests that an entity, be it an organization or individual, has an obligation to act for the benefit of society at large. _____ is a duty every individual has to perform so as to maintain a balance between the economy and the ecosystems. A trade-off may exist between economic development, in the material sense, and the welfare of the society and environment, though this has been challenged by many reports over the past decade. _____ means sustaining the equilibrium between the two. It pertains not only to business organizations but also to everyone whose any action impacts the environment. This responsibility can be passive, by avoiding engaging in socially harmful acts, or active, by performing activities that directly advance social goals. _____ must be intergenerational since the actions of one generation have consequences on those following.

Exam Probability: **Low**

24. *Answer choices:*

(see index for correct answer)

- a. Family and consumer science
- b. Social responsibility
- c. Euthenics
- d. Home economics

Guidance: level 1

:: Globalization-related theories ::

_____ is the process in which a nation is being improved in the sector of the economic, political, and social well-being of its people. The term has been used frequently by economists, politicians, and others in the 20th and 21st centuries. The concept, however, has been in existence in the West for centuries. "Modernization, "westernization", and especially "industrialization" are other terms often used while discussing _____ . _____ has a direct relationship with the environment and environmental issues. _____ is very often confused with industrial development, even in some academic sources.

Exam Probability: **Medium**

25. *Answer choices:*

(see index for correct answer)

- a. Economic Development
- b. postmodernism
- c. post-industrial

Guidance: level 1

:: Industrial Revolution ::

The _____, now also known as the First _____, was the transition to new manufacturing processes in Europe and the US, in the period from about 1760 to sometime between 1820 and 1840. This transition included going from hand production methods to machines, new chemical manufacturing and iron production processes, the increasing use of steam power and water power, the development of machine tools and the rise of the mechanized factory system. The _____ also led to an unprecedented rise in the rate of population growth.

Exam Probability: **Low**

26. *Answer choices:*

(see index for correct answer)

- a. Sykes Bleaching Company
- b. Blast furnace
- c. Industrial Revolution
- d. Line shaft

Guidance: level 1

:: Budgets ::

A _____ is a financial plan for a defined period, often one year. It may also include planned sales volumes and revenues, resource quantities, costs and expenses, assets, liabilities and cash flows. Companies, governments, families and other organizations use it to express strategic plans of activities or events in measurable terms.

Exam Probability: **Low**

27. *Answer choices:*

(see index for correct answer)

- a. Public budgeting
- b. Budget
- c. Film budgeting
- d. Budget set

Guidance: level 1

:: Income ::

_____ is a ratio between the net profit and cost of investment resulting from an investment of some resources. A high ROI means the investment's gains favorably to its cost. As a performance measure, ROI is used to evaluate the efficiency of an investment or to compare the efficiencies of several different investments. In purely economic terms, it is one way of relating profits to capital invested. _____ is a performance measure used by businesses to identify the efficiency of an investment or number of different investments.

Exam Probability: **High**

28. *Answer choices:*

(see index for correct answer)

- a. Signing bonus
- b. Mandatory tipping
- c. Return on investment
- d. Revenue management

Guidance: level 1

:: Critical thinking ::

> In psychology, _____ is regarded as the cognitive process resulting in the selection of a belief or a course of action among several alternative possibilities. Every _____ process produces a final choice, which may or may not prompt action.

Exam Probability: **Medium**

29. *Answer choices:*

(see index for correct answer)

- a. Inquiry
- b. Decision-making
- c. Proof
- d. Project Reason

Guidance: level 1

:: Supply chain management terms ::

In business and finance, _____ is a system of organizations, people, activities, information, and resources involved in moving a product or service from supplier to customer. _____ activities involve the transformation of natural resources, raw materials, and components into a finished product that is delivered to the end customer. In sophisticated _____ systems, used products may re-enter the _____ at any point where residual value is recyclable. _____ s link value chains.

Exam Probability: **Medium**

30. *Answer choices:*

(see index for correct answer)

- a. inventory management
- b. Last mile
- c. Supply chain
- d. Consumables

Guidance: level 1

:: Management accounting ::

_____s are costs that change as the quantity of the good or service that a business produces changes. _____s are the sum of marginal costs over all units produced. They can also be considered normal costs. Fixed costs and _____s make up the two components of total cost. Direct costs are costs that can easily be associated with a particular cost object. However, not all _____s are direct costs. For example, variable manufacturing overhead costs are _____s that are indirect costs, not direct costs. _____s are sometimes called unit-level costs as they vary with the number of units produced.

Exam Probability: **High**

31. *Answer choices:*

(see index for correct answer)

- a. Bridge life-cycle cost analysis
- b. Owner earnings
- c. Variable cost
- d. Managerial risk accounting

Guidance: level 1

:: Information systems ::

_____ are formal, sociotechnical, organizational systems designed to collect, process, store, and distribute information. In a sociotechnical perspective, _____ are composed by four components: task, people, structure, and technology.

Exam Probability: **Medium**

32. *Answer choices:*

(see index for correct answer)

- a. Social Study of Information Systems
- b. Laboratory information management system
- c. Expert system
- d. Information systems

Guidance: level 1

:: Management occupations ::

_____ is the process of designing, launching and running a new business, which is often initially a small business. The people who create these businesses are called entrepreneurs.

Exam Probability: **High**

33. *Answer choices:*

(see index for correct answer)

- a. Entrepreneurship
- b. Business magnate
- c. Hayward
- d. Comptroller

Guidance: level 1

:: Debt ::

_____ is when something, usually money, is owed by one party, the borrower or _____ or, to a second party, the lender or creditor. _____ is a deferred payment, or series of payments, that is owed in the future, which is what differentiates it from an immediate purchase. The _____ may be owed by sovereign state or country, local government, company, or an individual. Commercial _____ is generally subject to contractual terms regarding the amount and timing of repayments of principal and interest. Loans, bonds, notes, and mortgages are all types of _____. The term can also be used metaphorically to cover moral obligations and other interactions not based on economic value. For example, in Western cultures, a person who has been helped by a second person is sometimes said to owe a " _____ of gratitude" to the second person.

Exam Probability: **High**

34. *Answer choices:*
(see index for correct answer)

- a. Debt
- b. Exchangeable bond
- c. Consumer debt
- d. Arrears

Guidance: level 1

:: Commerce ::

_____ relates to "the exchange of goods and services, especially on a large scale". It includes legal, economic, political, social, cultural and technological systems that operate in a country or in international trade.

Exam Probability: **High**

35. *Answer choices:*

(see index for correct answer)

- a. Country commercial guides
- b. V-commerce
- c. Commerce
- d. Oxygen bar

Guidance: level 1

:: Project management ::

A _____ is a source or supply from which a benefit is produced and it has some utility. _____ s can broadly be classified upon their availability—they are classified into renewable and non-renewable _____ s. Examples of non renewable _____ s are coal, crude oil natural gas nuclear energy etc. Examples of renewable _____ s are air, water, wind, solar energy etc. They can also be classified as actual and potential on the basis of level of development and use, on the basis of origin they can be classified as biotic and abiotic, and on the basis of their distribution, as ubiquitous and localized. An item becomes a _____ with time and developing technology. Typically, _____ s are materials, energy, services, staff, knowledge, or other assets that are transformed to produce benefit and in the process may be consumed or made unavailable. Benefits of _____ utilization may include increased wealth, proper functioning of a system, or enhanced well-being. From a human perspective a natural _____ is anything obtained from the environment to satisfy human needs and wants. From a broader biological or ecological perspective a _____ satisfies the needs of a living organism.

Exam Probability: **High**

36. *Answer choices:*

(see index for correct answer)

- a. Budgeted cost of work performed
- b. Resource
- c. Expected commercial value
- d. Research program

Guidance: level 1

:: ::

_____ is the production of products for use or sale using labour and machines, tools, chemical and biological processing, or formulation. The term may refer to a range of human activity, from handicraft to high tech, but is most commonly applied to industrial design, in which raw materials are transformed into finished goods on a large scale. Such finished goods may be sold to other manufacturers for the production of other, more complex products, such as aircraft, household appliances, furniture, sports equipment or automobiles, or sold to wholesalers, who in turn sell them to retailers, who then sell them to end users and consumers.

Exam Probability: **Medium**

37. *Answer choices:*

(see index for correct answer)

- a. similarity-attraction theory
- b. Sarbanes-Oxley act of 2002
- c. Manufacturing
- d. Character

Guidance: level 1

:: Consumer theory ::

A _____ is a technical term in psychology, economics and philosophy usually used in relation to choosing between alternatives. For example, someone prefers A over B if they would rather choose A than B.

Exam Probability: **High**

38. *Answer choices:*

(see index for correct answer)

- a. Consumer service
- b. Marshallian demand function
- c. Preference
- d. Elasticity of intertemporal substitution

Guidance: level 1

:: Business process ::

A _____ or business method is a collection of related, structured activities or tasks by people or equipment which in a specific sequence produce a service or product for a particular customer or customers. _____ es occur at all organizational levels and may or may not be visible to the customers. A _____ may often be visualized as a flowchart of a sequence of activities with interleaving decision points or as a process matrix of a sequence of activities with relevance rules based on data in the process. The benefits of using _____ es include improved customer satisfaction and improved agility for reacting to rapid market change. Process-oriented organizations break down the barriers of structural departments and try to avoid functional silos.

Exam Probability: **Medium**

39. *Answer choices:*

(see index for correct answer)

- a. Joget Workflow
- b. Business process
- c. IDS Scheer
- d. Process mapping

Guidance: level 1

:: Business ::

_____ is a trade policy that does not restrict imports or exports; it can also be understood as the free market idea applied to international trade. In government, _____ is predominantly advocated by political parties that hold liberal economic positions while economically left-wing and nationalist political parties generally support protectionism, the opposite of _____ .

Exam Probability: **Low**

40. *Answer choices:*

(see index for correct answer)

- a. Policy capturing
- b. Religion and business
- c. Backward invention
- d. Free trade

Guidance: level 1

:: Organizational theory ::

_____ is the process of groups of organisms working or acting together for common, mutual, or some underlying benefit, as opposed to working in competition for selfish benefit. Many animal and plant species cooperate both with other members of their own species and with members of other species.

Exam Probability: **Low**

41. *Answer choices:*

(see index for correct answer)

- a. Resource dependence theory
- b. Organizational effectiveness
- c. Imprinting
- d. Cooperation

Guidance: level 1

:: Payments ::

A _____ is the trade of value from one party to another for goods, or services, or to fulfill a legal obligation.

Exam Probability: **Low**

42. *Answer choices:*

(see index for correct answer)

- a. Market transition payments
- b. County payments
- c. Subsidy
- d. Thirty pieces of silver

Guidance: level 1

:: Fraud ::

In law, _____ is intentional deception to secure unfair or unlawful gain, or to deprive a victim of a legal right. _____ can violate civil law, a criminal law, or it may cause no loss of money, property or legal right but still be an element of another civil or criminal wrong. The purpose of _____ may be monetary gain or other benefits, for example by obtaining a passport, travel document, or driver's license, or mortgage _____, where the perpetrator may attempt to qualify for a mortgage by way of false statements.

Exam Probability: **High**

43. *Answer choices:*

(see index for correct answer)

- a. Charity fraud
- b. Wangiri
- c. Fraud
- d. Employment fraud

Guidance: level 1

:: Business law ::

A _____ is a business entity created by two or more parties, generally characterized by shared ownership, shared returns and risks, and shared governance. Companies typically pursue _____ s for one of four reasons: to access a new market, particularly emerging markets; to gain scale efficiencies by combining assets and operations; to share risk for major investments or projects; or to access skills and capabilities.

Exam Probability: **High**

44. *Answer choices:*

(see index for correct answer)

- a. Joint venture
- b. Refusal to deal
- c. European Patent Convention
- d. Subordination

Guidance: level 1

:: Management ::

_____ is the process of thinking about the activities required to achieve a desired goal. It is the first and foremost activity to achieve desired results. It involves the creation and maintenance of a plan, such as psychological aspects that require conceptual skills. There are even a couple of tests to measure someone's capability of _____ well. As such, _____ is a fundamental property of intelligent behavior. An important further meaning, often just called " _____ " is the legal context of permitted building developments.

Exam Probability: **Low**

45. *Answer choices:*

(see index for correct answer)

- a. Mobile sales enablement
- b. Planning
- c. Shrinkage
- d. Reverse innovation

Guidance: level 1

:: Data collection ::

A _____ is an utterance which typically functions as a request for information. _____ s can thus be understood as a kind of illocutionary act in the field of pragmatics or as special kinds of propositions in frameworks of formal semantics such as alternative semantics or inquisitive semantics. The information requested is expected to be provided in the form of an answer. _____ s are often conflated with interrogatives, which are the grammatical forms typically used to achieve them. Rhetorical _____ s, for example, are interrogative in form but may not be considered true _____ s as they are not expected to be answered. Conversely, non-interrogative grammatical structures may be considered _____ s as in the case of the imperative sentence "tell me your name".

Exam Probability: **High**

46. *Answer choices:*

(see index for correct answer)

- a. Surveylab
- b. Question
- c. Paradata
- d. Physical test

Guidance: level 1

:: Business models ::

_____es are privately owned corporations, partnerships, or sole proprietorships that have fewer employees and/or less annual revenue than a regular-sized business or corporation. Businesses are defined as "small" in terms of being able to apply for government support and qualify for preferential tax policy varies depending on the country and industry. _____es range from fifteen employees under the Australian Fair Work Act 2009, fifty employees according to the definition used by the European Union, and fewer than five hundred employees to qualify for many U.S. _____ Administration programs. While _____es can also be classified according to other methods, such as annual revenues, shipments, sales, assets, or by annual gross or net revenue or net profits, the number of employees is one of the most widely used measures.

Exam Probability: **Low**

47. *Answer choices:*

(see index for correct answer)

- a. Small business
- b. Paid To Click
- c. Micro-enterprise
- d. Entreship

Guidance: level 1

:: National accounts ::

_____ is a monetary measure of the market value of all the final goods and services produced in a period of time, often annually. GDP per capita does not, however, reflect differences in the cost of living and the inflation rates of the countries; therefore using a basis of GDP per capita at purchasing power parity is arguably more useful when comparing differences in living standards between nations.

Exam Probability: **High**

48. *Answer choices:*

(see index for correct answer)

- a. capital formation
- b. Fixed capital
- c. National Income

Guidance: level 1

:: Auditing ::

_____, as defined by accounting and auditing, is a process for assuring of an organization's objectives in operational effectiveness and efficiency, reliable financial reporting, and compliance with laws, regulations and policies. A broad concept, _____ involves everything that controls risks to an organization.

Exam Probability: **High**

49. Answer choices:

(see index for correct answer)

- a. Internal control
- b. Auditor independence
- c. Circulation Verification Council
- d. International Federation of Audit Bureaux of Circulations

Guidance: level 1

:: Project management ::

Some scenarios associate "this kind of planning" with learning "life skills". _____ s are necessary, or at least useful, in situations where individuals need to know what time they must be at a specific location to receive a specific service, and where people need to accomplish a set of goals within a set time period.

Exam Probability: **High**

50. Answer choices:

(see index for correct answer)

- a. Starmad
- b. The Goal
- c. Schedule
- d. Resource leveling

Guidance: level 1

:: Management ::

The term _____ refers to measures designed to increase the degree of autonomy and self-determination in people and in communities in order to enable them to represent their interests in a responsible and self-determined way, acting on their own authority. It is the process of becoming stronger and more confident, especially in controlling one's life and claiming one's rights. _____ as action refers both to the process of self-_____ and to professional support of people, which enables them to overcome their sense of powerlessness and lack of influence, and to recognize and use their resources. To do work with power.

Exam Probability: **Medium**

51. *Answer choices:*

(see index for correct answer)

- a. Earned schedule
- b. Empowerment
- c. Business workflow analysis
- d. Coworking

Guidance: level 1

:: Management ::

A _____ is when two or more people come together to discuss one or more topics, often in a formal or business setting, but _____ s also occur in a variety of other environments. Many various types of _____ s exist.

Exam Probability: **Low**

52. *Answer choices:*

(see index for correct answer)

- a. Stovepipe
- b. Concept of the Corporation
- c. Downstream
- d. Meeting

Guidance: level 1

:: Critical thinking ::

An _____ is a set of statements usually constructed to describe a set of facts which clarifies the causes, context, and consequences of those facts. This description of the facts et cetera may establish rules or laws, and may clarify the existing rules or laws in relation to any objects, or phenomena examined. The components of an _____ can be implicit, and interwoven with one another.

Exam Probability: **High**

53. *Answer choices:*

(see index for correct answer)

- a. Inquiry: Critical Thinking Across the Disciplines
- b. Source credibility
- c. decision-making
- d. Explanation

Guidance: level 1

:: Debt ::

_____ is the trust which allows one party to provide money or resources to another party wherein the second party does not reimburse the first party immediately, but promises either to repay or return those resources at a later date. In other words, _____ is a method of making reciprocity formal, legally enforceable, and extensible to a large group of unrelated people.

Exam Probability: **High**

54. *Answer choices:*

(see index for correct answer)

- a. Credit
- b. Debt club
- c. Debt relief
- d. Extendible bond

Guidance: level 1

:: Energy and fuel journals ::

In physics, energy is the quantitative property that must be transferred to an object in order to perform work on, or to heat, the object. Energy is a conserved quantity; the law of conservation of energy states that energy can be converted in form, but not created or destroyed. The SI unit of energy is the joule, which is the energy transferred to an object by the work of moving it a distance of 1 metre against a force of 1 newton.

Exam Probability: **Low**

55. *Answer choices:*
(see index for correct answer)

- a. Heat and Mass Transfer
- b. Energy Procedia
- c. Energy and Environmental Science
- d. Energies

Guidance: level 1

:: Marketing ::

A _____ is a group of customers within a business's serviceable available market at which a business aims its marketing efforts and resources. A _____ is a subset of the total market for a product or service. The _____ typically consists of consumers who exhibit similar characteristics and are considered most likely to buy a business's market offerings or are likely to be the most profitable segments for the business to service.

Exam Probability: **High**

56. *Answer choices:*

(see index for correct answer)

- a. Aftermarket
- b. Target market
- c. Corporate capabilities package
- d. Digital billboard

Guidance: level 1

:: Market research ::

_____ is "the process or set of processes that links the producers, customers, and end users to the marketer through information used to identify and define marketing opportunities and problems; generate, refine, and evaluate marketing actions; monitor marketing performance; and improve understanding of marketing as a process. _____ specifies the information required to address these issues, designs the method for collecting information, manages and implements the data collection process, analyzes the results, and communicates the findings and their implications."

Exam Probability: **Low**

57. *Answer choices:*

(see index for correct answer)

- a. Virtual store research
- b. Media-Analyse
- c. INDEX
- d. Cume

Guidance: level 1

:: ::

Some scenarios associate "this kind of planning" with learning "life skills". Schedules are necessary, or at least useful, in situations where individuals need to know what time they must be at a specific location to receive a specific service, and where people need to accomplish a set of goals within a set time period.

Exam Probability: **Low**

58. *Answer choices:*

(see index for correct answer)

- a. Sarbanes-Oxley act of 2002
- b. corporate values

- c. deep-level diversity
- d. Scheduling

Guidance: level 1

:: Legal terms ::

An _____ is an action which is inaccurate or incorrect. In some usages, an _____ is synonymous with a mistake. In statistics, "_____" refers to the difference between the value which has been computed and the correct value. An _____ could result in failure or in a deviation from the intended performance or behaviour.

Exam Probability: **Low**

59. *Answer choices:*
(see index for correct answer)

- a. Estray
- b. Error
- c. Concurring opinion
- d. Prejudgment writ of attachment

Guidance: level 1

Management

   Management is the administration of an organization, whether it is a business, a not-for-profit organization, or government body. Management includes the activities of setting the strategy of an organization and coordinating the efforts of its employees (or of volunteers) to accomplish its objectives through the application of available resources, such as financial, natural, technological, and human resources.

:: Management ::

_____ is the process of thinking about the activities required to achieve a desired goal. It is the first and foremost activity to achieve desired results. It involves the creation and maintenance of a plan, such as psychological aspects that require conceptual skills. There are even a couple of tests to measure someone's capability of _____ well. As such, _____ is a fundamental property of intelligent behavior. An important further meaning, often just called " _____ " is the legal context of permitted building developments.

Exam Probability: **Medium**

1. *Answer choices:*

(see index for correct answer)

- a. Planning
- b. Knowledge ecosystem
- c. Communications management
- d. Flat organization

Guidance: level 1

:: Majority–minority relations ::

_____, also known as reservation in India and Nepal, positive discrimination / action in the United Kingdom, and employment equity in Canada and South Africa, is the policy of promoting the education and employment of members of groups that are known to have previously suffered from discrimination. Historically and internationally, support for _____ has sought to achieve goals such as bridging inequalities in employment and pay, increasing access to education, promoting diversity, and redressing apparent past wrongs, harms, or hindrances.

Exam Probability: **High**

2. *Answer choices:*

(see index for correct answer)

- a. cultural Relativism
- b. cultural dissonance
- c. Affirmative action

Guidance: level 1

:: Organizational behavior ::

_____ is the term now used more commonly in business management, particularly human resource management. _____ refers to the number of subordinates a supervisor has.

Exam Probability: **Low**

3. *Answer choices:*

(see index for correct answer)

- a. Satisficing
- b. Span of control
- c. Organizational Expedience
- d. Micro-initiative

Guidance: level 1

:: ::

_____ consists of using generic or ad hoc methods in an orderly manner to find solutions to problems. Some of the problem-solving techniques developed and used in philosophy, artificial intelligence, computer science, engineering, mathematics, or medicine are related to mental problem-solving techniques studied in psychology.

Exam Probability: **Low**

4. *Answer choices:*

(see index for correct answer)

- a. cultural
- b. co-culture
- c. process perspective
- d. Problem solving

Guidance: level 1

:: Socialism ::

In sociology, _____ is the process of internalizing the norms and ideologies of society. _____ encompasses both learning and teaching and is thus "the means by which social and cultural continuity are attained".

Exam Probability: **Low**

5. *Answer choices:*

(see index for correct answer)

- a. Nanosocialism
- b. Real socialism
- c. Participism
- d. Socialization

Guidance: level 1

:: ::

A _____ is a leader's method of providing direction, implementing plans, and motivating people. Various authors have proposed identifying many different _____ s as exhibited by leaders in the political, business or other fields. Studies on _____ are conducted in the military field, expressing an approach that stresses a holistic view of leadership, including how a leader's physical presence determines how others perceive that leader. The factors of physical presence in this context include military bearing, physical fitness, confidence, and resilience. The leader's intellectual capacity helps to conceptualize solutions and to acquire knowledge to do the job. A leader's conceptual abilities apply agility, judgment, innovation, interpersonal tact, and domain knowledge. Domain knowledge encompasses tactical and technical knowledge as well as cultural and geopolitical awareness. Daniel Goleman in his article "Leadership that Gets Results" talks about six styles of leadership.

Exam Probability: **High**

6. *Answer choices:*

(see index for correct answer)

- a. co-culture
- b. personal values
- c. surface-level diversity
- d. levels of analysis

Guidance: level 1

:: ::

_____ is the process of two or more people or organizations working together to complete a task or achieve a goal. _____ is similar to cooperation. Most _____ requires leadership, although the form of leadership can be social within a decentralized and egalitarian group. Teams that work collaboratively often access greater resources, recognition and rewards when facing competition for finite resources.

Exam Probability: **Medium**

7. *Answer choices:*

(see index for correct answer)

- a. process perspective
- b. similarity-attraction theory
- c. Collaboration
- d. Character

Guidance: level 1

:: ::

In organizational behavior and industrial/organizational psychology, proactivity or _____ behavior by individuals refers to anticipatory, change-oriented and self-initiated behavior in situations. _____ behavior involves acting in advance of a future situation, rather than just reacting. It means taking control and making things happen rather than just adjusting to a situation or waiting for something to happen. _____ employees generally do not need to be asked to act, nor do they require detailed instructions.

Exam Probability: **Low**

8. *Answer choices:*

(see index for correct answer)

- a. corporate values
- b. open system
- c. levels of analysis
- d. deep-level diversity

Guidance: level 1

:: ::

In production, research, retail, and accounting, a _____ is the value of money that has been used up to produce something or deliver a service, and hence is not available for use anymore. In business, the _____ may be one of acquisition, in which case the amount of money expended to acquire it is counted as _____. In this case, money is the input that is gone in order to acquire the thing. This acquisition _____ may be the sum of the _____ of production as incurred by the original producer, and further _____s of transaction as incurred by the acquirer over and above the price paid to the producer. Usually, the price also includes a mark-up for profit over the _____ of production.

Exam Probability: **High**

9. *Answer choices:*

(see index for correct answer)

- a. Cost
- b. corporate values
- c. empathy
- d. hierarchical perspective

Guidance: level 1

:: Game theory ::

To _____ is to make a deal between different parties where each party gives up part of their demand. In arguments, _____ is a concept of finding agreement through communication, through a mutual acceptance of terms—often involving variations from an original goal or desires.

Exam Probability: **Low**

10. *Answer choices:*

(see index for correct answer)

- a. Purification theorem
- b. Screening game
- c. Compromise
- d. Axiom of projective determinacy

Guidance: level 1

:: Organizational theory ::

_____ comprises the actual output or results of an organization as measured against its intended outputs.

Exam Probability: **Medium**

11. *Answer choices:*
(see index for correct answer)

- a. Organizational performance
- b. Aston Group
- c. Organizational communication
- d. Linking pin model

Guidance: level 1

:: Hospitality management ::

A _____ is an establishment that provides paid lodging on a short-term basis. Facilities provided may range from a modest-quality mattress in a small room to large suites with bigger, higher-quality beds, a dresser, a refrigerator and other kitchen facilities, upholstered chairs, a flat screen television, and en-suite bathrooms. Small, lower-priced _____ s may offer only the most basic guest services and facilities. Larger, higher-priced _____ s may provide additional guest facilities such as a swimming pool, business centre, childcare, conference and event facilities, tennis or basketball courts, gymnasium, restaurants, day spa, and social function services. _____ rooms are usually numbered to allow guests to identify their room. Some boutique, high-end _____ s have custom decorated rooms. Some _____ s offer meals as part of a room and board arrangement. In the United Kingdom, a _____ is required by law to serve food and drinks to all guests within certain stated hours. In Japan, capsule _____ s provide a tiny room suitable only for sleeping and shared bathroom facilities.

Exam Probability: **Low**

12. *Answer choices:*

(see index for correct answer)

- a. Group booking
- b. Birgit Zotz
- c. Hotel
- d. ChannelGain

Guidance: level 1

:: Management ::

In business, a _____ is the attribute that allows an organization to outperform its competitors. A _____ may include access to natural resources, such as high-grade ores or a low-cost power source, highly skilled labor, geographic location, high entry barriers, and access to new technology.

Exam Probability: **High**

13. *Answer choices:*

(see index for correct answer)

- a. Hierarchical organization
- b. Tacit knowledge
- c. Competitive advantage
- d. Relevance paradox

Guidance: level 1

:: Business models ::

A _____, _____ company or daughter company is a company that is owned or controlled by another company, which is called the parent company, parent, or holding company. The _____ can be a company, corporation, or limited liability company. In some cases it is a government or state-owned enterprise. In some cases, particularly in the music and book publishing industries, subsidiaries are referred to as imprints.

Exam Probability: **Medium**

14. *Answer choices:*

(see index for correct answer)

- a. Subsidiary
- b. Home business
- c. Cooperative
- d. Paid To Click

Guidance: level 1

:: Free trade agreements ::

A _____ is a wide-ranging taxes, tariff and trade treaty that often includes investment guarantees. It exists when two or more countries agree on terms that helps them trade with each other. The most common _____ s are of the preferential and free trade types are concluded in order to reduce tariffs, quotas and other trade restrictions on items traded between the signatories.

Exam Probability: **Low**

15. *Answer choices:*

(see index for correct answer)

- a. CISFTA
- b. Trade agreement
- c. European Union Central American Association Agreement
- d. Central Asian Union

Guidance: level 1

:: Management occupations ::

_____ is the process of designing, launching and running a new business, which is often initially a small business. The people who create these businesses are called entrepreneurs.

Exam Probability: **Medium**

16. *Answer choices:*
(see index for correct answer)

- a. Comprador
- b. Entrepreneurship
- c. General partner
- d. City manager

Guidance: level 1

:: Business law ::

A _____ is a group of people who jointly supervise the activities of an organization, which can be either a for-profit business, nonprofit organization, or a government agency. Such a board's powers, duties, and responsibilities are determined by government regulations and the organization's own constitution and bylaws. These authorities may specify the number of members of the board, how they are to be chosen, and how often they are to meet.

Exam Probability: **High**

17. *Answer choices:*

(see index for correct answer)

- a. Board of directors
- b. Output contract
- c. Consularization
- d. Company mortgage

Guidance: level 1

:: Classification systems ::

_____ is the practice of comparing business processes and performance metrics to industry bests and best practices from other companies. Dimensions typically measured are quality, time and cost.

Exam Probability: **Medium**

18. Answer choices:

(see index for correct answer)

- a. Structural Classification of Proteins database
- b. Benchmarking
- c. World Health Organisation Composite International Diagnostic Interview
- d. Active galactic nucleus

Guidance: level 1

:: ::

In logic and philosophy, an _____ is a series of statements, called the premises or premisses, intended to determine the degree of truth of another statement, the conclusion. The logical form of an _____ in a natural language can be represented in a symbolic formal language, and independently of natural language formally defined " _____ s" can be made in math and computer science.

Exam Probability: **Medium**

19. Answer choices:

(see index for correct answer)

- a. hierarchical
- b. Argument
- c. process perspective

- d. empathy

Guidance: level 1

:: Goods ::

In most contexts, the concept of _____ denotes the conduct that should be preferred when posed with a choice between possible actions. _____ is generally considered to be the opposite of evil, and is of interest in the study of morality, ethics, religion and philosophy. The specific meaning and etymology of the term and its associated translations among ancient and contemporary languages show substantial variation in its inflection and meaning depending on circumstances of place, history, religious, or philosophical context.

Exam Probability: **High**

20. *Answer choices:*

(see index for correct answer)

- a. Good
- b. Common good
- c. Private good
- d. Veblen good

Guidance: level 1

:: ::

_____ is the assignment of any responsibility or authority to another person to carry out specific activities. It is one of the core concepts of management leadership. However, the person who delegated the work remains accountable for the outcome of the delegated work. _____ empowers a subordinate to make decisions, i.e. it is a shifting of decision-making authority from one organizational level to a lower one. _____, if properly done, is not fabrication. The opposite of effective _____ is micromanagement, where a manager provides too much input, direction, and review of delegated work. In general, _____ is good and can save money and time, help in building skills, and motivate people. On the other hand, poor _____ might cause frustration and confusion to all the involved parties. Some agents, however, do not favour a _____ and consider the power of making a decision rather burdensome.

Exam Probability: **Medium**

21. *Answer choices:*

(see index for correct answer)

- a. open system
- b. hierarchical
- c. Delegation
- d. hierarchical perspective

Guidance: level 1

:: Organizational theory ::

_____ refers to both a body of non-elective government officials and an administrative policy-making group. Historically, a _____ was a government administration managed by departments staffed with non-elected officials. Today, _____ is the administrative system governing any large institution, whether publicly owned or privately owned. The public administration in many countries is an example of a _____, but so is the centralized hierarchical structure of a business firm.

Exam Probability: **Medium**

22. *Answer choices:*

(see index for correct answer)

- a. Bureaucracy
- b. Contingency theory
- c. Star Roles Model
- d. Solid line reporting

Guidance: level 1

:: Meetings ::

A _____ is a body of one or more persons that is subordinate to a deliberative assembly. Usually, the assembly sends matters into a _____ as a way to explore them more fully than would be possible if the assembly itself were considering them. _____ s may have different functions and their type of work differ depending on the type of the organization and its needs.

Exam Probability: **Low**

23. *Answer choices:*

(see index for correct answer)

- a. Over the Air
- b. Committee
- c. Annual general meeting
- d. AEI World Forum

Guidance: level 1

:: Organizational theory ::

_____ is the process of groups of organisms working or acting together for common, mutual, or some underlying benefit, as opposed to working in competition for selfish benefit. Many animal and plant species cooperate both with other members of their own species and with members of other species.

Exam Probability: **Low**

24. *Answer choices:*

(see index for correct answer)

- a. Organisational semiotics
- b. Conflict
- c. Solid line reporting

- d. Cooperation

Guidance: level 1

:: ::

_____ is the capacity of consciously making sense of things, establishing and verifying facts, applying logic, and changing or justifying practices, institutions, and beliefs based on new or existing information. It is closely associated with such characteristically human activities as philosophy, science, language, mathematics and art, and is normally considered to be a distinguishing ability possessed by humans. _____ , or an aspect of it, is sometimes referred to as rationality.

Exam Probability: **High**

25. *Answer choices:*

(see index for correct answer)

- a. imperative
- b. Reason
- c. corporate values
- d. similarity-attraction theory

Guidance: level 1

:: ::

The _____ or labour force is the labour pool in employment. It is generally used to describe those working for a single company or industry, but can also apply to a geographic region like a city, state, or country. Within a company, its value can be labelled as its "_____ in Place". The _____ of a country includes both the employed and the unemployed. The labour force participation rate, LFPR, is the ratio between the labour force and the overall size of their cohort. The term generally excludes the employers or management, and can imply those involved in manual labour. It may also mean all those who are available for work.

Exam Probability: **High**

26. *Answer choices:*

(see index for correct answer)

- a. imperative
- b. corporate values
- c. Sarbanes-Oxley act of 2002
- d. Workforce

Guidance: level 1

:: Management ::

A _____ is a formal written document containing business goals, the methods on how these goals can be attained, and the time frame within which these goals need to be achieved. It also describes the nature of the business, background information on the organization, the organization's financial projections, and the strategies it intends to implement to achieve the stated targets. In its entirety, this document serves as a road map that provides direction to the business.

Exam Probability: **High**

27. *Answer choices:*

(see index for correct answer)

- a. Business process interoperability
- b. Business plan
- c. Twelve leverage points
- d. Backsourcing

Guidance: level 1

:: Industrial Revolution ::

The _____, now also known as the First _____, was the transition to new manufacturing processes in Europe and the US, in the period from about 1760 to sometime between 1820 and 1840. This transition included going from hand production methods to machines, new chemical manufacturing and iron production processes, the increasing use of steam power and water power, the development of machine tools and the rise of the mechanized factory system. The _____ also led to an unprecedented rise in the rate of population growth.

Exam Probability: **Medium**

28. *Answer choices:*

(see index for correct answer)

- a. Luddite
- b. Industrial Revolution
- c. Stott and Sons
- d. Platt Brothers

Guidance: level 1

:: Product management ::

_____ s, also known as Shewhart charts or process-behavior charts, are a statistical process control tool used to determine if a manufacturing or business process is in a state of control.

Exam Probability: **Low**

29. *Answer choices:*

(see index for correct answer)

- a. Crossing the Chasm
- b. Whole product
- c. Trademark
- d. Control chart

Guidance: level 1

:: Summary statistics ::

_____ is the number of occurrences of a repeating event per unit of time. It is also referred to as temporal _____, which emphasizes the contrast to spatial _____ and angular _____. The period is the duration of time of one cycle in a repeating event, so the period is the reciprocal of the _____. For example: if a newborn baby's heart beats at a _____ of 120 times a minute, its period—the time interval between beats—is half a second. _____ is an important parameter used in science and engineering to specify the rate of oscillatory and vibratory phenomena, such as mechanical vibrations, audio signals, radio waves, and light.

Exam Probability: **High**

30. *Answer choices:*

(see index for correct answer)

- a. Scan statistic
- b. Nonparametric skew
- c. Quantile
- d. Frequency

Guidance: level 1

:: Management ::

In organizational studies, _____ is the efficient and effective development of an organization's resources when they are needed. Such resources may include financial resources, inventory, human skills, production resources, or information technology and natural resources.

Exam Probability: **High**

31. *Answer choices:*

(see index for correct answer)

- a. Resource management
- b. Organizational conflict
- c. Industrial democracy
- d. Innovation management

Guidance: level 1

:: Organizational theory ::

A _____ is an organizational theory that claims that there is no best way to organize a corporation, to lead a company, or to make decisions. Instead, the optimal course of action is contingent upon the internal and external situation. A contingent leader effectively applies their own style of leadership to the right situation.

Exam Probability: **Medium**

32. *Answer choices:*

(see index for correct answer)

- a. Stages of growth model
- b. Organizational ecology
- c. System 4
- d. Star Roles Model

Guidance: level 1

:: Outsourcing ::

_____ is the relocation of a business process from one country to another—typically an operational process, such as manufacturing, or supporting processes, such as accounting. Typically this refers to a company business, although state governments may also employ _____ . More recently, technical and administrative services have been offshored.

Exam Probability: **High**

33. *Answer choices:*

(see index for correct answer)

- a. Media Process Outsourcing
- b. Extengineering
- c. Counsel On Call
- d. Editorial process outsourcing

Guidance: level 1

:: Decision theory ::

Within economics the concept of _____ is used to model worth or value, but its usage has evolved significantly over time. The term was introduced initially as a measure of pleasure or satisfaction within the theory of utilitarianism by moral philosophers such as Jeremy Bentham and John Stuart Mill. But the term has been adapted and reapplied within neoclassical economics, which dominates modern economic theory, as a _____ function that represents a consumer's preference ordering over a choice set. As such, it is devoid of its original interpretation as a measurement of the pleasure or satisfaction obtained by the consumer from that choice.

Exam Probability: **Medium**

34. *Answer choices:*

(see index for correct answer)

- a. Utility
- b. Decision-theoretic rough sets
- c. Two-moment decision model
- d. Rational Focal Point

Guidance: level 1

:: ::

_____ or haggling is a type of negotiation in which the buyer and seller of a good or service debate the price and exact nature of a transaction. If the _____ produces agreement on terms, the transaction takes place. _____ is an alternative pricing strategy to fixed prices. Optimally, if it costs the retailer nothing to engage and allow _____ , s/he can divine the buyer's willingness to spend. It allows for capturing more consumer surplus as it allows price discrimination, a process whereby a seller can charge a higher price to one buyer who is more eager. Haggling has largely disappeared in parts of the world where the cost to haggle exceeds the gain to retailers for most common retail items. However, for expensive goods sold to uninformed buyers such as automobiles, _____ can remain commonplace.

Exam Probability: **Low**

35. *Answer choices:*

(see index for correct answer)

- a. imperative
- b. empathy
- c. information systems assessment
- d. open system

Guidance: level 1

:: Organizational structure ::

An _____ defines how activities such as task allocation, coordination, and supervision are directed toward the achievement of organizational aims.

Exam Probability: **High**

36. *Answer choices:*

(see index for correct answer)

- a. Organizational structure
- b. Unorganisation
- c. Automated Bureaucracy
- d. Followership

Guidance: level 1

:: Problem solving ::

In other words, _____ is a situation where a group of people meet to generate new ideas and solutions around a specific domain of interest by removing inhibitions. People are able to think more freely and they suggest as many spontaneous new ideas as possible. All the ideas are noted down and those ideas are not criticized and after _____ session the ideas are evaluated. The term was popularized by Alex Faickney Osborn in the 1953 book Applied Imagination.

Exam Probability: **Medium**

37. *Answer choices:*

(see index for correct answer)

- a. Problem finding

- b. Rogerian argument
- c. Rhetorical reason
- d. Brainstorming

Guidance: level 1

:: ::

_____ refers to the confirmation of certain characteristics of an object, person, or organization. This confirmation is often, but not always, provided by some form of external review, education, assessment, or audit. Accreditation is a specific organization's process of _____ . According to the National Council on Measurement in Education, a _____ test is a credentialing test used to determine whether individuals are knowledgeable enough in a given occupational area to be labeled "competent to practice" in that area.

Exam Probability: **Low**

38. *Answer choices:*

(see index for correct answer)

- a. Certification
- b. corporate values
- c. Sarbanes-Oxley act of 2002
- d. co-culture

Guidance: level 1

:: Asset ::

In financial accounting, an _____ is any resource owned by the business. Anything tangible or intangible that can be owned or controlled to produce value and that is held by a company to produce positive economic value is an _____ . Simply stated, _____ s represent value of ownership that can be converted into cash . The balance sheet of a firm records the monetary value of the _____ s owned by that firm. It covers money and other valuables belonging to an individual or to a business.

Exam Probability: **Medium**

39. *Answer choices:*

(see index for correct answer)

- a. Asset
- b. Current asset

Guidance: level 1

:: Marketing ::

_____ or stock control can be broadly defined as "the activity of checking a shop's stock." However, a more focused definition takes into account the more science-based, methodical practice of not only verifying a business` inventory but also focusing on the many related facets of inventory management "within an organisation to meet the demand placed upon that business economically." Other facets of _____ include supply chain management, production control, financial flexibility, and customer satisfaction. At the root of _____ , however, is the _____ problem, which involves determining when to order, how much to order, and the logistics of those decisions.

Exam Probability: **Medium**

40. *Answer choices:*

(see index for correct answer)

- a. Gift suite
- b. HyTrust
- c. Advertising media selection
- d. Inventory control

Guidance: level 1

:: ::

A _____ is the ability to carry out a task with determined results often within a given amount of time, energy, or both. _____ s can often be divided into domain-general and domain-specific _____ s. For example, in the domain of work, some general _____ s would include time management, teamwork and leadership, self-motivation and others, whereas domain-specific _____ s would be used only for a certain job. _____ usually requires certain environmental stimuli and situations to assess the level of _____ being shown and used.

Exam Probability: **Low**

41. *Answer choices:*

(see index for correct answer)

- a. co-culture
- b. levels of analysis
- c. similarity-attraction theory
- d. Skill

Guidance: level 1

:: ::

_____ is the amount of time someone works beyond normal working hours. The term is also used for the pay received for this time. Normal hours may be determined in several ways.

Exam Probability: **Medium**

42. *Answer choices:*

(see index for correct answer)

- a. similarity-attraction theory
- b. hierarchical
- c. open system
- d. Overtime

Guidance: level 1

:: Rhetoric ::

_____ is the pattern of narrative development that aims to make vivid a place, object, character, or group. _____ is one of four rhetorical modes, along with exposition, argumentation, and narration. In practice it would be difficult to write literature that drew on just one of the four basic modes.

Exam Probability: **Medium**

43. *Answer choices:*

(see index for correct answer)

- a. Ethos
- b. Colon
- c. Description
- d. Neo-Aristotelianism

Guidance: level 1

:: Management ::

A _____ is someone who engages in facilitation—any activity that makes a social process easy or easier. A _____ often helps a group of people to understand their common objectives and assists them to plan how to achieve these objectives; in doing so, the _____ remains "neutral", meaning he/she does not take a particular position in the discussion. Some _____ tools will try to assist the group in achieving a consensus on any disagreements that preexist or emerge in the meeting so that it has a strong basis for future action.

Exam Probability: **Low**

44. *Answer choices:*

(see index for correct answer)

- a. Formula for change
- b. Relevance paradox
- c. Data Item Descriptions
- d. Facilitator

Guidance: level 1

:: Autonomy ::

In developmental psychology and moral, political, and bioethical philosophy, _____ is the capacity to make an informed, uncoerced decision. Autonomous organizations or institutions are independent or self-governing. _____ can also be defined from a human resources perspective, where it denotes a level of discretion granted to an employee in his or her work. In such cases, _____ is known to generally increase job satisfaction. _____ is a term that is also widely used in the field of medicine — personal _____ is greatly recognized and valued in health care.

Exam Probability: **Medium**

45. *Answer choices:*

(see index for correct answer)

- a. Self-determination theory
- b. Accountable autonomy
- c. Autonomy
- d. Anti-individualism

Guidance: level 1

:: Evaluation ::

_____ solving consists of using generic or ad hoc methods in an orderly manner to find solutions to _____ s. Some of the _____ -solving techniques developed and used in philosophy, artificial intelligence, computer science, engineering, mathematics, or medicine are related to mental _____ -solving techniques studied in psychology.

Exam Probability: **Medium**

46. *Answer choices:*

(see index for correct answer)

- a. American Evaluation Association
- b. Career portfolio
- c. Problem
- d. Narrative evaluation

Guidance: level 1

:: Business terms ::

Centralisation or _____ is the process by which the activities of an organization, particularly those regarding planning and decision-making, framing strategy and policies become concentrated within a particular geographical location group. This moves the important decision-making and planning powers within the center of the organisation.

Exam Probability: **Low**

47. *Answer choices:*

(see index for correct answer)

- a. Owner Controlled Insurance Program
- b. organic growth

- c. back office
- d. Centralization

Guidance: level 1

:: Leadership ::

_____ /Management is a part of a style of leadership that focuses on supervision, organization, and performance; it is an integral part of the Full Range Leadership Model. _____ is a style of leadership in which leaders promote compliance by followers through both rewards and punishments. Through a rewards and punishments system, transactional leaders are able to keep followers motivated for the short-term. Unlike transformational leaders, those using the transactional approach are not looking to change the future, they look to keep things the same. Leaders using _____ as a model pay attention to followers' work in order to find faults and deviations.

Exam Probability: **Low**

48. *Answer choices:*

(see index for correct answer)

- a. Transformational leadership
- b. Leadership analysis
- c. Transactional leadership
- d. Strategic leadership

Guidance: level 1

:: International trade ::

_____ involves the transfer of goods or services from one person or entity to another, often in exchange for money. A system or network that allows _____ is called a market.

Exam Probability: **Low**

49. *Answer choices:*

(see index for correct answer)

- a. Ecumenical Advocacy Alliance
- b. Mutual recognition agreement
- c. Agreement on Technical Barriers to Trade
- d. Trade

Guidance: level 1

:: Manufacturing ::

A _____ is a building for storing goods. _____ s are used by manufacturers, importers, exporters, wholesalers, transport businesses, customs, etc. They are usually large plain buildings in industrial parks on the outskirts of cities, towns or villages.

Exam Probability: **Low**

50. *Answer choices:*

(see index for correct answer)

- a. Ashery
- b. Manufacturing engineering
- c. Supplier Risk Management
- d. Warehouse

Guidance: level 1

:: Income ::

In business and accounting, net income is an entity's income minus cost of goods sold, expenses and taxes for an accounting period. It is computed as the residual of all revenues and gains over all expenses and losses for the period, and has also been defined as the net increase in shareholders' equity that results from a company's operations. In the context of the presentation of financial statements, the IFRS Foundation defines net income as synonymous with profit and loss. The difference between revenue and the cost of making a product or providing a service, before deducting overheads, payroll, taxation, and interest payments. This is different from operating income.

Exam Probability: **High**

51. *Answer choices:*

(see index for correct answer)

- a. Real estate investing
- b. Imputed income
- c. Gratuity
- d. Bottom line

Guidance: level 1

:: Information systems ::

_____ is the process of creating, sharing, using and managing the knowledge and information of an organisation. It refers to a multidisciplinary approach to achieving organisational objectives by making the best use of knowledge.

Exam Probability: **Medium**

52. *Answer choices:*

(see index for correct answer)

- a. SAP Information Interchange OnDemand
- b. Cold start
- c. Knowledge management
- d. Dynamic Business Modeling

Guidance: level 1

:: Project management ::

_____ is a process of setting goals, planning and/or controlling the organizing and leading the execution of any type of activity, such as.

Exam Probability: **Medium**

53. *Answer choices:*

(see index for correct answer)

- a. Project portfolio management
- b. Theme-centered interaction
- c. Akihabara syndrome
- d. Management process

Guidance: level 1

:: ::

Some scenarios associate "this kind of planning" with learning "life skills". Schedules are necessary, or at least useful, in situations where individuals need to know what time they must be at a specific location to receive a specific service, and where people need to accomplish a set of goals within a set time period.

Exam Probability: **Low**

54. Answer choices:

(see index for correct answer)

- a. imperative
- b. Scheduling
- c. co-culture
- d. functional perspective

Guidance: level 1

:: ::

_____ refers to the overall process of attracting, shortlisting, selecting and appointing suitable candidates for jobs within an organization. _____ can also refer to processes involved in choosing individuals for unpaid roles. Managers, human resource generalists and _____ specialists may be tasked with carrying out _____, but in some cases public-sector employment agencies, commercial _____ agencies, or specialist search consultancies are used to undertake parts of the process. Internet-based technologies which support all aspects of _____ have become widespread.

Exam Probability: **High**

55. Answer choices:

(see index for correct answer)

- a. similarity-attraction theory
- b. empathy

- c. open system
- d. Recruitment

Guidance: level 1

:: Industrial agreements ::

_____ is a process of negotiation between employers and a group of employees aimed at agreements to regulate working salaries, working conditions, benefits, and other aspects of workers' compensation and rights for workers. The interests of the employees are commonly presented by representatives of a trade union to which the employees belong. The collective agreements reached by these negotiations usually set out wage scales, working hours, training, health and safety, overtime, grievance mechanisms, and rights to participate in workplace or company affairs.

Exam Probability: **High**

56. *Answer choices:*

(see index for correct answer)

- a. Bargaining unit
- b. Ex parte H.V. McKay
- c. Collective bargaining
- d. Workplace Authority

Guidance: level 1

:: Marketing ::

_____ is based on a marketing concept which can be adopted by an organization as a strategy for business expansion. Where implemented, a franchisor licenses its know-how, procedures, intellectual property, use of its business model, brand, and rights to sell its branded products and services to a franchisee. In return the franchisee pays certain fees and agrees to comply with certain obligations, typically set out in a Franchise Agreement.

Exam Probability: **Medium**

57. *Answer choices:*
(see index for correct answer)

- a. Albuquerque Craft Beer Market
- b. Product sabotage
- c. Cannibalization
- d. Franchising

Guidance: level 1

:: ::

In a supply chain, a _____ , or a seller, is an enterprise that contributes goods or services. Generally, a supply chain _____ manufactures inventory/stock items and sells them to the next link in the chain. Today, these terms refer to a supplier of any good or service.

Exam Probability: **Medium**

58. *Answer choices:*

(see index for correct answer)

- a. Vendor
- b. levels of analysis
- c. information systems assessment
- d. Character

Guidance: level 1

:: Project management ::

_____ is the right to exercise power, which can be formalized by a state and exercised by way of judges, appointed executives of government, or the ecclesiastical or priestly appointed representatives of a God or other deities.

Exam Probability: **High**

59. *Answer choices:*

(see index for correct answer)

- a. Starmad
- b. Hart Mason Index
- c. The Transformation Project

- d. Authority

Guidance: level 1

Business law

Corporate law (also known as business law) is the body of law governing the rights, relations, and conduct of persons, companies, organizations and businesses. It refers to the legal practice relating to, or the theory of corporations. Corporate law often describes the law relating to matters which derive directly from the life-cycle of a corporation. It thus encompasses the formation, funding, governance, and death of a corporation.

:: ::

A _____ , in law, is a set of facts sufficient to justify a right to sue to obtain money, property, or the enforcement of a right against another party. The term also refers to the legal theory upon which a plaintiff brings suit . The legal document which carries a claim is often called a `statement of claim` in English law, or a `complaint` in U.S. federal practice and in many U.S. states. It can be any communication notifying the party to whom it is addressed of an alleged fault which resulted in damages, often expressed in amount of money the receiving party should pay/reimburse.

Exam Probability: **High**

1. *Answer choices:*

(see index for correct answer)

- a. Cause of action
- b. corporate values
- c. similarity-attraction theory
- d. empathy

Guidance: level 1

:: Commerce ::

_____ relates to "the exchange of goods and services, especially on a large scale". It includes legal, economic, political, social, cultural and technological systems that operate in a country or in international trade.

Exam Probability: **High**

2. *Answer choices:*

(see index for correct answer)

- a. Group buying
- b. Commerce
- c. Acquiring bank
- d. Card association

Guidance: level 1

:: Contract law ::

An _____ —or acceleration covenant— in the law of contracts, is a term that fully matures the performance due from a party upon a breach of the contract. Such clauses are most prevalent in mortgages and similar contracts to purchase real estate in installments.

Exam Probability: **High**

3. *Answer choices:*

(see index for correct answer)

- a. Fundamental breach
- b. Acceleration clause
- c. Contract lifecycle management
- d. Force majeure

Guidance: level 1

:: Generally Accepted Accounting Principles ::

Expenditure is an outflow of money to another person or group to pay for an item or service, or for a category of costs. For a tenant, rent is an _____ . For students or parents, tuition is an _____ . Buying food, clothing, furniture or an automobile is often referred to as an _____ . An _____ is a cost that is "paid" or "remitted", usually in exchange for something of value. Something that seems to cost a great deal is "expensive". Something that seems to cost little is "inexpensive". "_____ s of the table" are _____ s of dining, refreshments, a feast, etc.

Exam Probability: **High**

4. *Answer choices:*

(see index for correct answer)

- a. Revenue recognition
- b. Expense
- c. Normal balance
- d. Contributed capital

Guidance: level 1

:: Personal property law ::

Bailment describes a legal relationship in common law where physical possession of personal property, or a chattel, is transferred from one person to another person who subsequently has possession of the property. It arises when a person gives property to someone else for safekeeping, and is a cause of action independent of contract or tort.

Exam Probability: **Low**

5. *Answer choices:*

(see index for correct answer)

- a. Bailee
- b. bailor

Guidance: level 1

:: Euthenics ::

_____ is an ethical framework and suggests that an entity, be it an organization or individual, has an obligation to act for the benefit of society at large. _____ is a duty every individual has to perform so as to maintain a balance between the economy and the ecosystems. A trade-off may exist between economic development, in the material sense, and the welfare of the society and environment, though this has been challenged by many reports over the past decade. _____ means sustaining the equilibrium between the two. It pertains not only to business organizations but also to everyone whose any action impacts the environment. This responsibility can be passive, by avoiding engaging in socially harmful acts, or active, by performing activities that directly advance social goals. _____ must be intergenerational since the actions of one generation have consequences on those following.

Exam Probability: **High**

6. *Answer choices:*

(see index for correct answer)

- a. Euthenics
- b. Social responsibility
- c. Home economics
- d. Family and consumer science

Guidance: level 1

:: ::

A _____ is a sworn body of people convened to render an impartial verdict officially submitted to them by a court, or to set a penalty or judgment. Modern juries tend to be found in courts to ascertain the guilt or lack thereof in a crime. In Anglophone jurisdictions, the verdict may be guilty or not guilty. The old institution of grand juries still exists in some places, particularly the United States, to investigate whether enough evidence of a crime exists to bring someone to trial.

Exam Probability: **High**

7. *Answer choices:*

(see index for correct answer)

- a. deep-level diversity
- b. Jury
- c. functional perspective
- d. process perspective

Guidance: level 1

:: ::

Competition law is a law that promotes or seeks to maintain market competition by regulating anti-competitive conduct by companies. Competition law is implemented through public and private enforcement. Competition law is known as "_____ law" in the United States for historical reasons, and as "anti-monopoly law" in China and Russia. In previous years it has been known as trade practices law in the United Kingdom and Australia. In the European Union, it is referred to as both _____ and competition law.

Exam Probability: **Medium**

8. *Answer choices:*

(see index for correct answer)

- a. Antitrust
- b. open system
- c. hierarchical perspective
- d. Sarbanes-Oxley act of 2002

Guidance: level 1

:: Business models ::

A _____, _____ company or daughter company is a company that is owned or controlled by another company, which is called the parent company, parent, or holding company. The _____ can be a company, corporation, or limited liability company. In some cases it is a government or state-owned enterprise. In some cases, particularly in the music and book publishing industries, subsidiaries are referred to as imprints.

Exam Probability: **High**

9. *Answer choices:*

(see index for correct answer)

- a. Very small business
- b. Subsidiary
- c. Market game
- d. Copy to China

Guidance: level 1

:: Contract law ::

Coercion is the practice of forcing another party to act in an involuntary manner by use of threats or force. It involves a set of various types of forceful actions that violate the free will of an individual to induce a desired response, for example: a bully demanding lunch money from a student or the student gets beaten. These actions may include extortion, blackmail, torture, threats to induce favors, or even sexual assault. In law, coercion is codified as a _____ crime. Such actions are used as leverage, to force the victim to act in a way contrary to their own interests. Coercion may involve the actual infliction of physical pain/injury or psychological harm in order to enhance the credibility of a threat. The threat of further harm may lead to the cooperation or obedience of the person being coerced.

Exam Probability: **High**

10. *Answer choices:*

(see index for correct answer)

- a. Contract price
- b. Duress
- c. Formal contract
- d. Mirror image rule

Guidance: level 1

_____ is the assignment of any responsibility or authority to another person to carry out specific activities. It is one of the core concepts of management leadership. However, the person who delegated the work remains accountable for the outcome of the delegated work. _____ empowers a subordinate to make decisions, i.e. it is a shifting of decision-making authority from one organizational level to a lower one. _____, if properly done, is not fabrication. The opposite of effective _____ is micromanagement, where a manager provides too much input, direction, and review of delegated work. In general, _____ is good and can save money and time, help in building skills, and motivate people. On the other hand, poor _____ might cause frustration and confusion to all the involved parties. Some agents, however, do not favour a _____ and consider the power of making a decision rather burdensome.

Exam Probability: **Low**

11. *Answer choices:*
(see index for correct answer)

- a. Delegation
- b. cultural
- c. Sarbanes-Oxley act of 2002
- d. corporate values

Guidance: level 1

:: ::

_____, also referred to as orthostasis, is a human position in which the body is held in an upright position and supported only by the feet.

Exam Probability: **High**

12. *Answer choices:*

(see index for correct answer)

- a. hierarchical perspective
- b. similarity-attraction theory
- c. Character
- d. Standing

Guidance: level 1

:: Clauses of the United States Constitution ::

The _____ describes an enumerated power listed in the United States Constitution. The clause states that the United States Congress shall have power "To regulate Commerce with foreign Nations, and among the several States, and with the Indian Tribes." Courts and commentators have tended to discuss each of these three areas of commerce as a separate power granted to Congress. It is common to see the individual components of the _____ referred to under specific terms: the Foreign _____, the Interstate _____, and the Indian _____.

Exam Probability: **Medium**

13. *Answer choices:*

(see index for correct answer)

- a. Full Faith and Credit Clause
- b. Commerce Clause
- c. Double Jeopardy Clause

Guidance: level 1

:: Business ethics ::

Banking secrecy, alternately known as _____, banking discretion, or bank safety, is a conditional agreement between a bank and its clients that all foregoing activities remain secure, confidential, and private. While some banking institutions voluntarily impose banking secrecy institutionally, others operate in regions where the practice is legally mandated and protected. Almost all banking secrecy standards prohibit the disclosure of client information to third parties without consent or an accepted criminal complaint. Additional privacy is provided to select clients via numbered bank accounts or underground bank vaults. Most often associated with banking in Switzerland, banking secrecy is prevalent in Luxembourg, Monaco, Hong Kong, Singapore, Ireland, Lebanon and the Cayman Islands, among other off-shore banking institutions.

Exam Probability: **Low**

14. *Answer choices:*

(see index for correct answer)

- a. Rules of the garage

- b. Evolution of corporate social responsibility in India
- c. Financial privacy
- d. Institute for Business and Professional Ethics

Guidance: level 1

:: Business ::

An _____ is a key document used by limited liability companies to outline the business' financial and functional decisions including rules, regulations and provisions. The purpose of the document is to govern the internal operations of the business in a way that suits the specific needs of the business owners. Once the document is signed by the members of the limited liability company, it acts as an official contract binding them to its terms. _____ is mandatory as per laws only in 5 states - California, Delaware, Maine, Missouri, and New York LLCs operating without an _____ are governed by the state's default rules contained in the relevant statute and developed through state court decisions. An _____ is similar in function to corporate by-laws, or analogous to a partnership agreement in multi-member LLCs. In single-member LLCs, an _____ is a declaration of the structure that the member has chosen for the company and sometimes used to prove in court that the LLC structure is separate from that of the individual owner and thus necessary so that the owner has documentation to prove that he or she is indeed separate from the entity itself.

Exam Probability: **Medium**

15. *Answer choices:*

(see index for correct answer)

- a. Operating agreement

- b. Intangible asset finance
- c. Counter trade
- d. Business mileage reimbursement rate

Guidance: level 1

:: Mereology ::

_____ , in the abstract, is what belongs to or with something, whether as an attribute or as a component of said thing. In the context of this article, it is one or more components , whether physical or incorporeal, of a person's estate; or so belonging to, as in being owned by, a person or jointly a group of people or a legal entity like a corporation or even a society. Depending on the nature of the _____ , an owner of _____ has the right to consume, alter, share, redefine, rent, mortgage, pawn, sell, exchange, transfer, give away or destroy it, or to exclude others from doing these things, as well as to perhaps abandon it; whereas regardless of the nature of the _____ , the owner thereof has the right to properly use it , or at the very least exclusively keep it.

Exam Probability: **Medium**

16. *Answer choices:*

(see index for correct answer)

- a. Property
- b. Mereotopology
- c. Non-wellfounded mereology
- d. Mereological essentialism

Guidance: level 1

:: Manufacturing ::

A _____ is a building for storing goods. _____ s are used by manufacturers, importers, exporters, wholesalers, transport businesses, customs, etc. They are usually large plain buildings in industrial parks on the outskirts of cities, towns or villages.

Exam Probability: **Medium**

17. *Answer choices:*

(see index for correct answer)

- a. Warehouse
- b. Optical comparator
- c. Diamond turning
- d. Universal gateway

Guidance: level 1

:: ::

_____s and acquisitions are transactions in which the ownership of companies, other business organizations, or their operating units are transferred or consolidated with other entities. As an aspect of strategic management, M&A can allow enterprises to grow or downsize, and change the nature of their business or competitive position.

Exam Probability: **Medium**

18. *Answer choices:*

(see index for correct answer)

- a. deep-level diversity
- b. Merger
- c. interpersonal communication
- d. hierarchical perspective

Guidance: level 1

:: Contract law ::

_____ is a legal process for collecting a monetary judgment on behalf of a plaintiff from a defendant. _____ allows the plaintiff to take the money or property of the debtor from the person or institution that holds that property. A similar legal mechanism called execution allows the seizure of money or property held directly by the debtor.

Exam Probability: **Medium**

19. *Answer choices:*

(see index for correct answer)

- a. Garnishment
- b. Force majeure
- c. Executory contract
- d. French contract law

Guidance: level 1

:: Business law ::

A _____ is a legal right granted by a debtor to a creditor over the debtor's property which enables the creditor to have recourse to the property if the debtor defaults in making payment or otherwise performing the secured obligations. One of the most common examples of a _____ is a mortgage: When person, by the action of an expressed conveyance, pledges by a promise to pay a certain sum of money, with certain conditions, on a said date or dates for a said period, that action on the page with wet ink applied on the part of the one wishing the exchange creates the original funds and negotiable Instrument. That action of pledging conveys a promise binding upon the mortgagee which creates a face value upon the Instrument of the amount of currency being asked for in exchange. It is therein in good faith offered to the Bank in exchange for local currency from the Bank to buy a house. The particular country's Bank Acts usually requires the Banks to deliver such fund bearing negotiable instruments to the Countries Main Bank such as is the case in Canada. This creates a _____ in the land the house sits on for the Bank and they file a caveat at land titles on the house as evidence of that _____ . If the mortgagee fails to pay defaulting in his promise to repay the exchange, the bank then applies to the court to for-close on your property to eventually sell the house and apply the proceeds to the outstanding exchange.

Exam Probability: **Medium**

20. *Answer choices:*

(see index for correct answer)

- a. Tacit relocation
- b. Negotiable instrument
- c. Security interest
- d. Inslaw

Guidance: level 1

:: ::

> Business is the activity of making one's living or making money by producing or buying and selling products . Simply put, it is "any activity or enterprise entered into for profit. It does not mean it is a company, a corporation, partnership, or have any such formal organization, but it can range from a street peddler to General Motors."

Exam Probability: **Low**

21. *Answer choices:*

(see index for correct answer)

- a. process perspective
- b. cultural

- c. Firm
- d. imperative

Guidance: level 1

:: Advertising ::

In law, _____ is speech or writing on behalf of a business with the intent of earning revenue or a profit. It is economic in nature and usually attempts to persuade consumers to purchase the business's product or service. The Supreme Court of the United States defines _____ as speech that "proposes a commercial transaction".

Exam Probability: **High**

22. *Answer choices:*

(see index for correct answer)

- a. Retail media
- b. Advertising to children
- c. Storyboard artist
- d. Conquesting

Guidance: level 1

:: United States securities law ::

_____ is a legal term for intent or knowledge of wrongdoing. An offending party then has knowledge of the "wrongness" of an act or event prior to committing it.

Exam Probability: **Low**

23. *Answer choices:*

(see index for correct answer)

- a. Scienter
- b. Securities regulation in the United States
- c. Uniform Securities Agent State Law Exam
- d. Series 7 Exam

Guidance: level 1

_____ is widespread, interconnected digital technology. The term entered the popular culture from science fiction and the arts but is now used by technology strategists, security professionals, government, military and industry leaders and entrepreneurs to describe the domain of the global technology environment. Others consider _____ to be just a notional environment in which communication over computer networks occurs. The word became popular in the 1990s when the uses of the Internet, networking, and digital communication were all growing dramatically and the term "_____" was able to represent the many new ideas and phenomena that were emerging. It has been called the largest unregulated and uncontrolled domain in the history of mankind, and is also unique because it is a domain created by people vice the traditional physical domains.

Exam Probability: **High**

24. *Answer choices:*

(see index for correct answer)

- a. functional perspective
- b. cultural
- c. Character
- d. deep-level diversity

Guidance: level 1

_____ is a concept of English common law and is a necessity for simple contracts but not for special contracts. The concept has been adopted by other common law jurisdictions, including the US.

Exam Probability: **Low**

25. *Answer choices:*

(see index for correct answer)

- a. corporate values
- b. deep-level diversity
- c. Consideration
- d. empathy

Guidance: level 1

:: Contract law ::

In contract law, a _____ is a promise which is not a condition of the contract or an innominate term: it is a term "not going to the root of the contract", and which only entitles the innocent party to damages if it is breached: i.e. the _____ is not true or the defaulting party does not perform the contract in accordance with the terms of the _____. A _____ is not guarantee. It is a mere promise. It may be enforced if it is breached by an award for the legal remedy of damages.

Exam Probability: **Medium**

26. Answer choices:

(see index for correct answer)

- a. Collateral contract
- b. Franchisor
- c. Warranty
- d. English clause

Guidance: level 1

:: Insolvency ::

_____ is the state of being unable to pay the money owed, by a person or company, on time; those in a state of _____ are said to be insolvent. There are two forms: cash-flow _____ and balance-sheet _____ .

Exam Probability: **Low**

27. Answer choices:

(see index for correct answer)

- a. Official Committee of Equity Security Holders
- b. Financial distress
- c. United Kingdom insolvency law
- d. Insolvency

Guidance: level 1

:: Sureties ::

In finance, a _____, _____ bond or guaranty involves a promise by one party to assume responsibility for the debt obligation of a borrower if that borrower defaults. The person or company providing the promise is also known as a " _____ " or as a "guarantor".

Exam Probability: **Low**

28. *Answer choices:*

(see index for correct answer)

- a. Aval
- b. Miller Act
- c. Estreature
- d. Little Miller Act

Guidance: level 1

:: ::

In common law legal systems, _____ is a principle or rule established in a previous legal case that is either binding on or persuasive for a court or other tribunal when deciding subsequent cases with similar issues or facts. Common-law legal systems place great value on deciding cases according to consistent principled rules, so that similar facts will yield similar and predictable outcomes, and observance of _____ is the mechanism by which that goal is attained. The principle by which judges are bound to _____s is known as stare decisis. Common-law _____ is a third kind of law, on equal footing with statutory law and delegated legislation or regulatory law.

Exam Probability: **Medium**

29. *Answer choices:*

(see index for correct answer)

- a. Precedent
- b. Sarbanes-Oxley act of 2002
- c. interpersonal communication
- d. hierarchical perspective

Guidance: level 1

:: ::

An _____ is a formal or official change made to a law, contract, constitution, or other legal document. It is based on the verb to amend, which means to change for better. _____ s can add, remove, or update parts of these agreements. They are often used when it is better to change the document than to write a new one.

Exam Probability: **Low**

30. *Answer choices:*
(see index for correct answer)

- a. Amendment
- b. levels of analysis
- c. Character
- d. hierarchical

Guidance: level 1

:: Legal procedure ::

An _____ is generally the first occasion that the trier of fact has to hear from a lawyer in a trial, aside possibly from questioning during voir dire. The _____ is generally constructed to serve as a "road map" for the fact-finder. This is especially essential, in many jury trials, since jurors know nothing at all about the case before the trial, . Though such statements may be dramatic and vivid, they must be limited to the evidence reasonably expected to be presented during the trial. Attorneys generally conclude _____ s with a reminder that at the conclusion of evidence, the attorney will return to ask the fact-finder to find in his or her client's favor.

Exam Probability: **High**

31. *Answer choices:*

(see index for correct answer)

- a. Closing argument
- b. appellate
- c. Procedural law
- d. civil procedure

Guidance: level 1

:: Legal doctrines and principles ::

_____ is a doctrine that a party is responsible for acts of their agents. For example, in the United States, there are circumstances when an employer is liable for acts of employees performed within the course of their employment. This rule is also called the master-servant rule, recognized in both common law and civil law jurisdictions.

Exam Probability: **High**

32. *Answer choices:*

(see index for correct answer)

- a. Mutual mistake
- b. Attractive nuisance
- c. Assumption of risk
- d. unconscionable contract

Guidance: level 1

:: Business models ::

A _____ is "an autonomous association of persons united voluntarily to meet their common economic, social, and cultural needs and aspirations through a jointly-owned and democratically-controlled enterprise". _____ s may include.

Exam Probability: **High**

33. Answer choices:

(see index for correct answer)

- a. Praenumeration
- b. Parent company
- c. One stop shop
- d. Cooperative

Guidance: level 1

:: ::

A contract is a legally-binding agreement which recognises and governs the rights and duties of the parties to the agreement. A contract is legally enforceable because it meets the requirements and approval of the law. An agreement typically involves the exchange of goods, services, money, or promises of any of those. In the event of breach of contract, the law awards the injured party access to legal remedies such as damages and cancellation.

Exam Probability: **High**

34. Answer choices:

(see index for correct answer)

- a. surface-level diversity
- b. co-culture
- c. Character
- d. Contract law

Guidance: level 1

:: Fraud ::

In law, _____ is intentional deception to secure unfair or unlawful gain, or to deprive a victim of a legal right. _____ can violate civil law, a criminal law, or it may cause no loss of money, property or legal right but still be an element of another civil or criminal wrong. The purpose of _____ may be monetary gain or other benefits, for example by obtaining a passport, travel document, or driver's license, or mortgage _____, where the perpetrator may attempt to qualify for a mortgage by way of false statements.

Exam Probability: **High**

35. *Answer choices:*

(see index for correct answer)

- a. Fraud
- b. Age fabrication
- c. Lottery scam
- d. Drug fraud

Guidance: level 1

:: Legal doctrines and principles ::

_____ is a defense in the law of torts, which bars or reduces a plaintiff's right to recovery against a negligent tortfeasor if the defendant can demonstrate that the plaintiff voluntarily and knowingly assumed the risks at issue inherent to the dangerous activity in which he was participating at the time of his or her injury.

Exam Probability: **Medium**

36. *Answer choices:*

(see index for correct answer)

- a. Mutual mistake
- b. negligence
- c. Attractive nuisance doctrine
- d. Assumption of risk

Guidance: level 1

:: Meetings ::

A _____ is a body of one or more persons that is subordinate to a deliberative assembly. Usually, the assembly sends matters into a _____ as a way to explore them more fully than would be possible if the assembly itself were considering them. _____ s may have different functions and their type of work differ depending on the type of the organization and its needs.

Exam Probability: **High**

37. *Answer choices:*

(see index for correct answer)

- a. Unconference
- b. Program book
- c. Committee
- d. Over the Air

Guidance: level 1

⠒⠒

> Punishment is the imposition of an undesirable or unpleasant outcome upon a group or individual, meted out by an authority—in contexts ranging from child discipline to criminal law—as a response and deterrent to a particular action or behaviour that is deemed undesirable or unacceptable. The reasoning may be to condition a child to avoid self-endangerment, to impose social conformity , to defend norms, to protect against future harms , and to maintain the law—and respect for rule of law—under which the social group is governed. Punishment may be self-inflicted as with self-flagellation and mortification of the flesh in the religious setting, but is most often a form of social coercion.

Exam Probability: **High**

38. *Answer choices:*

(see index for correct answer)

- a. Punitive
- b. Character

- c. empathy
- d. personal values

Guidance: level 1

:: Real estate ::

_____, real estate, realty, or immovable property In English common law refers to landed properties belonging to some person. It include all structures, crops, buildings, machinery, wells, dams, ponds, mines, canals, and roads, among other things. The term is historic, arising from the now-discontinued form of action, which distinguish between _____ disputes and personal property disputes. Personal property was, and continues to refer to all properties that are not real properties.

Exam Probability: **Low**

39. *Answer choices:*

(see index for correct answer)

- a. Finca
- b. Seniors Real Estate Specialist
- c. 3D floor plan
- d. Real property

Guidance: level 1

:: Contract law ::

_____, also called an anticipatory breach, is a term in the law of contracts that describes a declaration by the promising party to a contract that he or she does not intend to live up to his or her obligations under the contract.

Exam Probability: **Low**

40. *Answer choices:*

(see index for correct answer)

- a. Neo-classical contract
- b. Quantum meruit
- c. Anticipatory repudiation
- d. Unjust enrichment

Guidance: level 1

:: ::

In general, _____ is a form of dishonesty or criminal activity undertaken by a person or organization entrusted with a position of authority, often to acquire illicit benefit. _____ may include many activities including bribery and embezzlement, though it may also involve practices that are legal in many countries. Political _____ occurs when an office-holder or other governmental employee acts in an official capacity for personal gain. _____ is most commonplace in kleptocracies, oligarchies, narco-states and mafia states.

Exam Probability: **High**

41. *Answer choices:*

(see index for correct answer)

- a. Corruption
- b. open system
- c. Character
- d. process perspective

Guidance: level 1

:: ::

In logic and philosophy, an _____ is a series of statements, called the premises or premisses, intended to determine the degree of truth of another statement, the conclusion. The logical form of an _____ in a natural language can be represented in a symbolic formal language, and independently of natural language formally defined " _____ s" can be made in math and computer science.

Exam Probability: **Low**

42. *Answer choices:*

(see index for correct answer)

- a. co-culture
- b. similarity-attraction theory
- c. corporate values
- d. Character

Guidance: level 1

:: Utilitarianism ::

_____ is a family of consequentialist ethical theories that promotes actions that maximize happiness and well-being for the majority of a population. Although different varieties of _____ admit different characterizations, the basic idea behind all of them is to in some sense maximize utility, which is often defined in terms of well-being or related concepts. For instance, Jeremy Bentham, the founder of _____ , described utility as

Exam Probability: **High**

43. *Answer choices:*

(see index for correct answer)

- a. Utilitarianism

- b. Mohism
- c. Equal consideration of interests
- d. Iain King

Guidance: level 1

:: Business law ::

A _____ is a document guaranteeing the payment of a specific amount of money, either on demand, or at a set time, with the payer usually named on the document. More specifically, it is a document contemplated by or consisting of a contract, which promises the payment of money without condition, which may be paid either on demand or at a future date. The term can have different meanings, depending on what law is being applied and what country and context it is used in.

Exam Probability: **Medium**

44. *Answer choices:*

(see index for correct answer)

- a. Doing business as
- b. Articles of partnership
- c. Extraordinary resolution
- d. Negotiable instrument

Guidance: level 1

:: ::

A _____ is a person who trades in commodities produced by other people. Historically, a _____ is anyone who is involved in business or trade. _____ s have operated for as long as industry, commerce, and trade have existed. During the 16th-century, in Europe, two different terms for _____ s emerged: One term, meerseniers, described local traders such as bakers, grocers, etc.; while a new term, koopman (Dutch: koopman, described _____ s who operated on a global stage, importing and exporting goods over vast distances, and offering added-value services such as credit and finance.

Exam Probability: **High**

45. *Answer choices:*

(see index for correct answer)

- a. Sarbanes-Oxley act of 2002
- b. corporate values
- c. process perspective
- d. Character

Guidance: level 1

:: Consumer theory ::

A _____ is a technical term in psychology, economics and philosophy usually used in relation to choosing between alternatives. For example, someone prefers A over B if they would rather choose A than B.

Exam Probability: **Medium**

46. *Answer choices:*

(see index for correct answer)

- a. Expenditure function
- b. Induced consumption
- c. Income elasticity of demand
- d. Preference

Guidance: level 1

:: Legal doctrines and principles ::

In the common law of torts, _____ loquitur is a doctrine that infers negligence from the very nature of an accident or injury in the absence of direct evidence on how any defendant behaved. Although modern formulations differ by jurisdiction, common law originally stated that the accident must satisfy the necessary elements of negligence: duty, breach of duty, causation, and injury. In _____ loquitur, the elements of duty of care, breach, and causation are inferred from an injury that does not ordinarily occur without negligence.

Exam Probability: **Medium**

47. *Answer choices:*

(see index for correct answer)

- a. Assumption of risk
- b. Eminent domain
- c. Res ipsa
- d. Unilateral mistake

Guidance: level 1

:: Marketing ::

_____ or stock is the goods and materials that a business holds for the ultimate goal of resale .

Exam Probability: **Medium**

48. *Answer choices:*

(see index for correct answer)

- a. MaxDiff
- b. Back to school
- c. Franchise fee
- d. Inventory

Guidance: level 1

:: American legal terms ::

The phrase "by _____" is a legal term that indicates that a right or liability has been created for a party, irrespective of the intent of that party, because it is dictated by existing legal principles. For example, if a person dies without a will, his or her heirs are determined by _____. Similarly, if a person marries or has a child after his or her will has been executed, the law writes this pretermitted spouse or pretermitted heir into the will if no provision for this situation was specifically included. Adverse possession, in which title to land passes because non-owners have occupied it for a certain period of time, is another important right that vests by _____.

Exam Probability: **High**

49. *Answer choices:*

(see index for correct answer)

- a. Reasonable time
- b. Chilling effect

Guidance: level 1

:: ::

A _____ is a request to do something, most commonly addressed to a government official or public entity. _____s to a deity are a form of prayer called supplication.

Exam Probability: **Low**

50. *Answer choices:*

(see index for correct answer)

- a. imperative
- b. similarity-attraction theory
- c. information systems assessment
- d. levels of analysis

Guidance: level 1

:: Money market instruments ::

_____ , in the global financial market, is an unsecured promissory note with a fixed maturity of not more than 270 days.

Exam Probability: **High**

51. *Answer choices:*

(see index for correct answer)

- a. Commercial paper in India
- b. Banker's acceptance

Guidance: level 1

:: Film production ::

_____ is a legal term more comprehensive and of higher import than either warranty or "security". It most commonly designates a private transaction by means of which one person, to obtain some trust, confidence or credit for another, engages to be answerable for him. It may also designate a treaty through which claims, rights or possessions are secured. It is to be differentiated from the colloquial "personal _____" in that a _____ is a legal concept which produces an economic effect. A personal _____ by contrast is often used to refer to a promise made by an individual which is supported by, or assured through, the word of the individual. In the same way, a _____ produces a legal effect wherein one party affirms the promise of another by promising to themselves pay if default occurs.

Exam Probability: **Medium**

52. *Answer choices:*

(see index for correct answer)

- a. Pan and scan
- b. Staged reading
- c. Made in NY
- d. Temp track

Guidance: level 1

:: Business law ::

In the United States, the United Kingdom, Australia, Canada and South Africa, _____ relates to the doctrines of the law of agency. It is relevant particularly in corporate law and constitutional law. _____ refers to a situation where a reasonable third party would understand that an agent had authority to act. This means a principal is bound by the agent's actions, even if the agent had no actual authority, whether express or implied. It raises an estoppel because the third party is given an assurance, which he relies on and would be inequitable for the principal to deny the authority given. _____ can legally be found, even if actual authority has not been given.

Exam Probability: **Medium**

53. *Answer choices:*

(see index for correct answer)

- a. Teck Corp. Ltd. v. Millar
- b. Output contract
- c. Bulk sale
- d. Board of directors

Guidance: level 1

:: Legal procedure ::

_____, adjective law, or rules of court comprises the rules by which a court hears and determines what happens in civil, lawsuit, criminal or administrative proceedings. The rules are designed to ensure a fair and consistent application of due process or fundamental justice to all cases that come before a court.

Exam Probability: **Low**

54. Answer choices:

(see index for correct answer)

- a. civil procedure
- b. Opening statement
- c. Procedural law
- d. appellate

Guidance: level 1

:: ::

A _____ is an individual or institution that legally owns one or more shares of stock in a public or private corporation. _____ s may be referred to as members of a corporation. Legally, a person is not a _____ in a corporation until their name and other details are entered in the corporation's register of _____ s or members.

Exam Probability: **High**

55. Answer choices:

(see index for correct answer)

- a. imperative
- b. Shareholder

- c. cultural
- d. corporate values

Guidance: level 1

:: Fair use ::

_____ is a doctrine in the law of the United States that permits limited use of copyrighted material without having to first acquire permission from the copyright holder. _____ is one of the limitations to copyright intended to balance the interests of copyright holders with the public interest in the wider distribution and use of creative works by allowing as a defense to copyright infringement claims certain limited uses that might otherwise be considered infringement.

Exam Probability: **High**

56. *Answer choices:*

(see index for correct answer)

- a. Derivative work
- b. Fair Use Project
- c. Fair use
- d. Nominative use

Guidance: level 1

:: Commercial item transport and distribution ::

A _____ is a commitment or expectation to perform some action in general or if certain circumstances arise. A _____ may arise from a system of ethics or morality, especially in an honor culture. Many duties are created by law, sometimes including a codified punishment or liability for non-performance. Performing one's _____ may require some sacrifice of self-interest.

Exam Probability: **Low**

57. *Answer choices:*

(see index for correct answer)

- a. Truck
- b. Affreightment
- c. Shipbroking
- d. Duty

Guidance: level 1

:: ::

A concept of English law, a _____ is an untrue or misleading statement of fact made during negotiations by one party to another, the statement then inducing that other party into the contract. The misled party may normally rescind the contract, and sometimes may be awarded damages as well

Exam Probability: **Low**

58. *Answer choices:*

(see index for correct answer)

- a. Misrepresentation
- b. functional perspective
- c. interpersonal communication
- d. corporate values

Guidance: level 1

:: Commercial crimes ::

In law, _____ is the unauthorized use of another's name, likeness, or identity without that person's permission, resulting in harm to that person.

Exam Probability: **Low**

59. *Answer choices:*

(see index for correct answer)

- a. United States antitrust law
- b. Offshore leaks
- c. Misappropriation
- d. Embezzlement

Guidance: level 1

Finance

Finance is a field that is concerned with the allocation (investment) of assets and liabilities over space and time, often under conditions of risk or uncertainty. Finance can also be defined as the science of money management. Participants in the market aim to price assets based on their risk level, fundamental value, and their expected rate of return. Finance can be split into three sub-categories: public finance, corporate finance and personal finance.

:: Accounting journals and ledgers ::

_____ is a daybook or journal which is used to record transactions relating to adjustment entries, opening stock, accounting errors etc. The source documents of this prime entry book are journal voucher, copy of management reports and invoices.

Exam Probability: **Medium**

1. *Answer choices:*

(see index for correct answer)

- a. Check register
- b. Sales journal
- c. General journal
- d. Journal entry

Guidance: level 1

:: Accounting terminology ::

A _____ contains all the accounts for recording transactions relating to a company's assets, liabilities, owners' equity, revenue, and expenses. In modern accounting software or ERP, the _____ works as a central repository for accounting data transferred from all subledgers or modules like accounts payable, accounts receivable, cash management, fixed assets, purchasing and projects. The _____ is the backbone of any accounting system which holds financial and non-financial data for an organization. The collection of all accounts is known as the _____ . Each account is known as a ledger account. In a manual or non-computerized system this may be a large book. The statement of financial position and the statement of income and comprehensive income are both derived from the _____ . Each account in the _____ consists of one or more pages. The _____ is where posting to the accounts occurs. Posting is the process of recording amounts as credits , and amounts as debits , in the pages of the _____ . Additional columns to the right hold a running activity total .

Exam Probability: **Low**

2. *Answer choices:*

(see index for correct answer)

- a. revenue recognition principle
- b. Internal auditing
- c. Double-entry accounting
- d. General ledger

Guidance: level 1

:: Generally Accepted Accounting Principles ::

In accounting, _____ is the income that a business have from its normal business activities, usually from the sale of goods and services to customers. _____ is also referred to as sales or turnover. Some companies receive _____ from interest, royalties, or other fees. _____ may refer to business income in general, or it may refer to the amount, in a monetary unit, earned during a period of time, as in "Last year, Company X had _____ of $42 million". Profits or net income generally imply total _____ minus total expenses in a given period. In accounting, in the balance statement it is a subsection of the Equity section and _____ increases equity, it is often referred to as the "top line" due to its position on the income statement at the very top. This is to be contrasted with the "bottom line" which denotes net income .

Exam Probability: **Medium**

3. *Answer choices:*

(see index for correct answer)

- a. Revenue
- b. Income statement
- c. Revenue recognition
- d. Deprival value

Guidance: level 1

:: ::

_____ is the process whereby a business sets the price at which it will sell its products and services, and may be part of the business's marketing plan. In setting prices, the business will take into account the price at which it could acquire the goods, the manufacturing cost, the market place, competition, market condition, brand, and quality of product.

Exam Probability: **High**

4. *Answer choices:*

(see index for correct answer)

- a. Pricing
- b. personal values
- c. open system
- d. imperative

Guidance: level 1

:: ::

_____ is the consumption and saving opportunity gained by an entity within a specified timeframe, which is generally expressed in monetary terms. For households and individuals, " _____ is the sum of all the wages, salaries, profits, interest payments, rents, and other forms of earnings received in a given period of time."

Exam Probability: **Medium**

5. *Answer choices:*

(see index for correct answer)

- a. information systems assessment
- b. process perspective
- c. imperative
- d. similarity-attraction theory

Guidance: level 1

:: Personal finance ::

_____ is income not spent, or deferred consumption. Methods of _____ include putting money aside in, for example, a deposit account, a pension account, an investment fund, or as cash. _____ also involves reducing expenditures, such as recurring costs. In terms of personal finance, _____ generally specifies low-risk preservation of money, as in a deposit account, versus investment, wherein risk is a lot higher; in economics more broadly, it refers to any income not used for immediate consumption.

Exam Probability: **Medium**

6. *Answer choices:*

(see index for correct answer)

- a. Benefactor
- b. Credit history
- c. Courtesy signing
- d. Saving

Guidance: level 1

:: Inventory ::

_____ is a system of inventory in which updates are made on a periodic basis. This differs from perpetual inventory systems, where updates are made as seen fit.

Exam Probability: **Medium**

7. *Answer choices:*

(see index for correct answer)

- a. Spare part
- b. Stock mix
- c. Stock keeping unit
- d. Periodic inventory

Guidance: level 1

:: Management accounting ::

_____ accounting is a traditional cost accounting method introduced in the 1920s, as an alternative for the traditional cost accounting method based on historical costs.

Exam Probability: **Medium**

8. *Answer choices:*

(see index for correct answer)

- a. Contribution margin
- b. Direct material total variance
- c. Operating profit margin
- d. Standard cost

Guidance: level 1

:: ::

A _____, in the word's original meaning, is a sheet of paper on which one performs work. They come in many forms, most commonly associated with children's school work assignments, tax forms, and accounting or other business environments. Software is increasingly taking over the paper-based _____.

Exam Probability: **High**

9. *Answer choices:*

(see index for correct answer)

- a. Worksheet
- b. deep-level diversity
- c. co-culture
- d. empathy

Guidance: level 1

:: ::

_____ is the study and management of exchange relationships. _____ is the business process of creating relationships with and satisfying customers. With its focus on the customer, _____ is one of the premier components of business management.

Exam Probability: **Low**

10. *Answer choices:*

(see index for correct answer)

- a. information systems assessment
- b. process perspective
- c. Marketing
- d. empathy

Guidance: level 1

:: International trade ::

In finance, an _____ is the rate at which one currency will be exchanged for another. It is also regarded as the value of one country's currency in relation to another currency. For example, an interbank _____ of 114 Japanese yen to the United States dollar means that ¥114 will be exchanged for each US$1 or that US$1 will be exchanged for each ¥114. In this case it is said that the price of a dollar in relation to yen is ¥114, or equivalently that the price of a yen in relation to dollars is $1/114.

Exam Probability: **Low**

11. *Answer choices:*

(see index for correct answer)

- a. Export-oriented

- b. Exchange rate
- c. Export function
- d. Trade creation

Guidance: level 1

:: ::

An _____ is an asset that lacks physical substance. It is defined in opposition to physical assets such as machinery and buildings. An _____ is usually very hard to evaluate. Patents, copyrights, franchises, goodwill, trademarks, and trade names. The general interpretation also includes software and other intangible computer based assets are all examples of _____ s. _____ s generally—though not necessarily—suffer from typical market failures of non-rivalry and non-excludability.

Exam Probability: **Low**

12. *Answer choices:*

(see index for correct answer)

- a. hierarchical
- b. Intangible asset
- c. Character
- d. imperative

Guidance: level 1

:: ::

_____ is a costing method that identifies activities in an organization and assigns the cost of each activity to all products and services according to the actual consumption by each. This model assigns more indirect costs into direct costs compared to conventional costing.

Exam Probability: **Medium**

13. *Answer choices:*

(see index for correct answer)

- a. Activity-based costing
- b. hierarchical
- c. Sarbanes-Oxley act of 2002
- d. personal values

Guidance: level 1

:: Data management ::

_____ is a form of intellectual property that grants the creator of an original creative work an exclusive legal right to determine whether and under what conditions this original work may be copied and used by others, usually for a limited term of years. The exclusive rights are not absolute but limited by limitations and exceptions to _____ law, including fair use. A major limitation on _____ on ideas is that _____ protects only the original expression of ideas, and not the underlying ideas themselves.

Exam Probability: **Medium**

14. *Answer choices:*

(see index for correct answer)

- a. Copyright
- b. Data Transformation Services
- c. Data governance
- d. Commit

Guidance: level 1

:: ::

_____ focuses on ratios, equities and debts. It is useful for portfolio management, distribution of dividend, capital raising, hedging and looking after fluctuations in foreign currency and product cycles. Financial managers are the people who will do research and based on the research, decide what sort of capital to obtain in order to fund the company's assets as well as maximizing the value of the firm for all the stakeholders. It also refers to the efficient and effective management of money in such a manner as to accomplish the objectives of the organization. It is the specialized function directly associated with the top management. The significance of this function is not seen in the `Line` but also in the capacity of the `Staff` in overall of a company. It has been defined differently by different experts in the field.

Exam Probability: **High**

15. *Answer choices:*

(see index for correct answer)

- a. Financial management
- b. levels of analysis
- c. process perspective
- d. open system

Guidance: level 1

:: ::

A shareholder is an individual or institution that legally owns one or more shares of stock in a public or private corporation. Shareholders may be referred to as members of a corporation. Legally, a person is not a shareholder in a corporation until their name and other details are entered in the corporation's register of shareholders or members.

Exam Probability: **Medium**

16. *Answer choices:*

(see index for correct answer)

- a. hierarchical perspective
- b. functional perspective
- c. surface-level diversity
- d. Stockholder

Guidance: level 1

:: Debt ::

_____ , in finance and economics, is payment from a borrower or deposit-taking financial institution to a lender or depositor of an amount above repayment of the principal sum , at a particular rate. It is distinct from a fee which the borrower may pay the lender or some third party. It is also distinct from dividend which is paid by a company to its shareholders from its profit or reserve, but not at a particular rate decided beforehand, rather on a pro rata basis as a share in the reward gained by risk taking entrepreneurs when the revenue earned exceeds the total costs.

Exam Probability: **High**

17. *Answer choices:*
(see index for correct answer)

- a. Least developed country
- b. Interest
- c. Debit commission
- d. Default trap

Guidance: level 1

:: ::

An _____, for United States federal income tax, is a closely held corporation that makes a valid election to be taxed under Subchapter S of Chapter 1 of the Internal Revenue Code. In general, _____ s do not pay any income taxes. Instead, the corporation's income or losses are divided among and passed through to its shareholders. The shareholders must then report the income or loss on their own individual income tax returns.

Exam Probability: **Medium**

18. *Answer choices:*

(see index for correct answer)

- a. levels of analysis
- b. open system
- c. interpersonal communication
- d. S corporation

Guidance: level 1

:: Debt ::

A _____ is a monetary amount owed to a creditor that is unlikely to be paid and, or which the creditor is not willing to take action to collect for various reasons, often due to the debtor not having the money to pay, for example due to a company going into liquidation or insolvency. There are various technical definitions of what constitutes a _____ , depending on accounting conventions, regulatory treatment and the institution provisioning. In the USA, bank loans with more than ninety days' arrears become "problem loans". Accounting sources advise that the full amount of a _____ be written off to the profit and loss account or a provision for _____ s as soon as it is foreseen.

Exam Probability: **High**

19. *Answer choices:*

(see index for correct answer)

- a. External financing
- b. Crown debt
- c. Credit cycle
- d. Bad debt

Guidance: level 1

:: Basic financial concepts ::

_____ is a sustained increase in the general price level of goods and services in an economy over a period of time. When the general price level rises, each unit of currency buys fewer goods and services; consequently, _____ reflects a reduction in the purchasing power per unit of money a loss of real value in the medium of exchange and unit of account within the economy. The measure of _____ is the _____ rate, the annualized percentage change in a general price index, usually the consumer price index, over time. The opposite of _____ is deflation.

Exam Probability: **High**

20. *Answer choices:*

(see index for correct answer)

- a. Inflation
- b. Future-oriented
- c. Base effect
- d. Eurodollar

Guidance: level 1

:: Debt ::

_____ is when something, usually money, is owed by one party, the borrower or _____ or, to a second party, the lender or creditor. _____ is a deferred payment, or series of payments, that is owed in the future, which is what differentiates it from an immediate purchase. The _____ may be owed by sovereign state or country, local government, company, or an individual. Commercial _____ is generally subject to contractual terms regarding the amount and timing of repayments of principal and interest. Loans, bonds, notes, and mortgages are all types of _____ . The term can also be used metaphorically to cover moral obligations and other interactions not based on economic value. For example, in Western cultures, a person who has been helped by a second person is sometimes said to owe a " _____ of gratitude" to the second person.

Exam Probability: **Medium**

21. *Answer choices:*

(see index for correct answer)

- a. Creditor
- b. External debt
- c. Exchangeable bond
- d. Debt

Guidance: level 1

:: Generally Accepted Accounting Principles ::

The term _____ is most often used to describe a practice or document that is provided as a courtesy or satisfies minimum requirements, conforms to a norm or doctrine, tends to be performed perfunctorily or is considered a formality.

Exam Probability: **Low**

22. *Answer choices:*

(see index for correct answer)

- a. Pro forma
- b. Gross income
- c. Construction in progress
- d. Liability

Guidance: level 1

:: ::

_____ officially refers to an administrative area of the Principality of Monaco, specifically the ward of _____ /Spélugues, where the _____ Casino is located. Informally the name also refers to a larger district, the _____ Quarter, which besides _____ /Spélugues also includes the wards of La Rousse/Saint Roman, Larvotto/Bas Moulins, and Saint Michel. The permanent population of the ward of _____ is about 3,500, while that of the quarter is about 15,000. Monaco has four traditional quarters. From west to east they are: Fontvieille, Monaco-Ville, La Condamine, and _____ .

Exam Probability: **Medium**

23. *Answer choices:*

(see index for correct answer)

- a. process perspective
- b. Monte Carlo
- c. similarity-attraction theory
- d. Sarbanes-Oxley act of 2002

Guidance: level 1

:: Business law ::

_____ is where a person's financial liability is limited to a fixed sum, most commonly the value of a person's investment in a company or partnership. If a company with _____ is sued, then the claimants are suing the company, not its owners or investors. A shareholder in a limited company is not personally liable for any of the debts of the company, other than for the amount already invested in the company and for any unpaid amount on the shares in the company, if any. The same is true for the members of a _____ partnership and the limited partners in a limited partnership. By contrast, sole proprietors and partners in general partnerships are each liable for all the debts of the business.

Exam Probability: **Medium**

24. *Answer choices:*

(see index for correct answer)

- a. Leave of absence
- b. Limited liability
- c. Holder
- d. Starting a Business Index

Guidance: level 1

:: ::

A _____ is the process of presenting a topic to an audience. It is typically a demonstration, introduction, lecture, or speech meant to inform, persuade, inspire, motivate, or to build good will or to present a new idea or product. The term can also be used for a formal or ritualized introduction or offering, as with the _____ of a debutante. _____ s in certain formats are also known as keynote address.

Exam Probability: **Low**

25. *Answer choices:*

(see index for correct answer)

- a. Presentation
- b. deep-level diversity
- c. empathy
- d. interpersonal communication

Guidance: level 1

:: Notes (finance) ::

A _____ , sometimes referred to as a note payable, is a legal instrument , in which one party promises in writing to pay a determinate sum of money to the other , either at a fixed or determinable future time or on demand of the payee, under specific terms.

Exam Probability: **Low**

26. *Answer choices:*

(see index for correct answer)

- a. Equity-linked note
- b. Circular note
- c. Surplus note
- d. A notes

Guidance: level 1

:: ::

_____ is a concept of English common law and is a necessity for simple contracts but not for special contracts . The concept has been adopted by other common law jurisdictions, including the US.

Exam Probability: **High**

27. *Answer choices:*

(see index for correct answer)

- a. Consideration
- b. similarity-attraction theory
- c. deep-level diversity
- d. surface-level diversity

Guidance: level 1

:: Cash flow ::

_____ s are narrowly interconnected with the concepts of value, interest rate and liquidity. A _____ that shall happen on a future day tN can be transformed into a _____ of the same value in t0.

Exam Probability: **High**

28. *Answer choices:*

(see index for correct answer)

- a. Discounted payback period
- b. Cash flow loan
- c. Valuation using discounted cash flows
- d. Cash flow

Guidance: level 1

:: Financial ratios ::

The _____ or dividend-price ratio of a share is the dividend per share, divided by the price per share. It is also a company's total annual dividend payments divided by its market capitalization, assuming the number of shares is constant. It is often expressed as a percentage.

Exam Probability: **Medium**

29. *Answer choices:*

(see index for correct answer)

- a. Social return on investment
- b. Dividend yield
- c. Debt service ratio
- d. Price-to-earnings ratio

Guidance: level 1

:: Financial ratios ::

_____ is a financial ratio that indicates the percentage of a company's assets that are provided via debt. It is the ratio of total debt and total assets.

Exam Probability: **Low**

30. *Answer choices:*

(see index for correct answer)

- a. Capital recovery factor
- b. PB ratio
- c. Days payable outstanding
- d. stock turnover

Guidance: level 1

:: Subprime mortgage crisis ::

The _____ Group, Inc., is an American multinational investment bank and financial services company headquartered in New York City. It offers services in investment management, securities, asset management, prime brokerage, and securities underwriting.

Exam Probability: **Low**

31. *Answer choices:*

(see index for correct answer)

- a. Goldman Sachs
- b. Foreclosure rescue
- c. Home Affordable Modification Program

- d. Homeowners Affordability and Stability Plan

Guidance: level 1

:: Financial ratios ::

A _____ or accounting ratio is a relative magnitude of two selected numerical values taken from an enterprise's financial statements. Often used in accounting, there are many standard ratios used to try to evaluate the overall financial condition of a corporation or other organization. _____ s may be used by managers within a firm, by current and potential shareholders of a firm, and by a firm's creditors. Financial analysts use _____ s to compare the strengths and weaknesses in various companies. If shares in a company are traded in a financial market, the market price of the shares is used in certain _____ s.

Exam Probability: **Medium**

32. *Answer choices:*

(see index for correct answer)

- a. PE ratio
- b. Total expense ratio
- c. Sharpe ratio
- d. Financial ratio

Guidance: level 1

:: Costs ::

_____ is the sum of costs of all resources consumed in the process of making a product. The _____ is classified into three categories: direct materials cost, direct labor cost and manufacturing overhead.

Exam Probability: **Low**

33. *Answer choices:*

(see index for correct answer)

- a. Search cost
- b. Manufacturing cost
- c. Direct materials cost
- d. Road Logistics Costing in South Africa

Guidance: level 1

:: ::

Pharmaceutical _____ is the creation of a particular pharmaceutical product to fit the unique need of a patient. To do this, _____ pharmacists combine or process appropriate ingredients using various tools.

Exam Probability: **Low**

34. *Answer choices:*

(see index for correct answer)

- a. empathy
- b. surface-level diversity
- c. personal values
- d. Character

Guidance: level 1

:: Accounting terminology ::

_____ is money owed by a business to its suppliers shown as a liability on a company's balance sheet. It is distinct from notes payable liabilities, which are debts created by formal legal instrument documents.

Exam Probability: **Medium**

35. *Answer choices:*

(see index for correct answer)

- a. Chart of accounts
- b. Accounts payable
- c. Capital appreciation
- d. Internal auditing

Guidance: level 1

:: Goods ::

In most contexts, the concept of _____ denotes the conduct that should be preferred when posed with a choice between possible actions. _____ is generally considered to be the opposite of evil, and is of interest in the study of morality, ethics, religion and philosophy. The specific meaning and etymology of the term and its associated translations among ancient and contemporary languages show substantial variation in its inflection and meaning depending on circumstances of place, history, religious, or philosophical context.

Exam Probability: **High**

36. *Answer choices:*

(see index for correct answer)

- a. Necessity good
- b. Case
- c. Positional good
- d. Giffen good

Guidance: level 1

:: Accounting in the United States ::

The _____ is a private-sector, nonprofit corporation created by the Sarbanes–Oxley Act of 2002 to oversee the audits of public companies and other issuers in order to protect the interests of investors and further the public interest in the preparation of informative, accurate and independent audit reports. The PCAOB also oversees the audits of broker-dealers, including compliance reports filed pursuant to federal securities laws, to promote investor protection. All PCAOB rules and standards must be approved by the U.S. Securities and Exchange Commission .

Exam Probability: **High**

37. *Answer choices:*

(see index for correct answer)

- a. Adjusted basis
- b. Other postemployment benefits
- c. Federal Accounting Standards Advisory Board
- d. Public Company Accounting Oversight Board

Guidance: level 1

:: Accounting ::

It is the period for which books are balanced and the financial statements are prepared. Generally, the _____ consists of 12 months. However the beginning of the _____ differs according to the jurisdiction. For example, one entity may follow the regular calendar year, i.e. January to December as the accounting year, while another entity may follow April to March as the _____ .

Exam Probability: **High**

38. *Answer choices:*

(see index for correct answer)

- a. Part exchange
- b. Russian GAAP
- c. Accounting period
- d. FreeAgent

Guidance: level 1

:: Expense ::

A company's _____, or As a result, the computation of the _____ is considerably more complex. Tax law may provide for different treatment of items of income and expenses as a result of tax policy. The differences may be of permanent or temporary nature. Permanent items are in the form of non taxable income and non taxable expenses. Things such as expenses considered not deductible by taxing authorities, the range of tax rates applicable to various levels of income, different tax rates in different jurisdictions, multiple layers of tax on income, and other issues.

Exam Probability: **Medium**

39. *Answer choices:*

(see index for correct answer)

- a. Tax expense
- b. expenditure
- c. Corporate travel
- d. Expense account

Guidance: level 1

:: Budgets ::

A _____ is a financial plan for a defined period, often one year. It may also include planned sales volumes and revenues, resource quantities, costs and expenses, assets, liabilities and cash flows. Companies, governments, families and other organizations use it to express strategic plans of activities or events in measurable terms.

Exam Probability: **Low**

40. *Answer choices:*

(see index for correct answer)

- a. Programme budgeting
- b. Operating budget
- c. Budgeted cost of work scheduled
- d. Public budgeting

Guidance: level 1

:: Asset ::

In accounting, a _____ is any asset which can reasonably be expected to be sold, consumed, or exhausted through the normal operations of a business within the current fiscal year or operating cycle. Typical _____ s include cash, cash equivalents, short-term investments, accounts receivable, stock inventory, supplies, and the portion of prepaid liabilities which will be paid within a year. In simple words, assets which are held for a short period are known as _____ s. Such assets are expected to be realised in cash or consumed during the normal operating cycle of the business.

Exam Probability: **High**

41. *Answer choices:*

(see index for correct answer)

- a. Fixed asset
- b. Asset

Guidance: level 1

:: Generally Accepted Accounting Principles ::

In accounting, an economic item's _____ is the original nominal monetary value of that item. _____ accounting involves reporting assets and liabilities at their _____ s, which are not updated for changes in the items' values. Consequently, the amounts reported for these balance sheet items often differ from their current economic or market values.

Exam Probability: **High**

42. *Answer choices:*

(see index for correct answer)

- a. Fin 48
- b. Indian Accounting Standards
- c. Historical cost
- d. Liability

Guidance: level 1

:: Pension funds ::

_____ s typically have large amounts of money to invest and are the major investors in listed and private companies. They are especially important to the stock market where large institutional investors dominate. The largest 300 _____ s collectively hold about $6 trillion in assets. In January 2008, The Economist reported that Morgan Stanley estimates that _____ s worldwide hold over US$20 trillion in assets, the largest for any category of investor ahead of mutual funds, insurance companies, currency reserves, sovereign wealth funds, hedge funds, or private equity.

Exam Probability: **Medium**

43. *Answer choices:*

(see index for correct answer)

- a. Pension buyout
- b. Pension led funding
- c. Texas Municipal Retirement System

Guidance: level 1

:: Financial ratios ::

The _____ is a liquidity ratio that measures whether a firm has enough resources to meet its short-term obligations. It compares a firm's current assets to its current liabilities, and is expressed as follows.

Exam Probability: **Medium**

44. *Answer choices:*

(see index for correct answer)

- a. Current ratio
- b. Financial result
- c. Rate of return on a portfolio
- d. Risk-adjusted return on capital

Guidance: level 1

:: Fixed income analysis ::

The _____, book yield or redemption yield of a bond or other fixed-interest security, such as gilts, is the internal rate of return earned by an investor who buys the bond today at the market price, assuming that the bond is held until maturity, and that all coupon and principal payments are made on schedule. _____ is the discount rate at which the sum of all future cash flows from the bond is equal to the current price of the bond. The YTM is often given in terms of Annual Percentage Rate, but more often market convention is followed. In a number of major markets the convention is to quote annualized yields with semi-annual compounding; thus, for example, an annual effective yield of 10.25% would be quoted as 10.00%, because $1.05 \times 1.05 = 1.1025$ and $2 \times 5 = 10$.

Exam Probability: **Low**

45. *Answer choices:*

(see index for correct answer)

- a. Bond convexity closed-form formula
- b. Yield to maturity
- c. Market yield
- d. Embedded option

Guidance: level 1

:: Decision theory ::

A _____ is a deliberate system of principles to guide decisions and achieve rational outcomes. A _____ is a statement of intent, and is implemented as a procedure or protocol. Policies are generally adopted by a governance body within an organization. Policies can assist in both subjective and objective decision making. Policies to assist in subjective decision making usually assist senior management with decisions that must be based on the relative merits of a number of factors, and as a result are often hard to test objectively, e.g. work-life balance _____ . In contrast policies to assist in objective decision making are usually operational in nature and can be objectively tested, e.g. password _____ .

Exam Probability: **Medium**

46. *Answer choices:*

(see index for correct answer)

- a. Group decision-making
- b. Utility
- c. Policy
- d. Lock-in

Guidance: level 1

:: Valuation (finance) ::

_____ refers to an assessment of the viability, stability, and profitability of a business, sub-business or project.

Exam Probability: **High**

47. *Answer choices:*

(see index for correct answer)

- a. Value-in-use
- b. Turnaround stock
- c. Appraisal value
- d. Financial analysis

Guidance: level 1

:: Legal terms ::

_____ s may be governments, corporations or investment trusts.
_____ s are legally responsible for the obligations of the issue and for reporting financial conditions, material developments and any other operational activities as required by the regulations of their jurisdictions.

Exam Probability: **Low**

48. *Answer choices:*

(see index for correct answer)

- a. Issuer
- b. Arraignment
- c. Gag order

- d. Literary executor

Guidance: level 1

:: ::

Business is the activity of making one's living or making money by producing or buying and selling products. Simply put, it is "any activity or enterprise entered into for profit. It does not mean it is a company, a corporation, partnership, or have any such formal organization, but it can range from a street peddler to General Motors."

Exam Probability: **High**

49. *Answer choices:*

(see index for correct answer)

- a. functional perspective
- b. open system
- c. Sarbanes-Oxley act of 2002
- d. similarity-attraction theory

Guidance: level 1

:: Real estate ::

Amortisation is paying off an amount owed over time by making planned, incremental payments of principal and interest. To amortise a loan means "to kill it off". In accounting, amortisation refers to charging or writing off an intangible asset's cost as an operational expense over its estimated useful life to reduce a company's taxable income.

Exam Probability: **Low**

50. *Answer choices:*

(see index for correct answer)

- a. Property ladder
- b. RealtyCompass
- c. Land trust
- d. Warrant of possession

Guidance: level 1

:: ::

An _____ is the production of goods or related services within an economy. The major source of revenue of a group or company is the indicator of its relevant _____ . When a large group has multiple sources of revenue generation, it is considered to be working in different industries.
Manufacturing _____ became a key sector of production and labour in European and North American countries during the Industrial Revolution, upsetting previous mercantile and feudal economies. This came through many successive rapid advances in technology, such as the production of steel and coal.

Exam Probability: **Low**

51. *Answer choices:*

(see index for correct answer)

- a. information systems assessment
- b. Industry
- c. hierarchical perspective
- d. open system

Guidance: level 1

:: Bonds (finance) ::

A _____ is a fund established by an economic entity by setting aside revenue over a period of time to fund a future capital expense, or repayment of a long-term debt.

Exam Probability: **High**

52. *Answer choices:*

(see index for correct answer)

- a. Current yield
- b. Catastrophe bond
- c. 360-day calendar
- d. Sinking fund

Guidance: level 1

:: Management ::

The _____ is a strategy performance management tool – a semi-standard structured report, that can be used by managers to keep track of the execution of activities by the staff within their control and to monitor the consequences arising from these actions.

Exam Probability: **Medium**

53. *Answer choices:*
(see index for correct answer)

- a. Planning fallacy
- b. manager's right to manage
- c. Balanced scorecard
- d. Quick response manufacturing

Guidance: level 1

:: Financial ratios ::

_____ is a measure of how revenue growth translates into growth in operating income. It is a measure of leverage, and of how risky, or volatile, a company's operating income is.

Exam Probability: **Medium**

54. *Answer choices:*

(see index for correct answer)

- a. Operating leverage
- b. Infection ratio
- c. Expense ratio
- d. Return on capital

Guidance: level 1

:: Income ::

_____ is a ratio between the net profit and cost of investment resulting from an investment of some resources. A high ROI means the investment's gains favorably to its cost. As a performance measure, ROI is used to evaluate the efficiency of an investment or to compare the efficiencies of several different investments. In purely economic terms, it is one way of relating profits to capital invested. _____ is a performance measure used by businesses to identify the efficiency of an investment or number of different investments.

Exam Probability: **Low**

55. Answer choices:

(see index for correct answer)

- a. Return on investment
- b. Private income
- c. Independent income
- d. Return of investment

Guidance: level 1

:: Interest rates ::

An _____ is the amount of interest due per period, as a proportion of the amount lent, deposited or borrowed. The total interest on an amount lent or borrowed depends on the principal sum, the _____ , the compounding frequency, and the length of time over which it is lent, deposited or borrowed.

Exam Probability: **Low**

56. Answer choices:

(see index for correct answer)

- a. Rate
- b. Interest rate
- c. Foreign exchange swap
- d. Notional amount

Guidance: level 1

:: Financial markets ::

In economics and finance, _____ is the practice of taking advantage of a price difference between two or more markets: striking a combination of matching deals that capitalize upon the imbalance, the profit being the difference between the market prices. When used by academics, an _____ is a transaction that involves no negative cash flow at any probabilistic or temporal state and a positive cash flow in at least one state; in simple terms, it is the possibility of a risk-free profit after transaction costs. For example, an _____ opportunity is present when there is the opportunity to instantaneously buy something for a low price and sell it for a higher price.

Exam Probability: **Low**

57. *Answer choices:*

(see index for correct answer)

- a. Arbitrage
- b. Long/short equity
- c. Secondary market
- d. Marketcetera

Guidance: level 1

:: Global systemically important banks ::

_____ Inc. or Citi is an American multinational investment bank and financial services corporation headquartered in New York City. The company was formed by the merger of banking giant Citicorp and financial conglomerate Travelers Group in 1998; Travelers was subsequently spun off from the company in 2002. _____ owns Citicorp, the holding company for Citibank, as well as several international subsidiaries.

Exam Probability: **Low**

58. *Answer choices:*

(see index for correct answer)

- a. Citigroup
- b. Commerzbank
- c. Groupe BPCE
- d. The Royal Bank of Scotland

Guidance: level 1

:: Derivatives (finance) ::

In finance, a _____ or simply a forward is a non-standardized contract between two parties to buy or to sell an asset at a specified future time at a price agreed upon today, making it a type of derivative instrument. The party agreeing to buy the underlying asset in the future assumes a long position, and the party agreeing to sell the asset in the future assumes a short position. The price agreed upon is called the delivery price, which is equal to the forward price at the time the contract is entered into.

Exam Probability: **Medium**

59. *Answer choices:*

(see index for correct answer)

- a. Forward contract
- b. STIRT
- c. Weather derivative
- d. Options arbitrage

Guidance: level 1

Human resource management

Human resource (HR) management is the strategic approach to the effective management of organization workers so that they help the business gain a competitive advantage. It is designed to maximize employee performance in service of an employer's strategic objectives. HR is primarily concerned with the management of people within organizations, focusing on policies and on systems. HR departments are responsible for overseeing employee-benefits design, employee recruitment, training and development, performance appraisal, and rewarding (e.g., managing pay and benefit systems). HR also concerns itself with organizational change and industrial relations, that is, the balancing of organizational practices with requirements arising from collective bargaining and from governmental laws.

_____ is defined by sociologist John R. Schermerhorn as the "...degree to which the people affected by decision are treated by dignity and respect. The theory focuses on the interpersonal treatment people receive when procedures are implemented.

Exam Probability: **High**

1. *Answer choices:*

(see index for correct answer)

- a. co-culture
- b. hierarchical
- c. corporate values
- d. process perspective

Guidance: level 1

:: Human resource management ::

_____ , also known as management by results , was first popularized by Peter Drucker in his 1954 book The Practice of Management. _____ is the process of defining specific objectives within an organization that management can convey to organization members, then deciding on how to achieve each objective in sequence. This process allows managers to take work that needs to be done one step at a time to allow for a calm, yet productive work environment. This process also helps organization members to see their accomplishments as they achieve each objective, which reinforces a positive work environment and a sense of achievement. An important part of MBO is the measurement and comparison of an employee's actual performance with the standards set. Ideally, when employees themselves have been involved with the goal-setting and choosing the course of action to be followed by them, they are more likely to fulfill their responsibilities. According to George S. Odiorne, the system of _____ can be described as a process whereby the superior and subordinate jointly identify common goals, define each individual's major areas of responsibility in terms of the results expected of him or her, and use these measures as guides for operating the unit and assessing the contribution of each of its members.

Exam Probability: **Medium**

2. *Answer choices:*

(see index for correct answer)

- a. Human resource consulting
- b. Human resources
- c. Human resource management in public administration
- d. Management by objectives

Guidance: level 1

:: Employment compensation ::

_____ is time off from work that workers can use to stay home to address their health and safety needs without losing pay. Paid _____ is a statutory requirement in many nations. Most European, many Latin American, a few African and a few Asian countries have legal requirements for paid _____ .

Exam Probability: **High**

3. *Answer choices:*
(see index for correct answer)

- a. Labour code
- b. Basic Income Earth Network
- c. Sick leave
- d. Stock appreciation right

Guidance: level 1

:: Power (social and political) ::

In a notable study of power conducted by social psychologists John R. P. French and Bertram Raven in 1959, power is divided into five separate and distinct forms. In 1965 Raven revised this model to include a sixth form by separating the informational power base as distinct from the _____ base.

Exam Probability: **Medium**

4. *Answer choices:*

(see index for correct answer)

- a. Expert power
- b. need for power
- c. Hard power

Guidance: level 1

:: Employee relations ::

_____ are tools used by organizational leadership to gain feedback on and measure employee engagement, employee morale, and performance. Usually answered anonymously, surveys are also used to gain a holistic picture of employees' feelings on such areas as working conditions, supervisory impact, and motivation that regular channels of communication may not. Surveys are considered effective in this regard provided they are well-designed, effectively administered, have validity, and evoke changes and improvements.

Exam Probability: **Low**

5. *Answer choices:*

(see index for correct answer)

- a. Fringe benefit
- b. Industry Federation of the State of Rio de Janeiro

- c. Employee engagement
- d. Employee handbook

Guidance: level 1

:: Management ::

A _____ describes the rationale of how an organization creates, delivers, and captures value, in economic, social, cultural or other contexts. The process of _____ construction and modification is also called _____ innovation and forms a part of business strategy.

Exam Probability: **Low**

6. *Answer choices:*

(see index for correct answer)

- a. Reval
- b. Completed Staff Work
- c. Business model
- d. Virtual customer environment

Guidance: level 1

:: Business law ::

A _____ is an arrangement where parties, known as partners, agree to cooperate to advance their mutual interests. The partners in a _____ may be individuals, businesses, interest-based organizations, schools, governments or combinations. Organizations may partner to increase the likelihood of each achieving their mission and to amplify their reach. A _____ may result in issuing and holding equity or may be only governed by a contract.

Exam Probability: **High**

7. *Answer choices:*

(see index for correct answer)

- a. Certificate of incorporation
- b. Unfair business practices
- c. Valuation using the Market Penetration Model
- d. Partnership

Guidance: level 1

:: Industrial agreements ::

A _____, in labor relations, is a group of employees with a clear and identifiable community of interests who are represented by a single labor union in collective bargaining and other dealings with management. Examples would be non-management professors, law enforcement professionals, blue-collar workers, clerical and administrative employees, etc. Geographic location as well as the number of facilities included in _____ s can be at issue during representation cases.

Exam Probability: **High**

8. *Answer choices:*

(see index for correct answer)

- a. Workplace Authority
- b. Australian workplace agreement
- c. Ex parte H.V. McKay
- d. Industrial Disputes Act 1947

Guidance: level 1

:: Employment ::

_____ is measuring the output of a particular business process or procedure, then modifying the process or procedure to increase the output, increase efficiency, or increase the effectiveness of the process or procedure. _____ can be applied to either individual performance such as an athlete or organizational performance such as a racing team or a commercial business.

Exam Probability: **Medium**

9. *Answer choices:*

(see index for correct answer)

- a. Executive Order 10925
- b. Birch index

- c. Liza Wright
- d. Performance improvement

Guidance: level 1

:: United States employment discrimination case law ::

_____ , 557 U.S. 557 , is a US labor law case of the United States Supreme Court on unlawful discrimination through disparate impact under the Civil Rights Act of 1964.

Exam Probability: **Medium**

10. *Answer choices:*

(see index for correct answer)

- a. Ricci v. DeStefano
- b. Vance v. Ball State University
- c. Hosanna-Tabor Evangelical Lutheran Church and School v. Equal Employment Opportunity Commission
- d. Glenn v. Brumby

Guidance: level 1

:: Employment compensation ::

An _____ is an employee benefit program that assists employees with personal problems and/or work-related problems that may impact their job performance, health, mental and emotional well-being. EAPs generally offer free and confidential assessments, short-term counseling, referrals, and follow-up services for employees and their household members. EAP counselors also work in a consultative role with managers and supervisors to address employee and organizational challenges and needs. Many corporations, academic institution and/or government agencies are active in helping organizations prevent and cope with workplace violence, trauma, and other emergency response situations. There is a variety of support programs offered for employees. Even though EAPs are mainly aimed at work-related problems, there are a variety of programs that can assist with problems outside of the workplace. EAPs have grown over the years, and are more desirable economically and socially.

Exam Probability: **Medium**

11. *Answer choices:*

(see index for correct answer)

- a. Pay scale
- b. The Theory of Wages
- c. Employee assistance program
- d. My Family Care

Guidance: level 1

An _____ is a person temporarily or permanently residing in a country other than their native country. In common usage, the term often refers to professionals, skilled workers, or artists taking positions outside their home country, either independently or sent abroad by their employers, who can be companies, universities, governments, or non-governmental organisations. Effectively migrant workers, they usually earn more than they would at home, and less than local employees. However, the term ` _____ ` is also used for retirees and others who have chosen to live outside their native country. Historically, it has also referred to exiles.

Exam Probability: **Medium**

12. *Answer choices:*

(see index for correct answer)

- a. levels of analysis
- b. cultural
- c. process perspective
- d. Expatriate

Guidance: level 1

:: Production and manufacturing ::

_____ consists of organization-wide efforts to "install and make permanent climate where employees continuously improve their ability to provide on demand products and services that customers will find of particular value." "Total" emphasizes that departments in addition to production are obligated to improve their operations; "management" emphasizes that executives are obligated to actively manage quality through funding, training, staffing, and goal setting. While there is no widely agreed-upon approach, TQM efforts typically draw heavily on the previously developed tools and techniques of quality control. TQM enjoyed widespread attention during the late 1980s and early 1990s before being overshadowed by ISO 9000, Lean manufacturing, and Six Sigma.

Exam Probability: **Low**

13. *Answer choices:*

(see index for correct answer)

- a. Total Quality Management
- b. Nuffield Tools and Gauges
- c. Corrective and preventive action
- d. Economic region of production

Guidance: level 1

:: Employment compensation ::

A _____ is the minimum income necessary for a worker to meet their basic needs. Needs are defined to include food, housing, and other essential needs such as clothing. The goal of a _____ is to allow a worker to afford a basic but decent standard of living. Due to the flexible nature of the term "needs", there is not one universally accepted measure of what a _____ is and as such it varies by location and household type.

Exam Probability: **High**

14. *Answer choices:*

(see index for correct answer)

- a. Salary calculator
- b. Employee stock purchase plan
- c. Uninsured employer
- d. Living wage

Guidance: level 1

:: Belief ::

_____ is an umbrella term of influence. _____ can attempt to influence a person's beliefs, attitudes, intentions, motivations, or behaviors. In business, _____ is a process aimed at changing a person's attitude or behavior toward some event, idea, object, or other person, by using written, spoken words or visual tools to convey information, feelings, or reasoning, or a combination thereof. _____ is also an often used tool in the pursuit of personal gain, such as election campaigning, giving a sales pitch, or in trial advocacy. _____ can also be interpreted as using one's personal or positional resources to change people's behaviors or attitudes. Systematic _____ is the process through which attitudes or beliefs are leveraged by appeals to logic and reason. Heuristic _____ on the other hand is the process through which attitudes or beliefs are leveraged by appeals to habit or emotion.

Exam Probability: **High**

15. *Answer choices:*

(see index for correct answer)

- a. Eschatological verification
- b. Urdoxa
- c. Political myth
- d. Popular belief

Guidance: level 1

:: Learning methods ::

_____ is an approach to problem solving. It involves taking action and reflecting upon the results. This helps improve the problem-solving process as well as simplify the solutions developed by the team.

Exam Probability: **Low**

16. *Answer choices:*

(see index for correct answer)

- a. Audience response system
- b. double loop learning
- c. Collaborative learning
- d. Action learning

Guidance: level 1

:: United States employment discrimination case law ::

_____ , 524 U.S. 775 , is a US labor law case of the United States Supreme Court in which the Court identified the circumstances under which an employer may be held liable under Title VII of the Civil Rights Act of 1964 for the acts of a supervisory employee whose sexual harassment of subordinates has created a hostile work environment amounting to employment discrimination. The court held that "an employer is vicariously liable for actionable discrimination caused by a supervisor, but subject to an affirmative defense looking to the reasonableness of the employer's conduct as well as that of a plaintiff victim."

Exam Probability: **High**

17. *Answer choices:*

(see index for correct answer)

- a. Faragher v. City of Boca Raton
- b. Reeves v. Sanderson Plumbing Products, Inc.
- c. Kloeckner v. Solis
- d. Ricci v. DeStefano

Guidance: level 1

:: Teams ::

A _____ usually refers to a group of individuals who work together from different geographic locations and rely on communication technology such as email, FAX, and video or voice conferencing services in order to collaborate. The term can also refer to groups or teams that work together asynchronously or across organizational levels. Powell, Piccoli and Ives define _____ s as "groups of geographically, organizationally and/or time dispersed workers brought together by information and telecommunication technologies to accomplish one or more organizational tasks." According to Ale Ebrahim et. al., _____ s can also be defined as "small temporary groups of geographically, organizationally and/or time dispersed knowledge workers who coordinate their work predominantly with electronic information and communication technologies in order to accomplish one or more organization tasks."

Exam Probability: **Low**

18. *Answer choices:*

(see index for correct answer)

- a. Virtual team
- b. Team-building

Guidance: level 1

:: ::

_____ is an enduring pattern of romantic or sexual attraction to persons of the opposite sex or gender, the same sex or gender, or to both sexes or more than one gender. These attractions are generally subsumed under heterosexuality, homosexuality, and bisexuality, while asexuality is sometimes identified as the fourth category.

Exam Probability: **Low**

19. *Answer choices:*

(see index for correct answer)

- a. hierarchical perspective
- b. Character
- c. functional perspective
- d. cultural

Guidance: level 1

:: ::

An _____ is a process where candidates are examined to determine their suitability for specific types of employment, especially management or military command. The candidates' personality and aptitudes are determined by techniques including interviews, group exercises, presentations, examinations and psychometric testing.

Exam Probability: **High**

20. *Answer choices:*

(see index for correct answer)

- a. cultural
- b. Assessment center
- c. surface-level diversity
- d. co-culture

Guidance: level 1

:: Social psychology ::

_____ is a type of nonverbal communication in which physical behaviors, as opposed to words, are used to express or convey information. Such behavior includes facial expressions, body posture, gestures, eye movement, touch and the use of space. _____ exists in both animals and humans, but this article focuses on interpretations of human _____. It is also known as kinesics.

Exam Probability: **Low**

21. *Answer choices:*

(see index for correct answer)

- a. Prosocial
- b. social loafing
- c. indoctrination
- d. objectification

Guidance: level 1

:: ::

A _____ is the ability to carry out a task with determined results often within a given amount of time, energy, or both. _____ s can often be divided into domain-general and domain-specific _____ s. For example, in the domain of work, some general _____ s would include time management, teamwork and leadership, self-motivation and others, whereas domain-specific _____ s would be used only for a certain job. _____ usually requires certain environmental stimuli and situations to assess the level of _____ being shown and used.

Exam Probability: **High**

22. *Answer choices:*

(see index for correct answer)

- a. imperative
- b. similarity-attraction theory
- c. empathy
- d. Skill

Guidance: level 1

:: Human resource management ::

_____ is an institutional process that maximizes performance levels and competency for an organization. The process includes all the activities needed to maintain a productive workforce, such as field service management, human resource management, performance and training management, data collection, recruiting, budgeting, forecasting, scheduling and analytics.

Exam Probability: **Medium**

23. *Answer choices:*

(see index for correct answer)

- a. Expense management
- b. Workforce management

- c. CEO succession
- d. Organizational orientations

Guidance: level 1

:: Self ::

_____ is a conscious or subconscious process in which people attempt to influence the perceptions of other people about a person, object or event. They do so by regulating and controlling information in social interaction. It was first conceptualized by Erving Goffman in 1959 in The Presentation of Self in Everyday Life, and then was expanded upon in 1967. An example of _____ theory in play is in sports such as soccer. At an important game, a player would want to showcase themselves in the best light possible, because there are college recruiters watching. This person would have the flashiest pair of cleats and try and perform their best to show off their skills. Their main goal may be to impress the college recruiters in a way that maximizes their chances of being chosen for a college team rather than winning the game.

Exam Probability: **Medium**

24. *Answer choices:*

(see index for correct answer)

- a. Impression management
- b. Generalized other
- c. Narcissism
- d. Self-actualization

Guidance: level 1

:: ::

A _____, covering letter, motivation letter, motivational letter or a letter of motivation is a letter of introduction attached to, or accompanying another document such as a résumé or curriculum vitae.

Exam Probability: **Medium**

25. *Answer choices:*

(see index for correct answer)

- a. Character
- b. similarity-attraction theory
- c. open system
- d. cultural

Guidance: level 1

:: ::

A _____ seeks to further a particular profession, the interests of individuals engaged in that profession and the public interest. In the United States, such an association is typically a nonprofit organization for tax purposes.

Exam Probability: **Medium**

26. *Answer choices:*

(see index for correct answer)

- a. imperative
- b. similarity-attraction theory
- c. personal values
- d. Professional association

Guidance: level 1

:: United States federal labor legislation ::

The _____ of 1967 is a US labor law that forbids employment discrimination against anyone at least 40 years of age in the United States. In 1967, the bill was signed into law by President Lyndon B. Johnson. The ADEA prevents age discrimination and provides equal employment opportunity under conditions that were not explicitly covered in Title VII of the Civil Rights Act of 1964. It also applies to the standards for pensions and benefits provided by employers, and requires that information concerning the needs of older workers be provided to the general public.

Exam Probability: **High**

27. *Answer choices:*

(see index for correct answer)

- a. National Industrial Recovery Act
- b. Age Discrimination in Employment Act
- c. Anti-Pinkerton Act
- d. Contract Work Hours and Safety Standards Act

Guidance: level 1

:: Lean manufacturing ::

> _____ is the Sino-Japanese word for "improvement". In business, _____ refers to activities that continuously improve all functions and involve all employees from the CEO to the assembly line workers. It also applies to processes, such as purchasing and logistics, that cross organizational boundaries into the supply chain. It has been applied in healthcare, psychotherapy, life-coaching, government, and banking.

Exam Probability: **Low**

28. *Answer choices:*

(see index for correct answer)

- a. Kaizen
- b. Production leveling

- c. Continuous improvement
- d. JobShopLean

Guidance: level 1

:: Organizational structure ::

An _____ defines how activities such as task allocation, coordination, and supervision are directed toward the achievement of organizational aims.

Exam Probability: **Low**

29. *Answer choices:*

(see index for correct answer)

- a. Organizational structure
- b. Organization of the New York City Police Department
- c. The Starfish and the Spider
- d. Unorganisation

Guidance: level 1

:: Business ::

_____ is a trade policy that does not restrict imports or exports; it can also be understood as the free market idea applied to international trade. In government, _____ is predominantly advocated by political parties that hold liberal economic positions while economically left-wing and nationalist political parties generally support protectionism, the opposite of _____ .

Exam Probability: **High**

30. *Answer choices:*

(see index for correct answer)

- a. Professional conference organiser
- b. Business development
- c. Business tourism
- d. GoCardless

Guidance: level 1

_____ is the combination of structured planning and the active management choice of one's own professional career. _____ was first defined in a social work doctoral thesis by Mary Valentich as the implementation of a career strategy through application of career tactics in relation to chosen career orientation . Career orientation referred to the overall design or pattern of one's career, shaped by particular goals and interests and identifiable by particular positions that embody these goals and interests. Career strategy pertains to the individual's general approach to the realization of career goals, and to the specificity of the goals themselves. Two general strategy approaches are adaptive and planned. Career tactics are actions to maintain oneself in a satisfactory employment situation. Tactics may be more or less assertive, with assertiveness in the work situation referring to actions taken to advance one's career interests or to exercise one's legitimate rights while respecting the rights of others.

Exam Probability: **High**

31. *Answer choices:*

(see index for correct answer)

- a. information systems assessment
- b. Career management
- c. empathy
- d. interpersonal communication

Guidance: level 1

:: Telecommuting ::

_____, also called telework, teleworking, working from home, mobile work, remote work, and flexible workplace, is a work arrangement in which employees do not commute or travel to a central place of work, such as an office building, warehouse, or store. Teleworkers in the 21st century often use mobile telecommunications technology such as Wi-Fi-equipped laptop or tablet computers and smartphones to work from coffee shops; others may use a desktop computer and a landline phone at their home. According to a Reuters poll, approximately "one in five workers around the globe, particularly employees in the Middle East, Latin America and Asia, telecommute frequently and nearly 10 percent work from home every day." In the 2000s, annual leave or vacation in some organizations was seen as absence from the workplace rather than ceasing work, and some office employees used telework to continue to check work e-mails while on vacation.

Exam Probability: **Low**

32. *Answer choices:*

(see index for correct answer)

- a. VenueGen
- b. Collaborative working environment
- c. Canadian Telework Association
- d. Calliflower

Guidance: level 1

:: Human resource management ::

A _____ is a form of payment from an employer to an employee, which may be specified in an employment contract. It is contrasted with piece wages, where each job, hour or other unit is paid separately, rather than on a periodic basis. From the point of view of running a business, _____ can also be viewed as the cost of acquiring and retaining human resources for running operations, and is then termed personnel expense or _____ expense. In accounting, salaries are recorded in payroll accounts.

Exam Probability: **Low**

33. *Answer choices:*

(see index for correct answer)

- a. Experticity
- b. Dr. Marri Channa Reddy Human Resource Development Institute of Andhra Pradesh
- c. Upward communication
- d. Salary

Guidance: level 1

:: Cognitive biases ::

In personality psychology, _____ is the degree to which people believe that they have control over the outcome of events in their lives, as opposed to external forces beyond their control. Understanding of the concept was developed by Julian B. Rotter in 1954, and has since become an aspect of personality studies. A person's "locus" is conceptualized as internal or external.

Exam Probability: **Medium**

34. *Answer choices:*

(see index for correct answer)

- a. Congruence bias
- b. Self-persuasion
- c. Locus of control
- d. Implicit cognition

Guidance: level 1

:: Training ::

_____ refers to practicing newly acquired skills beyond the point of initial mastery. The term is also often used to refer to the pedagogical theory that this form of practice leads to automaticity or other beneficial consequences.

Exam Probability: **High**

35. Answer choices:

(see index for correct answer)

- a. Overlearning
- b. Head coach
- c. National Occupational Standards
- d. Compliance training

Guidance: level 1

:: Human resource management ::

A _____ is a group of people with different functional expertise working toward a common goal. It may include people from finance, marketing, operations, and human resources departments. Typically, it includes employees from all levels of an organization. Members may also come from outside an organization.

Exam Probability: **High**

36. Answer choices:

(see index for correct answer)

- a. Job enlargement
- b. Voluntary redundancy
- c. Cross-functional team
- d. Chartered Institute of Personnel and Development

Guidance: level 1

:: Free market ::

Piece work is any type of employment in which a worker is paid a fixed _____ for each unit produced or action performed regardless of time.

Exam Probability: **Medium**

37. *Answer choices:*
(see index for correct answer)

- a. Piece rate
- b. Regulated market

Guidance: level 1

:: Training ::

_____ is a phase of training needs analysis directed at identifying which individuals within an organization should receive training.

Exam Probability: **Medium**

38. *Answer choices:*

(see index for correct answer)

- a. National Occupational Standards
- b. Person Analysis
- c. Officer training
- d. ISpring Suite

Guidance: level 1

:: Supply chain management terms ::

In business and finance, _____ is a system of organizations, people, activities, information, and resources involved in moving a product or service from supplier to customer. _____ activities involve the transformation of natural resources, raw materials, and components into a finished product that is delivered to the end customer. In sophisticated _____ systems, used products may re-enter the _____ at any point where residual value is recyclable. _____ s link value chains.

Exam Probability: **High**

39. *Answer choices:*

(see index for correct answer)

- a. Price look-up code
- b. Overstock
- c. Will call

- d. Consumables

Guidance: level 1

:: ::

A _____, medical practitioner, medical doctor, or simply doctor, is a professional who practises medicine, which is concerned with promoting, maintaining, or restoring health through the study, diagnosis, prognosis and treatment of disease, injury, and other physical and mental impairments. _____ s may focus their practice on certain disease categories, types of patients, and methods of treatment—known as specialities—or they may assume responsibility for the provision of continuing and comprehensive medical care to individuals, families, and communities—known as general practice. Medical practice properly requires both a detailed knowledge of the academic disciplines, such as anatomy and physiology, underlying diseases and their treatment—the science of medicine—and also a decent competence in its applied practice—the art or craft of medicine.

Exam Probability: **Medium**

40. *Answer choices:*
(see index for correct answer)

- a. Physician
- b. Character
- c. functional perspective
- d. imperative

Guidance: level 1

:: Employee relations ::

_____ ownership, or employee share ownership, is an ownership interest in a company held by the company's workforce. The ownership interest may be facilitated by the company as part of employees' remuneration or incentive compensation for work performed, or the company itself may be employee owned.

Exam Probability: **Low**

41. *Answer choices:*

(see index for correct answer)

- a. Employee stock
- b. Fringe benefit
- c. Employee morale
- d. Employee surveys

Guidance: level 1

:: Business law ::

In professional sports, a _____ is a player who is eligible to freely sign with any club or franchise; i.e., not under contract to any specific team. The term is also used in reference to a player who is under contract at present but who is allowed to solicit offers from other teams. In some circumstances, the _____'s options are limited by league rules.

Exam Probability: **High**

42. *Answer choices:*

(see index for correct answer)

- a. Business.gov
- b. Free agent
- c. Closed shop
- d. Teck Corp. Ltd. v. Millar

Guidance: level 1

:: Employment ::

_____ s are experiential learning opportunities, similar to internships but generally shorter, provided by partnerships between educational institutions and employers to give students short practical experiences in their field of study. In medicine it may refer to a visiting physician who is not part of the regular staff. In law, it usually refers to rigorous legal work opportunities undertaken by law students for law school credit and pay, similar to that of a junior attorney. It is derived from Latin externus and from English -ship.

Exam Probability: **Medium**

43. *Answer choices:*

(see index for correct answer)

- a. Fly-in fly-out
- b. Externship
- c. Virtual Student Foreign Service
- d. WorkKeys

Guidance: level 1

:: Validity (statistics) ::

_____ is a type of evidence that can be gathered to defend the use of a test for predicting other outcomes. It is a parameter used in sociology, psychology, and other psychometric or behavioral sciences. _____ is demonstrated when a test correlates well with a measure that has previously been validated. The two measures may be for the same construct, but more often used for different, but presumably related, constructs.

Exam Probability: **Medium**

44. *Answer choices:*

(see index for correct answer)

- a. Concurrent validity
- b. Nomological network

- c. External validity
- d. Statistical conclusion

Guidance: level 1

:: Business terms ::

A _____ is a short statement of why an organization exists, what its overall goal is, identifying the goal of its operations: what kind of product or service it provides, its primary customers or market, and its geographical region of operation. It may include a short statement of such fundamental matters as the organization's values or philosophies, a business's main competitive advantages, or a desired future state—the "vision".

Exam Probability: **Low**

45. *Answer choices:*

(see index for correct answer)

- a. churn rate
- b. Personal selling
- c. Mission statement
- d. strategic plan

Guidance: level 1

:: Training ::

A _____ is commonly known as an individual taking part in a _____ program or a graduate program within a company after having graduated from university or college.

Exam Probability: **High**

46. *Answer choices:*

(see index for correct answer)

- a. Confidence-based learning
- b. Screencast
- c. Trainee
- d. Biography Work

Guidance: level 1

:: Employment of foreign-born ::

_____ refers to the international labor pool of workers, including those employed by multinational companies and connected through a global system of networking and production, immigrant workers, transient migrant workers, telecommuting workers, those in export-oriented employment, contingent work or other precarious employment. As of 2012, the global labor pool consisted of approximately 3 billion workers, around 200 million unemployed.

Exam Probability: **High**

47. Answer choices:

(see index for correct answer)

- a. Optional Practical Training
- b. L-1 visa
- c. Global workforce
- d. Human capital flight

Guidance: level 1

:: Human resource management ::

_____, also known as organizational socialization, is management jargon first created in 1988 that refers to the mechanism through which new employees acquire the necessary knowledge, skills, and behaviors in order to become effective organizational members and insiders.

Exam Probability: **Low**

48. Answer choices:

(see index for correct answer)

- a. Vendor management system
- b. Onboarding
- c. Talent management
- d. Adecco Group North America

Guidance: level 1

:: Employment ::

_____ is a relationship between two parties, usually based on a contract where work is paid for, where one party, which may be a corporation, for profit, not-for-profit organization, co-operative or other entity is the employer and the other is the employee. Employees work in return for payment, which may be in the form of an hourly wage, by piecework or an annual salary, depending on the type of work an employee does or which sector she or he is working in. Employees in some fields or sectors may receive gratuities, bonus payment or stock options. In some types of _____ , employees may receive benefits in addition to payment. Benefits can include health insurance, housing, disability insurance or use of a gym. _____ is typically governed by _____ laws, regulations or legal contracts.

Exam Probability: **Low**

49. *Answer choices:*

(see index for correct answer)

- a. Employment
- b. ThinkTalk
- c. Adoption-Friendly Workplace
- d. Nominative determinism

Guidance: level 1

:: Corporate governance ::

An _____ is generally a person responsible for running an organization, although the exact nature of the role varies depending on the organization. In many militaries, an _____ , or "XO," is the second-in-command, reporting to the commanding officer. The XO is typically responsible for the management of day-to-day activities, freeing the commander to concentrate on strategy and planning the unit's next move.

Exam Probability: **Low**

50. *Answer choices:*

(see index for correct answer)

- a. Executive officer
- b. Corporate immune system
- c. Model Audit Rule 205
- d. Institute of Directors

Guidance: level 1

:: Recruitment ::

_____ , also known as Recruitment communications and Recruitment agency, includes all communications used by an organization to attract talent to work within it. Recruitment advertisements may be the first impression of a company for many job seekers. In turn, the strength of employer branding in job postings can directly impact interest in job openings.

Exam Probability: **High**

51. *Answer choices:*

(see index for correct answer)

- a. Campus placement
- b. Recruitment advertising
- c. Employment agency
- d. Haigui

Guidance: level 1

:: Labour relations ::

_____ is a field of study that can have different meanings depending on the context in which it is used. In an international context, it is a subfield of labor history that studies the human relations with regard to work – in its broadest sense – and how this connects to questions of social inequality. It explicitly encompasses unregulated, historical, and non-Western forms of labor. Here, _____ define "for or with whom one works and under what rules. These rules determine the type of work, type and amount of remuneration, working hours, degrees of physical and psychological strain, as well as the degree of freedom and autonomy associated with the work."

Exam Probability: **Medium**

52. *Answer choices:*

(see index for correct answer)

- a. Labor relations
- b. Union Wallonne des Entreprises
- c. United Students Against Sweatshops
- d. European Trade Union Confederation

Guidance: level 1

:: Production and manufacturing ::

_____ is a set of techniques and tools for process improvement. Though as a shortened form it may be found written as 6S, it should not be confused with the methodology known as 6S.

Exam Probability: **Low**

53. *Answer choices:*

(see index for correct answer)

- a. ISO/TS 16949
- b. Economic region of production
- c. Production part approval process
- d. Memo motion

Guidance: level 1

:: Validity (statistics) ::

In psychometrics, criterion or concrete validity is the extent to which a measure is related to an outcome. _____ is often divided into concurrent and predictive validity. Concurrent validity refers to a comparison between the measure in question and an outcome assessed at the same time. In Standards for Educational & Psychological Tests, it states, "concurrent validity reflects only the status quo at a particular time." Predictive validity, on the other hand, compares the measure in question with an outcome assessed at a later time. Although concurrent and predictive validity are similar, it is cautioned to keep the terms and findings separated. "Concurrent validity should not be used as a substitute for predictive validity without an appropriate supporting rationale."

Exam Probability: **Low**

54. *Answer choices:*

(see index for correct answer)

- a. External validity
- b. Criterion validity
- c. Concurrent validity
- d. Validation

Guidance: level 1

:: United States employment discrimination case law ::

_____, 490 U.S. 228, was an important decision by the United States Supreme Court on the issues of prescriptive sex discrimination and employer liability for sex discrimination. The employee, Ann Hopkins, sued her former employer, the accounting firm Price Waterhouse. She argued that the firm denied her partnership because she didn't fit the partners' idea of what a female employee should look like and act like. The employer failed to prove that it would have denied her partnership anyway, and the Court held that constituted sex discrimination under Title VII of the Civil Rights Act of 1964. The significance of the Supreme Court's ruling was twofold. First, it established that gender stereotyping is actionable as sex discrimination. Second, it established the mixed-motive framework that enables employees to prove discrimination when other, lawful reasons for the adverse employment action exist alongside discriminatory motivations or reasons.

Exam Probability: **Low**

55. *Answer choices:*

(see index for correct answer)

- a. Ricci v. DeStefano
- b. Reeves v. Sanderson Plumbing Products, Inc.
- c. Faragher v. City of Boca Raton
- d. Price Waterhouse v. Hopkins

Guidance: level 1

:: Human resource management ::

_____ is athletic training in sports other than the athlete's usual sport. The goal is improving overall performance. It takes advantage of the particular effectiveness of one training method to negate the shortcomings of another.

Exam Probability: **Medium**

56. *Answer choices:*

(see index for correct answer)

- a. TPI-theory
- b. Cross-training
- c. Reward management
- d. Progressive discipline

Guidance: level 1

:: ::

Educational technology is "the study and ethical practice of facilitating learning and improving performance by creating, using, and managing appropriate technological processes and resources".

Exam Probability: **High**

57. *Answer choices:*

(see index for correct answer)

- a. E-learning
- b. personal values
- c. empathy
- d. similarity-attraction theory

Guidance: level 1

:: ::

The _____ of 1938 29 U.S.C. § 203 is a United States labor law that creates the right to a minimum wage, and "time-and-a-half" overtime pay when people work over forty hours a week. It also prohibits most employment of minors in "oppressive child labor". It applies to employees engaged in interstate commerce or employed by an enterprise engaged in commerce or in the production of goods for commerce, unless the employer can claim an exemption from coverage.

Exam Probability: **Low**

58. *Answer choices:*

(see index for correct answer)

- a. imperative
- b. information systems assessment
- c. process perspective
- d. surface-level diversity

Guidance: level 1

:: Psychometrics ::

Electronic assessment, also known as e-assessment, _____, computer assisted/mediated assessment and computer-based assessment, is the use of information technology in various forms of assessment such as educational assessment, health assessment, psychiatric assessment, and psychological assessment. This may utilize an online computer connected to a network. This definition embraces a wide range of student activity ranging from the use of a word processor to on-screen testing. Specific types of e-assessment include multiple choice, online/electronic submission, computerized adaptive testing and computerized classification testing.

Exam Probability: **High**

59. *Answer choices:*

(see index for correct answer)

- a. Borderline intellectual functioning
- b. Citizen survey
- c. Multistage testing
- d. Online assessment

Guidance: level 1

Information systems

Information systems (IS) are formal, sociotechnical, organizational systems designed to collect, process, store, and distribute information. In a sociotechnical perspective Information Systems are composed by four components: technology, process, people and organizational structure.

:: User interfaces ::

_____, keystroke biometrics, typing dynamics and lately typing biometrics, is the detailed timing information which describes exactly when each key was pressed and when it was released as a person is typing at a computer keyboard.

Exam Probability: **Medium**

1. *Answer choices:*

(see index for correct answer)

- a. System console
- b. User Research
- c. Ttyrec
- d. Keystroke dynamics

Guidance: level 1

:: Digital rights management ::

_____ tools or technological protection measures are a set of access control technologies for restricting the use of proprietary hardware and copyrighted works. DRM technologies try to control the use, modification, and distribution of copyrighted works , as well as systems within devices that enforce these policies.

Exam Probability: **Low**

2. *Answer choices:*

(see index for correct answer)

- a. Digital rights management
- b. Protected Media Path

- c. Active Directory Rights Management Services
- d. Perpetual access

Guidance: level 1

:: E-commerce ::

The phrase _____ was originally coined in 1997 by Kevin Duffey at the launch of the Global _____ Forum, to mean "the delivery of electronic commerce capabilities directly into the consumer's hand, anywhere, via wireless technology." Many choose to think of _____ as meaning "a retail outlet in your customer's pocket."

Exam Probability: **Low**

3. *Answer choices:*

(see index for correct answer)

- a. Zingiri
- b. Mobile commerce
- c. Electronic Payment Services
- d. Segundamano

Guidance: level 1

:: Data security ::

_____, sometimes shortened to InfoSec, is the practice of preventing unauthorized access, use, disclosure, disruption, modification, inspection, recording or destruction of information. The information or data may take any form, e.g. electronic or physical. _____'s primary focus is the balanced protection of the confidentiality, integrity and availability of data while maintaining a focus on efficient policy implementation, all without hampering organization productivity. This is largely achieved through a multi-step risk management process that identifies assets, threat sources, vulnerabilities, potential impacts, and possible controls, followed by assessment of the effectiveness of the risk management plan.

Exam Probability: **Low**

4. *Answer choices:*

(see index for correct answer)

- a. Security level management
- b. LogLogic
- c. Password fatigue
- d. Screening router

Guidance: level 1

:: Market research ::

_____ is the action of defining, gathering, analyzing, and distributing intelligence about products, customers, competitors, and any aspect of the environment needed to support executives and managers in strategic decision making for an organization.

Exam Probability: **Low**

5. *Answer choices:*

(see index for correct answer)

- a. Nielsen SoundScan
- b. Early adopter
- c. Customer satisfaction research
- d. Situation analysis

Guidance: level 1

:: ::

_____ is the fundamental facilities and systems serving a country, city, or other area, including the services and facilities necessary for its economy to function. _____ is composed of public and private physical improvements such as roads, bridges, tunnels, water supply, sewers, electrical grids, and telecommunications . In general, it has also been defined as "the physical components of interrelated systems providing commodities and services essential to enable, sustain, or enhance societal living conditions".

Exam Probability: **Medium**

6. *Answer choices:*

(see index for correct answer)

- a. Infrastructure

- b. imperative
- c. open system
- d. Sarbanes-Oxley act of 2002

Guidance: level 1

:: Management ::

> Porter's Five Forces Framework is a tool for analyzing competition of a business. It draws from industrial organization economics to derive five forces that determine the competitive intensity and, therefore, the attractiveness of an industry in terms of its profitability. An "unattractive" industry is one in which the effect of these five forces reduces overall profitability. The most unattractive industry would be one approaching "pure competition", in which available profits for all firms are driven to normal profit levels. The five-forces perspective is associated with its originator, Michael E. Porter of Harvard University. This framework was first published in Harvard Business Review in 1979.

Exam Probability: **High**

7. *Answer choices:*

(see index for correct answer)

- a. Porter five forces analysis
- b. Project stakeholder
- c. Double linking
- d. Matrix management

Guidance: level 1

:: Data modeling languages ::

An entity–relationship model describes interrelated things of interest in a specific domain of knowledge. A basic ER model is composed of entity types and specifies relationships that can exist between entities.

Exam Probability: **Low**

8. *Answer choices:*

(see index for correct answer)

- a. Entity-relationship
- b. Common Business Communication Language
- c. Information Object Class
- d. XSIL

Guidance: level 1

:: Distribution, retailing, and wholesaling ::

_____ measures the performance of a system. Certain goals are defined and the _____ gives the percentage to which those goals should be achieved. Fill rate is different from _____ .

Exam Probability: **Medium**

9. *Answer choices:*

(see index for correct answer)

- a. Filling station
- b. Foodservice distributor
- c. Independent Publishers Group
- d. Capital City Distribution

Guidance: level 1

:: Information science ::

_____ has been defined as "the branch of ethics that focuses on the relationship between the creation, organization, dissemination, and use of information, and the ethical standards and moral codes governing human conduct in society". It examines the morality that comes from information as a resource, a product, or as a target. It provides a critical framework for considering moral issues concerning informational privacy, moral agency, new environmental issues, problems arising from the life-cycle of information. It is very vital to understand that librarians, archivists, information professionals among others, really understand the importance of knowing how to disseminate proper information as well as being responsible with their actions when addressing information.

Exam Probability: **High**

10. *Answer choices:*

(see index for correct answer)

- a. Information ethics
- b. Investigative Data Warehouse
- c. Visual Paradigm for UML
- d. Browsing

Guidance: level 1

:: Satellite navigation systems ::

> _____ Galilei was an Italian astronomer, physicist and engineer, sometimes described as a polymath. _____ has been called the "father of observational astronomy", the "father of modern physics", the "father of the scientific method", and the "father of modern science".

Exam Probability: **High**

11. *Answer choices:*

(see index for correct answer)

- a. Dilution of precision
- b. Transit
- c. Galileo
- d. Quasi-Zenith Satellite System

Guidance: level 1

A web _____ or Internet _____ is a software system that is designed to carry out web search, which means to search the World Wide Web in a systematic way for particular information specified in a web search query. The search results are generally presented in a line of results, often referred to as _____ results pages. The information may be a mix of web pages, images, videos, infographics, articles, research papers and other types of files. Some _____ s also mine data available in databases or open directories. Unlike web directories, which are maintained only by human editors, _____ s also maintain real-time information by running an algorithm on a web crawler. Internet content that is not capable of being searched by a web _____ is generally described as the deep web.

Exam Probability: **High**

12. *Answer choices:*

(see index for correct answer)

- a. imperative
- b. similarity-attraction theory
- c. corporate values
- d. Search engine

Guidance: level 1

A _____ is a discussion or informational website published on the World Wide Web consisting of discrete, often informal diary-style text entries. Posts are typically displayed in reverse chronological order, so that the most recent post appears first, at the top of the web page. Until 2009, _____ s were usually the work of a single individual, occasionally of a small group, and often covered a single subject or topic. In the 2010s, "multi-author _____ s" emerged, featuring the writing of multiple authors and sometimes professionally edited. MABs from newspapers, other media outlets, universities, think tanks, advocacy groups, and similar institutions account for an increasing quantity of _____ traffic. The rise of Twitter and other "micro _____ ging" systems helps integrate MABs and single-author _____ s into the news media. _____ can also be used as a verb, meaning to maintain or add content to a _____ .

Exam Probability: **High**

13. *Answer choices:*

(see index for correct answer)

- a. levels of analysis
- b. interpersonal communication
- c. corporate values
- d. Character

Guidance: level 1

:: Strategic management ::

_____ is a management term for an element that is necessary for an organization or project to achieve its mission. Alternative terms are key result area and key success factor.

Exam Probability: **High**

14. *Answer choices:*

(see index for correct answer)

- a. Predictable surprise
- b. Critical success factor
- c. strategy implementation
- d. International business strategy

Guidance: level 1

:: Information technology management ::

_____s or pop-ups are forms of online advertising on the World Wide Web. A pop-up is a graphical user interface display area, usually a small window, that suddenly appears in the foreground of the visual interface. The pop-up window containing an advertisement is usually generated by JavaScript that uses cross-site scripting, sometimes with a secondary payload that uses Adobe Flash. They can also be generated by other vulnerabilities/security holes in browser security.

Exam Probability: **Medium**

15. *Answer choices:*

(see index for correct answer)

- a. Pop-up ad
- b. HP ePrint
- c. ISO/IEC JTC 1/SC 40
- d. Application Services Library

Guidance: level 1

:: Google services ::

A blog is a discussion or informational website published on the World Wide Web consisting of discrete, often informal diary-style text entries. Posts are typically displayed in reverse chronological order, so that the most recent post appears first, at the top of the web page. Until 2009, blogs were usually the work of a single individual, occasionally of a small group, and often covered a single subject or topic. In the 2010s, "multi-author blogs" emerged, featuring the writing of multiple authors and sometimes professionally edited. MABs from newspapers, other media outlets, universities, think tanks, advocacy groups, and similar institutions account for an increasing quantity of blog traffic. The rise of Twitter and other "microblogging" systems helps integrate MABs and single-author blogs into the news media. Blog can also be used as a verb, meaning to maintain or add content to a blog.

Exam Probability: **Medium**

16. *Answer choices:*

(see index for correct answer)

- a. Google Public DNS
- b. Google Grants
- c. Google Translator Toolkit
- d. Google Gadgets

Guidance: level 1

:: E-commerce ::

_____ is a method of e-commerce where shoppers' friends become involved in the shopping experience. _____ attempts to use technology to mimic the social interactions found in physical malls and stores. With the rise of mobile devices, _____ is now extending beyond the online world and into the offline world of shopping.

Exam Probability: **Medium**

17. *Answer choices:*

(see index for correct answer)

- a. Wildcard certificate
- b. Confinity
- c. Transactional Link
- d. Social shopping

Guidance: level 1

:: Information technology management ::

The term _____ is used to refer to periods when a system is unavailable. _____ or outage duration refers to a period of time that a system fails to provide or perform its primary function. Reliability, availability, recovery, and unavailability are related concepts. The unavailability is the proportion of a time-span that a system is unavailable or offline. This is usually a result of the system failing to function because of an unplanned event, or because of routine maintenance.

Exam Probability: **High**

18. *Answer choices:*

(see index for correct answer)

- a. Downtime
- b. ITIL security management
- c. Global Information Governance Day
- d. Wire data

Guidance: level 1

:: Credit cards ::

A _____ is a payment card issued to users to enable the cardholder to pay a merchant for goods and services based on the cardholder's promise to the card issuer to pay them for the amounts plus the other agreed charges. The card issuer creates a revolving account and grants a line of credit to the cardholder, from which the cardholder can borrow money for payment to a merchant or as a cash advance.

Exam Probability: **Medium**

19. *Answer choices:*

(see index for correct answer)

- a. Ingenico
- b. TaiwanMoney Card
- c. SBI Cards
- d. China UnionPay

Guidance: level 1

:: Data management ::

_____ , or OLAP , is an approach to answer multi-dimensional analytical queries swiftly in computing. OLAP is part of the broader category of business intelligence, which also encompasses relational databases, report writing and data mining. Typical applications of OLAP include business reporting for sales, marketing, management reporting, business process management , budgeting and forecasting, financial reporting and similar areas, with new applications emerging, such as agriculture. The term OLAP was created as a slight modification of the traditional database term online transaction processing .

Exam Probability: **High**

20. *Answer choices:*

(see index for correct answer)

- a. Online analytical processing
- b. Query language
- c. Paper data storage
- d. single sourcing

Guidance: level 1

:: Web analytics ::

A click path or _____ is the sequence of hyperlinks one or more website visitors follows on a given site, presented in the order viewed. A visitor's click path may start within the website or at a separate 3rd party website, often a search engine results page, and it continues as a sequence of successive webpages visited by the user. Click paths take call data and can match it to ad sources, keywords, and/or referring domains, in order to capture data.

Exam Probability: **High**

21. *Answer choices:*

(see index for correct answer)

- a. Clickstream

- b. PostRank
- c. Webtrends
- d. CrawlTrack

Guidance: level 1

:: Tag editors ::

_____ is a media player, media library, Internet radio broadcaster, and mobile device management application developed by Apple Inc. It was announced on January 9, 2001. It is used to play, download, and organize digital multimedia files, including music and video, on personal computers running the macOS and Windows operating systems. Content must be purchased through the _____ Store, whereas _____ is the software letting users manage their purchases.

Exam Probability: **High**

22. *Answer choices:*

(see index for correct answer)

- a. EasyTag
- b. ExifTool
- c. Foobar2000
- d. ITunes

Guidance: level 1

:: Internet advertising ::

_____ , according to the United States federal law known as the Anti _____ Consumer Protection Act, is registering, trafficking in, or using an Internet domain name with bad faith intent to profit from the goodwill of a trademark belonging to someone else. The cybersquatter then offers to sell the domain to the person or company who owns a trademark contained within the name at an inflated price.

Exam Probability: **High**

23. *Answer choices:*

(see index for correct answer)

- a. Cybersquatting
- b. Jason Harris
- c. Joe job
- d. LeadBolt

Guidance: level 1

:: Costs ::

In economics, _____ is the total economic cost of production and is made up of variable cost, which varies according to the quantity of a good produced and includes inputs such as labour and raw materials, plus fixed cost, which is independent of the quantity of a good produced and includes inputs that cannot be varied in the short term: fixed costs such as buildings and machinery, including sunk costs if any. Since cost is measured per unit of time, it is a flow variable.

Exam Probability: **Low**

24. *Answer choices:*

(see index for correct answer)

- a. Average cost
- b. Cost of products sold
- c. Direct labor cost
- d. Total cost

Guidance: level 1

:: E-commerce ::

Electronic governance or e-governance is the application of information and communication technology for delivering government services, exchange of information, communication transactions, integration of various stand-alone systems and services between government-to-citizen , _____ , government-to-government , government-to-employees as well as back-office processes and interactions within the entire government framework. Through e-governance, government services are made available to citizens in a convenient, efficient, and transparent manner. The three main target groups that can be distinguished in governance concepts are government, citizens, andbusinesses/interest groups. In e-governance, there are no distinct boundaries.

Exam Probability: **Low**

25. *Answer choices:*

(see index for correct answer)

- a. Electronic bill payment
- b. Business-to-manager
- c. IzzoNet
- d. Government-to-business

Guidance: level 1

:: Cloud storage ::

_____ was an online backup service for both Windows and macOS users. Linux support was made available in Q3, 2014. In 2007 _____ was acquired by EMC, and in 2013 _____ was included in the EMC Backup Recovery Systems division's product list.On September 7, 2016, Dell Inc. acquired EMC Corporation to form Dell Technologies, restructuring the original Dell Inc. as a subsidiary of Dell Technologies.. On March 19, 2018 Carbonite acquired _____ from Dell for $148.5 million in cash and in 2019 shut down the service, incorporating _____ 's clients into its own online backup service programs.

Exam Probability: **Medium**

26. *Answer choices:*

(see index for correct answer)

- a. Mozy
- b. GreenQloud
- c. Pdfvue
- d. The Linkup

Guidance: level 1

:: History of human–computer interaction ::

A _____, plural mice, is a small rodent characteristically having a pointed snout, small rounded ears, a body-length scaly tail and a high breeding rate. The best known _____ species is the common house _____. It is also a popular pet. In some places, certain kinds of field mice are locally common. They are known to invade homes for food and shelter.

Exam Probability: **Low**

27. *Answer choices:*

(see index for correct answer)

- a. Block-oriented terminal
- b. Eye tracking
- c. Mouse
- d. Sketchpad

Guidance: level 1

:: Data management ::

Data aggregation is the compiling of information from databases with intent to prepare combined datasets for data processing.

Exam Probability: **Low**

28. *Answer choices:*

(see index for correct answer)

- a. Clustered file system
- b. Conference on Innovative Data Systems Research
- c. Metadirectory
- d. Data aggregator

Guidance: level 1

:: Automatic identification and data capture ::

_____ is human–computer interaction in which a computer is expected to be transported during normal usage, which allows for transmission of data, voice and video. _____ involves mobile communication, mobile hardware, and mobile software. Communication issues include ad hoc networks and infrastructure networks as well as communication properties, protocols, data formats and concrete technologies. Hardware includes mobile devices or device components. Mobile software deals with the characteristics and requirements of mobile applications.

Exam Probability: **High**

29. *Answer choices:*

(see index for correct answer)

- a. Track and trace
- b. Digital Automated Identification SYstem
- c. Mobile computing
- d. Molecular computational identification

Guidance: level 1

:: ::

_____ is a kind of action that occur as two or more objects have an effect upon one another. The idea of a two-way effect is essential in the concept of _____, as opposed to a one-way causal effect. A closely related term is interconnectivity, which deals with the _____ s of _____ s within systems: combinations of many simple _____ s can lead to surprising emergent phenomena. _____ has different tailored meanings in various sciences. Changes can also involve _____.

Exam Probability: **Low**

30. *Answer choices:*
(see index for correct answer)

- a. Character
- b. empathy
- c. personal values
- d. Interaction

Guidance: level 1

:: Information systems ::

A _____ manages the creation and modification of digital content. It typically supports multiple users in a collaborative environment.

Exam Probability: **Low**

31. *Answer choices:*

(see index for correct answer)

- a. Policy appliances
- b. Social Study of Information Systems
- c. Content management system
- d. NESI

Guidance: level 1

:: ::

A _____ is a published declaration of the intentions, motives, or views of the issuer, be it an individual, group, political party or government. A _____ usually accepts a previously published opinion or public consensus or promotes a new idea with prescriptive notions for carrying out changes the author believes should be made. It often is political or artistic in nature, but may present an individual's life stance. _____ s relating to religious belief are generally referred to as creeds.

Exam Probability: **High**

32. *Answer choices:*

(see index for correct answer)

- a. open system
- b. empathy
- c. co-culture

- d. similarity-attraction theory

Guidance: level 1

:: Google services ::

_____ is a word processor included as part of a free, web-based software office suite offered by Google within its Google Drive service. This service also includes Google Sheets and Google Slides, a spreadsheet and presentation program respectively. _____ is available as a web application, mobile app for Android, iOS, Windows, BlackBerry, and as a desktop application on Google's ChromeOS. The app is compatible with Microsoft Office file formats. The application allows users to create and edit files online while collaborating with other users in real-time. Edits are tracked by user with a revision history presenting changes. An editor's position is highlighted with an editor-specific color and cursor. A permissions system regulates what users can do. Updates have introduced features using machine learning, including "Explore", offering search results based on the contents of a document, and "Action items", allowing users to assign tasks to other users.

Exam Probability: **Low**

33. *Answer choices:*

(see index for correct answer)

- a. Google News
- b. Google Friend Connect
- c. Google Docs
- d. Google Trends

Guidance: level 1

:: Contract law ::

_____ refers to a situation where a statement's author cannot successfully dispute its authorship or the validity of an associated contract. The term is often seen in a legal setting when the authenticity of a signature is being challenged. In such an instance, the authenticity is being "repudiated".

Exam Probability: **High**

34. *Answer choices:*

(see index for correct answer)

- a. Transmutation agreement
- b. Mandatory rule
- c. Non-repudiation
- d. Franchisor

Guidance: level 1

:: Marketing by medium ::

_____ , also called online marketing or Internet advertising or web advertising, is a form of marketing and advertising which uses the Internet to deliver promotional marketing messages to consumers. Many consumers find _____ disruptive and have increasingly turned to ad blocking for a variety of reasons. When software is used to do the purchasing, it is known as programmatic advertising.

Exam Probability: **Medium**

35. *Answer choices:*

(see index for correct answer)

- a. Social video marketing
- b. Brand infiltration
- c. Viral marketing
- d. Direct Text Marketing

Guidance: level 1

:: Network management ::

_____ is the process of administering and managing computer networks. Services provided by this discipline include fault analysis, performance management, provisioning of networks and maintaining the quality of service. Software that enables network administrators to perform their functions is called _____ software.

Exam Probability: **High**

36. *Answer choices:*

(see index for correct answer)

- a. Managed object
- b. Real user monitoring
- c. Oracle Enterprise Manager Ops Center
- d. Network management

Guidance: level 1

:: Computing input devices ::

In computing, an _____ is a piece of computer hardware equipment used to provide data and control signals to an information processing system such as a computer or information appliance. Examples of _____ s include keyboards, mouse, scanners, digital cameras and joysticks. Audio _____ s may be used for purposes including speech recognition. Many companies are utilizing speech recognition to help assist users to use their device.

Exam Probability: **Low**

37. *Answer choices:*

(see index for correct answer)

- a. Robotic book scanner
- b. Sign language glove
- c. Motion capture
- d. Input device

Guidance: level 1

:: Ubiquitous computing ::

A _____, chip card, or integrated circuit card is a physical electronic authorization device, used to control access to a resource. It is typically a plastic credit card sized card with an embedded integrated circuit. Many _____ s include a pattern of metal contacts to electrically connect to the internal chip. Others are contactless, and some are both. _____ s can provide personal identification, authentication, data storage, and application processing. Applications include identification, financial, mobile phones, public transit, computer security, schools, and healthcare. _____ s may provide strong security authentication for single sign-on within organizations. Several nations have deployed _____ s throughout their populations.

Exam Probability: **Low**

38. *Answer choices:*

(see index for correct answer)

- a. Automatic vehicle location
- b. Ubiquitous Communicator
- c. Calm technology
- d. Smart card

Guidance: level 1

:: Commerce websites ::

_____ is an American classified advertisements website with sections devoted to jobs, housing, for sale, items wanted, services, community service, gigs, résumés, and discussion forums.

Exam Probability: **Low**

39. *Answer choices:*

(see index for correct answer)

- a. Tocquigny
- b. TigerDirect
- c. Coast to Coast Tickets
- d. Square Meal

Guidance: level 1

:: Production and manufacturing ::

_____ is the manufacturing approach of using computers to control entire production process. This integration allows individual processes to exchange information with each other and initiate actions. Although manufacturing can be faster and less error-prone by the integration of computers, the main advantage is the ability to create automated manufacturing processes. Typically CIM relies of closed-loop control processes, based on real-time input from sensors. It is also known as flexible design and manufacturing.

Exam Probability: **Medium**

40. *Answer choices:*

(see index for correct answer)

- a. EFQM Excellence Model
- b. Rolled throughput yield
- c. Computer-integrated manufacturing
- d. Fab lab

Guidance: level 1

:: ::

A _____ , sometimes called a passcode, is a memorized secret used to confirm the identity of a user. Using the terminology of the NIST Digital Identity Guidelines, the secret is memorized by a party called the claimant while the party verifying the identity of the claimant is called the verifier. When the claimant successfully demonstrates knowledge of the _____ to the verifier through an established authentication protocol, the verifier is able to infer the claimant's identity.

Exam Probability: **High**

41. *Answer choices:*

(see index for correct answer)

- a. deep-level diversity

- b. Sarbanes-Oxley act of 2002
- c. Character
- d. Password

Guidance: level 1

:: Information technology management ::

> B2B is often contrasted with business-to-consumer. In B2B commerce, it is often the case that the parties to the relationship have comparable negotiating power, and even when they do not, each party typically involves professional staff and legal counsel in the negotiation of terms, whereas B2C is shaped to a far greater degree by economic implications of information asymmetry. However, within a B2B context, large companies may have many commercial, resource and information advantages over smaller businesses. The United Kingdom government, for example, created the post of Small Business Commissioner under the Enterprise Act 2016 to "enable small businesses to resolve disputes" and "consider complaints by small business suppliers about payment issues with larger businesses that they supply."

Exam Probability: **Medium**

42. *Answer choices:*
(see index for correct answer)

- a. Website promotion
- b. High Availability Application Architecture
- c. ITIL security management
- d. Business-to-business

Guidance: level 1

:: Internet privacy ::

An _____ is a private network accessible only to an organization's staff. Often, a wide range of information and services are available on an organization's internal _____ that are unavailable to the public, unlike the Internet. A company-wide _____ can constitute an important focal point of internal communication and collaboration, and provide a single starting point to access internal and external resources. In its simplest form, an _____ is established with the technologies for local area networks and wide area networks . Many modern _____ s have search engines, user profiles, blogs, mobile apps with notifications, and events planning within their infrastructure.

Exam Probability: **High**

43. *Answer choices:*

(see index for correct answer)

- a. Intranet
- b. Geolocation
- c. Proxify
- d. Cypherpunks

Guidance: level 1

:: Information systems ::

An _____, or a group of such silos, is an insular management system in which one information system or subsystem is incapable of reciprocal operation with others that are, or should be, related. Thus information is not adequately shared but rather remains sequestered within each system or subsystem, figuratively trapped within a container like grain is trapped within a silo: there may be a lot of it, and it may be stacked quite high and freely available within those limits, but it has no effect outside those limits. Such data silos are proving to be an obstacle for businesses wishing to use data mining to make productive use of their data.

Exam Probability: **Low**

44. *Answer choices:*

(see index for correct answer)

- a. Semantic desktop
- b. Strategic information system
- c. Research Objects
- d. Information engineering

Guidance: level 1

:: Payment systems ::

_____s are part of a payment system issued by financial institutions, such as a bank, to a customer that enables its owner to access the funds in the customer's designated bank accounts, or through a credit account and make payments by electronic funds transfer and access automated teller machines. Such cards are known by a variety of names including bank cards, ATM cards, MAC, client cards, key cards or cash cards.

Exam Probability: **Medium**

45. *Answer choices:*

(see index for correct answer)

- a. Manual fare collection
- b. Payment card
- c. GreenZap
- d. Money order

Guidance: level 1

:: Process management ::

When used in the context of communication networks, such as Ethernet or packet radio, _____ or network _____ is the rate of successful message delivery over a communication channel. The data these messages belong to may be delivered over a physical or logical link, or it can pass through a certain network node. _____ is usually measured in bits per second, and sometimes in data packets per second or data packets per time slot.

Exam Probability: **Medium**

46. *Answer choices:*

(see index for correct answer)

- a. Defects per million opportunities
- b. Artifact-centric business process model
- c. Throughput
- d. Revenue assurance

Guidance: level 1

:: ::

_____ is a free email service developed by Google. Users can access _____ on the web and using third-party programs that synchronize email content through POP or IMAP protocols. _____ started as a limited beta release on April 1, 2004 and ended its testing phase on July 7, 2009.

Exam Probability: **Low**

47. *Answer choices:*

(see index for correct answer)

- a. imperative
- b. information systems assessment
- c. similarity-attraction theory

- d. Gmail

Guidance: level 1

:: Business models ::

_____, or The Computer Utility, is a service provisioning model in which a service provider makes computing resources and infrastructure management available to the customer as needed, and charges them for specific usage rather than a flat rate. Like other types of on-demand computing, the utility model seeks to maximize the efficient use of resources and/or minimize associated costs. Utility is the packaging of system resources, such as computation, storage and services, as a metered service. This model has the advantage of a low or no initial cost to acquire computer resources; instead, resources are essentially rented.

Exam Probability: **High**

48. *Answer choices:*

(see index for correct answer)

- a. Freemium
- b. Component business model
- c. Lemonade stand
- d. Utility computing

Guidance: level 1

:: Payment systems ::

A _____ is any system used to settle financial transactions through the transfer of monetary value. This includes the institutions, instruments, people, rules, procedures, standards, and technologies that make it exchange possible. A common type of _____ is called an operational network that links bank accounts and provides for monetary exchange using bank deposits. Some _____ s also include credit mechanisms, which are essentially a different aspect of payment.

Exam Probability: **Low**

49. *Answer choices:*

(see index for correct answer)

- a. Payment system
- b. Honesty bar
- c. Lemon Wallet
- d. Payment service provider

Guidance: level 1

:: Classification systems ::

_____ is the practice of comparing business processes and performance metrics to industry bests and best practices from other companies. Dimensions typically measured are quality, time and cost.

Exam Probability: **Low**

50. *Answer choices:*

(see index for correct answer)

- a. Bautz-Morgan classification
- b. Carnegie Classification of Institutions of Higher Education
- c. Transformed cladistics
- d. Benchmarking

Guidance: level 1

:: Data analysis ::

_____ , also referred to as text data mining, roughly equivalent to text analytics, is the process of deriving high-quality information from text. High-quality information is typically derived through the devising of patterns and trends through means such as statistical pattern learning. _____ usually involves the process of structuring the input text , deriving patterns within the structured data, and finally evaluation and interpretation of the output. 'High quality' in _____ usually refers to some combination of relevance, novelty, and interest. Typical _____ tasks include text categorization, text clustering, concept/entity extraction, production of granular taxonomies, sentiment analysis, document summarization, and entity relation modeling .

Exam Probability: **Medium**

51. *Answer choices:*

(see index for correct answer)

- a. Data definition specification
- b. Limited dependent variable
- c. Oversampling and undersampling in data analysis
- d. Standard deviation

Guidance: level 1

:: Big data ::

_____ is the discovery, interpretation, and communication of meaningful patterns in data; and the process of applying those patterns towards effective decision making. In other words, _____ can be understood as the connective tissue between data and effective decision making, within an organization. Especially valuable in areas rich with recorded information, _____ relies on the simultaneous application of statistics, computer programming and operations research to quantify performance.

Exam Probability: **High**

52. *Answer choices:*

(see index for correct answer)

- a. Hue
- b. Analytics
- c. Data literacy
- d. Medopad

Guidance: level 1

:: Market research ::

_____s are many different distantly related animals that typically have a long cylindrical tube-like body and no limbs. _____s vary in size from microscopic to over 1 metre in length for marine polychaete _____s , 6.7 metres for the African giant earth _____, Microchaetus rappi, and 58 metres for the marine nemertean _____, Lineus longissimus. Various types of _____ occupy a small variety of parasitic niches, living inside the bodies of other animals. Free-living _____ species do not live on land, but instead, live in marine or freshwater environments, or underground by burrowing.In biology, "_____" refers to an obsolete taxon, vermes, used by Carolus Linnaeus and Jean-Baptiste Lamarck for all non-arthropod invertebrate animals, now seen to be paraphyletic. The name stems from the Old English word wyrm. Most animals called "_____s" are invertebrates, but the term is also used for the amphibian caecilians and the slow _____ Anguis, a legless burrowing lizard. Invertebrate animals commonly called "_____s" include annelids , nematodes , platyhelminthes , marine nemertean _____s , marine Chaetognatha , priapulid _____s, and insect larvae such as grubs and maggots.

Exam Probability: **Low**

53. *Answer choices:*
(see index for correct answer)

- a. The Ehrenberg-Bass Institute for Marketing Science
- b. Monroe Mendelsohn Research
- c. PreTesting Company
- d. Worm

Guidance: level 1

:: Management ::

A _____ defines or constrains some aspect of business and always resolves to either true or false. _____ s are intended to assert business structure or to control or influence the behavior of the business. _____ s describe the operations, definitions and constraints that apply to an organization. _____ s can apply to people, processes, corporate behavior and computing systems in an organization, and are put in place to help the organization achieve its goals.

Exam Probability: **High**

54. *Answer choices:*

(see index for correct answer)

- a. Business rule
- b. Toxic leader
- c. Remedial action
- d. Scenario planning

Guidance: level 1

:: Management ::

In business, a _____ is the attribute that allows an organization to outperform its competitors. A _____ may include access to natural resources, such as high-grade ores or a low-cost power source, highly skilled labor, geographic location, high entry barriers, and access to new technology.

Exam Probability: **Low**

55. *Answer choices:*

(see index for correct answer)

- a. Competitive advantage
- b. Place management
- c. SimulTrain
- d. Action item

Guidance: level 1

:: Procurement practices ::

_____ or commercially available off-the-shelf products are packaged solutions which are then adapted to satisfy the needs of the purchasing organization, rather than the commissioning of custom-made, or bespoke, solutions. A related term, Mil-COTS, refers to COTS products for use by the U.S. military.

Exam Probability: **Low**

56. Answer choices:

(see index for correct answer)

- a. Syndicated procurement
- b. Construction by configuration

Guidance: level 1

:: ::

_____, Inc. was a company that provided human resource management systems, Financial Management Solutions, supply chain management, customer relationship management, and enterprise performance management software, as well as software for manufacturing, and student administration to large corporations, governments, and organizations. It existed as an independent corporation until its acquisition by Oracle Corporation in 2005. The _____ name and product line are now marketed by Oracle.

Exam Probability: **High**

57. Answer choices:

(see index for correct answer)

- a. PeopleSoft
- b. levels of analysis
- c. imperative
- d. cultural

Guidance: level 1

:: Computer security standards ::

> The _____ for Information Technology Security Evaluation is an international standard for computer security certification. It is currently in version 3.1 revision 5.

Exam Probability: **High**

58. *Answer choices:*

(see index for correct answer)

- a. Common Criteria
- b. CTCPEC
- c. FIPS 140
- d. ISO 27799

Guidance: level 1

:: Teams ::

A _____ usually refers to a group of individuals who work together from different geographic locations and rely on communication technology such as email, FAX, and video or voice conferencing services in order to collaborate. The term can also refer to groups or teams that work together asynchronously or across organizational levels. Powell, Piccoli and Ives define _____ s as "groups of geographically, organizationally and/or time dispersed workers brought together by information and telecommunication technologies to accomplish one or more organizational tasks." According to Ale Ebrahim et. al., _____ s can also be defined as "small temporary groups of geographically, organizationally and/or time dispersed knowledge workers who coordinate their work predominantly with electronic information and communication technologies in order to accomplish one or more organization tasks."

Exam Probability: **High**

59. *Answer choices:*

(see index for correct answer)

- a. team composition
- b. Team-building

Guidance: level 1

Marketing

   Marketing is the study and management of exchange relationships. Marketing is the business process of creating relationships with and satisfying customers. With its focus on the customer, marketing is one of the premier components of business management.
  Marketing is defined by the American Marketing Association as "the activity, set of institutions, and processes for creating, communicating, delivering, and exchanging offerings that have value for customers, clients, partners, and society at large."

_____ characterises the behaviour of a system or model whose components interact in multiple ways and follow local rules, meaning there is no reasonable higher instruction to define the various possible interactions.

Exam Probability: **High**

1. *Answer choices:*

(see index for correct answer)

- a. hierarchical
- b. deep-level diversity
- c. Complexity
- d. similarity-attraction theory

Guidance: level 1

:: Monopoly (economics) ::

A _____ exists when a specific person or enterprise is the only supplier of a particular commodity. This contrasts with a monopsony which relates to a single entity's control of a market to purchase a good or service, and with oligopoly which consists of a few sellers dominating a market. Monopolies are thus characterized by a lack of economic competition to produce the good or service, a lack of viable substitute goods, and the possibility of a high _____ price well above the seller`s marginal cost that leads to a high _____ profit. The verb monopolise or monopolize refers to the process by which a company gains the ability to raise prices or exclude competitors. In economics, a _____ is a single seller. In law, a _____ is a business entity that has significant market power, that is, the power to charge overly high prices. Although monopolies may be big businesses, size is not a characteristic of a _____ . A small business may still have the power to raise prices in a small industry .

Exam Probability: **High**

2. *Answer choices:*

(see index for correct answer)

- a. Cost per procedure
- b. Complementary monopoly
- c. Barriers to exit
- d. Monopoly

Guidance: level 1

:: ::

Consumer behaviour is the study of individuals, groups, or organizations and all the activities associated with the purchase, use and disposal of goods and services, including the consumer's emotional, mental and behavioural responses that precede or follow these activities. Consumer behaviour emerged in the 1940s and 50s as a distinct sub-discipline in the marketing area.

Exam Probability: **Medium**

3. *Answer choices:*

(see index for correct answer)

- a. Character
- b. interpersonal communication
- c. Sarbanes-Oxley act of 2002
- d. Consumer behavior

Guidance: level 1

:: ::

In business and engineering, new _____ covers the complete process of bringing a new product to market. A central aspect of NPD is product design, along with various business considerations. New _____ is described broadly as the transformation of a market opportunity into a product available for sale. The product can be tangible or intangible, though sometimes services and other processes are distinguished from "products." NPD requires an understanding of customer needs and wants, the competitive environment, and the nature of the market. Cost, time and quality are the main variables that drive customer needs. Aiming at these three variables, innovative companies develop continuous practices and strategies to better satisfy customer requirements and to increase their own market share by a regular development of new products. There are many uncertainties and challenges which companies must face throughout the process. The use of best practices and the elimination of barriers to communication are the main concerns for the management of the NPD.

Exam Probability: **Low**

4. *Answer choices:*

(see index for correct answer)

- a. similarity-attraction theory
- b. corporate values
- c. Character
- d. Product development

Guidance: level 1

:: Product management ::

`_____` is a phrase used in the marketing industry which describes the value of having a well-known brand name, based on the idea that the owner of a well-known brand name can generate more revenue simply from brand recognition; that is from products with that brand name than from products with a less well known name, as consumers believe that a product with a well-known name is better than products with less well-known names.

Exam Probability: **High**

5. *Answer choices:*

(see index for correct answer)

- a. Product cost management
- b. Tipping point
- c. Brand equity
- d. Whole product

Guidance: level 1

:: ::

_____ is the means to see, hear, or become aware of something or someone through our fundamental senses. The term _____ derives from the Latin word perceptio, and is the organization, identification, and interpretation of sensory information in order to represent and understand the presented information, or the environment.

Exam Probability: **Low**

6. *Answer choices:*

(see index for correct answer)

- a. levels of analysis
- b. Perception
- c. interpersonal communication
- d. similarity-attraction theory

Guidance: level 1

:: Stock market ::

_____ is freedom from, or resilience against, potential harm caused by others. Beneficiaries of _____ may be of persons and social groups, objects and institutions, ecosystems or any other entity or phenomenon vulnerable to unwanted change by its environment.

Exam Probability: **High**

7. *Answer choices:*

(see index for correct answer)

- a. Microcap
- b. Shadow stock
- c. Initial public offering
- d. Security

Guidance: level 1

:: ::

A _____ is a graphic mark, emblem, or symbol used to aid and promote public identification and recognition. It may be of an abstract or figurative design or include the text of the name it represents as in a wordmark.

Exam Probability: **Low**

8. *Answer choices:*

(see index for correct answer)

- a. hierarchical
- b. personal values
- c. Sarbanes-Oxley act of 2002
- d. surface-level diversity

Guidance: level 1

:: Behaviorism ::

In behavioral psychology, _____ is a consequence applied that will strengthen an organism's future behavior whenever that behavior is preceded by a specific antecedent stimulus. This strengthening effect may be measured as a higher frequency of behavior, longer duration, greater magnitude, or shorter latency. There are two types of _____, known as positive _____ and negative _____; positive is where by a reward is offered on expression of the wanted behaviour and negative is taking away an undesirable element in the persons environment whenever the desired behaviour is achieved.

Exam Probability: **Low**

9. *Answer choices:*
(see index for correct answer)

- a. contingency management
- b. chaining
- c. Systematic desensitization
- d. Reinforcement

Guidance: level 1

:: Marketing ::

_____ is the marketing of products that are presumed to be environmentally safe. It incorporates a broad range of activities, including product modification, changes to the production process, sustainable packaging, as well as modifying advertising. Yet defining _____ is not a simple task where several meanings intersect and contradict each other; an example of this will be the existence of varying social, environmental and retail definitions attached to this term. Other similar terms used are environmental marketing and ecological marketing.

Exam Probability: **Medium**

10. *Answer choices:*

(see index for correct answer)

- a. Green marketing
- b. Servicescape
- c. Market environment
- d. City marketing

Guidance: level 1

:: Management accounting ::

_____s are costs that change as the quantity of the good or service that a business produces changes. _____s are the sum of marginal costs over all units produced. They can also be considered normal costs. Fixed costs and _____s make up the two components of total cost. Direct costs are costs that can easily be associated with a particular cost object. However, not all _____s are direct costs. For example, variable manufacturing overhead costs are _____s that are indirect costs, not direct costs. _____s are sometimes called unit-level costs as they vary with the number of units produced.

Exam Probability: **High**

11. *Answer choices:*

(see index for correct answer)

- a. Operating profit margin
- b. Throughput accounting
- c. Direct material total variance
- d. Variable cost

Guidance: level 1

:: ::

A _____ is an organization, usually a group of people or a company, authorized to act as a single entity and recognized as such in law. Early incorporated entities were established by charter. Most jurisdictions now allow the creation of new _____s through registration.

Exam Probability: **Medium**

12. *Answer choices:*

(see index for correct answer)

- a. Corporation
- b. surface-level diversity
- c. hierarchical perspective
- d. co-culture

Guidance: level 1

:: ::

In law, an _____ is the process in which cases are reviewed, where parties request a formal change to an official decision. _____ s function both as a process for error correction as well as a process of clarifying and interpreting law. Although appellate courts have existed for thousands of years, common law countries did not incorporate an affirmative right to _____ into their jurisprudence until the 19th century.

Exam Probability: **Low**

13. *Answer choices:*

(see index for correct answer)

- a. process perspective
- b. information systems assessment

- c. functional perspective
- d. deep-level diversity

Guidance: level 1

:: ::

A _____ consists of one people who live in the same dwelling and share meals. It may also consist of a single family or another group of people. A dwelling is considered to contain multiple _____ s if meals or living spaces are not shared. The _____ is the basic unit of analysis in many social, microeconomic and government models, and is important to economics and inheritance.

Exam Probability: **Low**

14. *Answer choices:*

(see index for correct answer)

- a. co-culture
- b. hierarchical
- c. Household
- d. interpersonal communication

Guidance: level 1

:: ::

Employment is a relationship between two parties, usually based on a contract where work is paid for, where one party, which may be a corporation, for profit, not-for-profit organization, co-operative or other entity is the employer and the other is the employee. Employees work in return for payment, which may be in the form of an hourly wage, by piecework or an annual salary, depending on the type of work an employee does or which sector she or he is working in. Employees in some fields or sectors may receive gratuities, bonus payment or stock options. In some types of employment, employees may receive benefits in addition to payment. Benefits can include health insurance, housing, disability insurance or use of a gym. Employment is typically governed by employment laws, regulations or legal contracts.

Exam Probability: **High**

15. *Answer choices:*

(see index for correct answer)

- a. co-culture
- b. hierarchical
- c. Personnel
- d. process perspective

Guidance: level 1

:: Direct marketing ::

_____ is a form of direct marketing using databases of customers or potential customers to generate personalized communications in order to promote a product or service for marketing purposes. The method of communication can be any addressable medium, as in direct marketing.

Exam Probability: **High**

16. *Answer choices:*

(see index for correct answer)

- a. Large-group awareness training
- b. Database marketing
- c. Direct marketing
- d. Ginsu

Guidance: level 1

:: Commerce ::

A _____ is a company or individual that purchases goods or services with the intention of selling them rather than consuming or using them. This is usually done for profit. One example can be found in the industry of telecommunications, where companies buy excess amounts of transmission capacity or call time from other carriers and resell it to smaller carriers.

Exam Probability: **Medium**

17. Answer choices:

(see index for correct answer)

- a. Reseller
- b. Staple right
- c. Global Commerce Initiative
- d. Social dumping

Guidance: level 1

:: ::

_____ s are formal, sociotechnical, organizational systems designed to collect, process, store, and distribute information. In a sociotechnical perspective, _____ s are composed by four components: task, people, structure, and technology.

Exam Probability: **Low**

18. Answer choices:

(see index for correct answer)

- a. Sarbanes-Oxley act of 2002
- b. hierarchical
- c. hierarchical perspective
- d. functional perspective

Guidance: level 1

:: Management ::

_____ is the organizational discipline which focuses on the practical application of marketing orientation, techniques and methods inside enterprises and organizations and on the management of a firm's marketing resources and activities.

Exam Probability: **Medium**

19. *Answer choices:*

(see index for correct answer)

- a. Stakeholder
- b. Continuous monitoring
- c. Scenario planning
- d. Supply chain sustainability

Guidance: level 1

:: ::

Distribution is one of the four elements of the marketing mix. Distribution is the process of making a product or service available for the consumer or business user who needs it. This can be done directly by the producer or service provider, or using indirect channels with distributors or intermediaries. The other three elements of the marketing mix are product, pricing, and promotion.

Exam Probability: **Medium**

20. *Answer choices:*

(see index for correct answer)

- a. hierarchical perspective
- b. process perspective
- c. Distribution channel
- d. personal values

Guidance: level 1

:: Competition (economics) ::

_____ arises whenever at least two parties strive for a goal which cannot be shared: where one's gain is the other's loss.

Exam Probability: **Medium**

21. *Answer choices:*

(see index for correct answer)

- a. Economic forces
- b. National Competitiveness Report of Armenia
- c. Self-competition
- d. Currency competition

Guidance: level 1

:: Advertising ::

A _____ is a document used by creative professionals and agencies to develop creative deliverables: visual design, copy, advertising, web sites, etc. The document is usually developed by the requestor and approved by the creative team of designers, writers, and project managers. In some cases, the project's _____ may need creative director approval before work will commence.

Exam Probability: **High**

22. *Answer choices:*

(see index for correct answer)

- a. Reply marketing
- b. Advertising Standards Authority
- c. Creative brief
- d. Superstudio

Guidance: level 1

:: Data interchange standards ::

_____ is the concept of businesses electronically communicating information that was traditionally communicated on paper, such as purchase orders and invoices. Technical standards for EDI exist to facilitate parties transacting such instruments without having to make special arrangements.

Exam Probability: **Medium**

23. *Answer choices:*

(see index for correct answer)

- a. Data Interchange Standards Association
- b. Electronic data interchange
- c. Common Alerting Protocol
- d. Uniform Communication Standard

Guidance: level 1

:: Income ::

_____ is a ratio between the net profit and cost of investment resulting from an investment of some resources. A high ROI means the investment's gains favorably to its cost. As a performance measure, ROI is used to evaluate the efficiency of an investment or to compare the efficiencies of several different investments. In purely economic terms, it is one way of relating profits to capital invested. _____ is a performance measure used by businesses to identify the efficiency of an investment or number of different investments.

Exam Probability: **High**

24. *Answer choices:*

(see index for correct answer)

- a. Net national income
- b. Return on investment
- c. Implied level of government service
- d. Pay grade

Guidance: level 1

:: Decision theory ::

A _____ is a deliberate system of principles to guide decisions and achieve rational outcomes. A _____ is a statement of intent, and is implemented as a procedure or protocol. Policies are generally adopted by a governance body within an organization. Policies can assist in both subjective and objective decision making. Policies to assist in subjective decision making usually assist senior management with decisions that must be based on the relative merits of a number of factors, and as a result are often hard to test objectively, e.g. work-life balance _____ . In contrast policies to assist in objective decision making are usually operational in nature and can be objectively tested, e.g. password _____ .

Exam Probability: **High**

25. *Answer choices:*

(see index for correct answer)

- a. Rademacher complexity
- b. Dominance-based rough set approach
- c. Policy
- d. Taguchi loss function

Guidance: level 1

:: Project management ::

Contemporary business and science treat as a _____ any undertaking, carried out individually or collaboratively and possibly involving research or design, that is carefully planned to achieve a particular aim.

Exam Probability: **High**

26. *Answer choices:*

(see index for correct answer)

- a. Operational bill
- b. Libyan Project Management Association
- c. Transport Initiatives Edinburgh
- d. Project

Guidance: level 1

:: ::

In regulatory jurisdictions that provide for it , _____ is a group of laws and organizations designed to ensure the rights of consumers as well as fair trade, competition and accurate information in the marketplace. The laws are designed to prevent the businesses that engage in fraud or specified unfair practices from gaining an advantage over competitors. They may also provides additional protection for those most vulnerable in society. _____ laws are a form of government regulation that aim to protect the rights of consumers. For example, a government may require businesses to disclose detailed information about products—particularly in areas where safety or public health is an issue, such as food.

Exam Probability: **Medium**

27. *Answer choices:*

(see index for correct answer)

- a. interpersonal communication
- b. open system
- c. Consumer Protection
- d. Sarbanes-Oxley act of 2002

Guidance: level 1

:: Credit cards ::

> The _____ Company, also known as Amex, is an American multinational financial services corporation headquartered in Three World Financial Center in New York City. The company was founded in 1850 and is one of the 30 components of the Dow Jones Industrial Average. The company is best known for its charge card, credit card, and traveler's cheque businesses.

Exam Probability: **High**

28. *Answer choices:*

(see index for correct answer)

- a. Ingenico
- b. Fuel card
- c. SBI Cards
- d. American Express

Guidance: level 1

:: Goods ::

In most contexts, the concept of _____ denotes the conduct that should be preferred when posed with a choice between possible actions. _____ is generally considered to be the opposite of evil, and is of interest in the study of morality, ethics, religion and philosophy. The specific meaning and etymology of the term and its associated translations among ancient and contemporary languages show substantial variation in its inflection and meaning depending on circumstances of place, history, religious, or philosophical context.

Exam Probability: **Low**

29. *Answer choices:*

(see index for correct answer)

- a. Necessity good
- b. Private good
- c. Good
- d. Normal good

Guidance: level 1

:: Business ::

The seller, or the provider of the goods or services, completes a sale in response to an acquisition, appropriation, requisition or a direct interaction with the buyer at the point of sale. There is a passing of title of the item, and the settlement of a price, in which agreement is reached on a price for which transfer of ownership of the item will occur. The seller, not the purchaser typically executes the sale and it may be completed prior to the obligation of payment. In the case of indirect interaction, a person who sells goods or service on behalf of the owner is known as a salesman or saleswoman or salesperson, but this often refers to someone _____ goods in a store/shop, in which case other terms are also common, including salesclerk, shop assistant, and retail clerk.

Exam Probability: **Medium**

30. *Answer choices:*

(see index for correct answer)

- a. Corporate social media
- b. Selling
- c. Post-transaction marketing
- d. Procurement PunchOut

Guidance: level 1

:: Television commercials ::

_____ is a characteristic that distinguishes physical entities that have biological processes, such as signaling and self-sustaining processes, from those that do not, either because such functions have ceased, or because they never had such functions and are classified as inanimate. Various forms of _____ exist, such as plants, animals, fungi, protists, archaea, and bacteria. The criteria can at times be ambiguous and may or may not define viruses, viroids, or potential synthetic _____ as "living". Biology is the science concerned with the study of _____ .

Exam Probability: **High**

31. *Answer choices:*

(see index for correct answer)

- a. Life
- b. Surfer
- c. Blipvert
- d. Little Mikey

Guidance: level 1

:: Marketing ::

_____ , in marketing, manufacturing, call centres and management, is the use of flexible computer-aided manufacturing systems to produce custom output. Such systems combine the low unit costs of mass production processes with the flexibility of individual customization.

Exam Probability: **Low**

32. *Answer choices:*

(see index for correct answer)

- a. Customer lifetime value
- b. Mass customization
- c. Generic brand
- d. Buy one, get one free

Guidance: level 1

:: Business terms ::

A _____ is a short statement of why an organization exists, what its overall goal is, identifying the goal of its operations: what kind of product or service it provides, its primary customers or market, and its geographical region of operation. It may include a short statement of such fundamental matters as the organization's values or philosophies, a business's main competitive advantages, or a desired future state—the "vision".

Exam Probability: **Medium**

33. *Answer choices:*

(see index for correct answer)

- a. centralization
- b. noncommercial

- c. Mission statement
- d. year-to-date

Guidance: level 1

:: ::

Market segmentation is the activity of dividing a broad consumer or business market, normally consisting of existing and potential customers, into sub-groups of consumers based on some type of shared characteristics. In dividing or segmenting markets, researchers typically look for common characteristics such as shared needs, common interests, similar lifestyles or even similar demographic profiles. The overall aim of segmentation is to identify high yield segments – that is, those segments that are likely to be the most profitable or that have growth potential – so that these can be selected for special attention.

Exam Probability: **Medium**

34. *Answer choices:*

(see index for correct answer)

- a. open system
- b. cultural
- c. levels of analysis
- d. process perspective

Guidance: level 1

:: Product management ::

A _____ is a professional role which is responsible for the development of products for an organization, known as the practice of product management. _____ s own the business strategy behind a product, specify its functional requirements and generally manage the launch of features. They coordinate work done by many other functions and are ultimately responsible for the business success of the product.

Exam Probability: **High**

35. *Answer choices:*

(see index for correct answer)

- a. Swing tag
- b. Pareto chart
- c. Consumer adoption of technological innovations
- d. Discontinuation

Guidance: level 1

:: Industrial design ::

In physics and mathematics, the _____ of a mathematical space is informally defined as the minimum number of coordinates needed to specify any point within it. Thus a line has a _____ of one because only one coordinate is needed to specify a point on it for example, the point at 5 on a number line. A surface such as a plane or the surface of a cylinder or sphere has a _____ of two because two coordinates are needed to specify a point on it for example, both a latitude and longitude are required to locate a point on the surface of a sphere. The inside of a cube, a cylinder or a sphere is three-_____ al because three coordinates are needed to locate a point within these spaces.

Exam Probability: **High**

36. *Answer choices:*

(see index for correct answer)

- a. Projection augmented model
- b. The Design of Everyday Things
- c. Dimension
- d. Industrial design right

Guidance: level 1

:: Commercial item transport and distribution ::

In commerce, supply-chain management, the management of the flow of goods and services, involves the movement and storage of raw materials, of work-in-process inventory, and of finished goods from point of origin to point of consumption. Interconnected or interlinked networks, channels and node businesses combine in the provision of products and services required by end customers in a supply chain. Supply-chain management has been defined as the "design, planning, execution, control, and monitoring of supply-chain activities with the objective of creating net value, building a competitive infrastructure, leveraging worldwide logistics, synchronizing supply with demand and measuring performance globally." SCM practice draws heavily from the areas of industrial engineering, systems engineering, operations management, logistics, procurement, information technology, and marketing and strives for an integrated approach. Marketing channels play an important role in supply-chain management. Current research in supply-chain management is concerned with topics related to sustainability and risk management, among others. Some suggest that the "people dimension" of SCM, ethical issues, internal integration, transparency/visibility, and human capital/talent management are topics that have, so far, been underrepresented on the research agenda.

Exam Probability: **High**

37. *Answer choices:*

(see index for correct answer)

- a. Haulage exchange
- b. Weigh station
- c. Supply chain management
- d. Gas carrier

Guidance: level 1

:: ::

In communications and information processing, _____ is a system of rules to convert information—such as a letter, word, sound, image, or gesture—into another form or representation, sometimes shortened or secret, for communication through a communication channel or storage in a storage medium. An early example is the invention of language, which enabled a person, through speech, to communicate what they saw, heard, felt, or thought to others. But speech limits the range of communication to the distance a voice can carry, and limits the audience to those present when the speech is uttered. The invention of writing, which converted spoken language into visual symbols, extended the range of communication across space and time.

Exam Probability: **Medium**

38. *Answer choices:*

(see index for correct answer)

- a. Code
- b. similarity-attraction theory
- c. cultural
- d. functional perspective

Guidance: level 1

:: Asset ::

In financial accounting, an _____ is any resource owned by the business. Anything tangible or intangible that can be owned or controlled to produce value and that is held by a company to produce positive economic value is an _____. Simply stated, _____s represent value of ownership that can be converted into cash. The balance sheet of a firm records the monetary value of the _____s owned by that firm. It covers money and other valuables belonging to an individual or to a business.

Exam Probability: **Medium**

39. *Answer choices:*

(see index for correct answer)

- a. Fixed asset
- b. Current asset

Guidance: level 1

:: Marketing ::

A _____ is the people, organizations, and activities necessary to transfer the ownership of goods from the point of production to the point of consumption. It is the way products get to the end-user, the consumer; and is also known as a distribution channel. A _____ is a useful tool for management, and is crucial to creating an effective and well-planned marketing strategy.

Exam Probability: **Medium**

40. *Answer choices:*

(see index for correct answer)

- a. Decoy effect
- b. Enterprise relationship management
- c. Business-to-government
- d. Intent scale translation

Guidance: level 1

:: ::

_____, or auditory perception, is the ability to perceive sounds by detecting vibrations, changes in the pressure of the surrounding medium through time, through an organ such as the ear. The academic field concerned with _____ is auditory science.

Exam Probability: **High**

41. *Answer choices:*

(see index for correct answer)

- a. interpersonal communication
- b. Hearing
- c. process perspective
- d. co-culture

Guidance: level 1

:: Management ::

In business, a _____ is the attribute that allows an organization to outperform its competitors. A _____ may include access to natural resources, such as high-grade ores or a low-cost power source, highly skilled labor, geographic location, high entry barriers, and access to new technology.

Exam Probability: **High**

42. *Answer choices:*

(see index for correct answer)

- a. Reverse innovation
- b. Organizational hologram
- c. Competitive advantage
- d. Managing stage boundaries

Guidance: level 1

:: ::

_____ involves decision making. It can include judging the merits of multiple options and selecting one or more of them. One can make a _____ between imagined options or between real options followed by the corresponding action. For example, a traveler might choose a route for a journey based on the preference of arriving at a given destination as soon as possible. The preferred route can then follow from information such as the length of each of the possible routes, traffic conditions, etc. The arrival at a _____ can include more complex motivators such as cognition, instinct, and feeling.

Exam Probability: **Low**

43. *Answer choices:*

(see index for correct answer)

- a. similarity-attraction theory
- b. functional perspective
- c. personal values
- d. Choice

Guidance: level 1

:: Marketing techniques ::

_____, also known as embedded marketing, is a marketing technique where references to specific brands or products are incorporated into another work, such as a film or television program, with specific promotional intent.

Exam Probability: **Medium**

44. *Answer choices:*

(see index for correct answer)

- a. Channel stuffing
- b. Stunt casting
- c. Product placement
- d. Real-time marketing

Guidance: level 1

:: Production economics ::

In microeconomics, _____ are the cost advantages that enterprises obtain due to their scale of operation, with cost per unit of output decreasing with increasing scale.

Exam Probability: **Medium**

45. *Answer choices:*

(see index for correct answer)

- a. Economies of scale
- b. Choice of techniques
- c. short run
- d. Returns to scale

Guidance: level 1

:: Marketing ::

_____ comes from the Latin neg and otsia referring to businessmen who, unlike the patricians, had no leisure time in their industriousness; it held the meaning of business until the 17th century when it took on the diplomatic connotation as a dialogue between two or more people or parties intended to reach a beneficial outcome over one or more issues where a conflict exists with respect to at least one of these issues. Thus, _____ is a process of combining divergent positions into a joint agreement under a decision rule of unanimity.

Exam Probability: **High**

46. *Answer choices:*

(see index for correct answer)

- a. Negotiation
- b. Product lining
- c. Adobe Marketing Cloud
- d. Gift suite

Guidance: level 1

:: Investment ::

In finance, the benefit from an _____ is called a return. The return may consist of a gain realised from the sale of property or an _____, unrealised capital appreciation, or _____ income such as dividends, interest, rental income etc., or a combination of capital gain and income. The return may also include currency gains or losses due to changes in foreign currency exchange rates.

Exam Probability: **Low**

47. *Answer choices:*

(see index for correct answer)

- a. Investment
- b. Legal Alpha
- c. Fundrise
- d. Investment Securities

Guidance: level 1

:: Product development ::

_____ is the understanding of the dynamics of the product in order to showcase the best qualities and maximum features of the product. Marketers spend a lot of time and research in order to target their attended audience. Marketers will look into a _____ before marketing a product towards their customers.

Exam Probability: **High**

48. *Answer choices:*

(see index for correct answer)

- a. WhiteBoard Product Solutions
- b. Product concept
- c. Product line extension
- d. Virtual prototyping

Guidance: level 1

:: Marketing ::

_____ s are structured marketing strategies designed by merchants to encourage customers to continue to shop at or use the services of businesses associated with each program. These programs exist covering most types of commerce, each one having varying features and rewards-schemes.

Exam Probability: **Medium**

49. *Answer choices:*

(see index for correct answer)

- a. Loyalty program
- b. Online research community
- c. Product requirements document
- d. Price skimming

Guidance: level 1

:: Direct marketing ::

_____ is a form of advertising where organizations communicate directly to customers through a variety of media including cell phone text messaging, email, websites, online adverts, database marketing, fliers, catalog distribution, promotional letters, targeted television, newspapers, magazine advertisements, and outdoor advertising. Among practitioners, it is also known as direct response marketing.

Exam Probability: **Low**

50. *Answer choices:*

(see index for correct answer)

- a. Solo Ads
- b. Direct marketing
- c. Stream Energy
- d. American Family Publishers

Guidance: level 1

:: Human resource management ::

_____ encompasses values and behaviors that contribute to the unique social and psychological environment of a business. The _____ influences the way people interact, the context within which knowledge is created, the resistance they will have towards certain changes, and ultimately the way they share knowledge. _____ represents the collective values, beliefs and principles of organizational members and is a product of factors such as history, product, market, technology, strategy, type of employees, management style, and national culture; culture includes the organization's vision, values, norms, systems, symbols, language, assumptions, environment, location, beliefs and habits.

Exam Probability: **High**

51. *Answer choices:*

(see index for correct answer)

- a. Organizational culture
- b. Occupational Information Network
- c. Training and development
- d. Perceived organizational support

Guidance: level 1

:: Generally Accepted Accounting Principles ::

Expenditure is an outflow of money to another person or group to pay for an item or service, or for a category of costs. For a tenant, rent is an _____. For students or parents, tuition is an _____. Buying food, clothing, furniture or an automobile is often referred to as an _____. An _____ is a cost that is "paid" or "remitted", usually in exchange for something of value. Something that seems to cost a great deal is "expensive". Something that seems to cost little is "inexpensive". "_____s of the table" are _____s of dining, refreshments, a feast, etc.

Exam Probability: **High**

52. *Answer choices:*

(see index for correct answer)

- a. Standard Business Reporting
- b. Expense
- c. Reserve
- d. Income statement

Guidance: level 1

:: Marketing ::

_____ is "commercial competition characterized by the repeated cutting of prices below those of competitors". One competitor will lower its price, then others will lower their prices to match. If one of them reduces their price again, a new round of reductions starts. In the short term, _____ s are good for buyers, who can take advantage of lower prices. Often they are not good for the companies involved because the lower prices reduce profit margins and can threaten their survival.

Exam Probability: **Low**

53. *Answer choices:*

(see index for correct answer)

- a. Kidification
- b. Price war
- c. Joseph E. Grosberg
- d. Mobile marketing research

Guidance: level 1

:: Debt ::

_____, in finance and economics, is payment from a borrower or deposit-taking financial institution to a lender or depositor of an amount above repayment of the principal sum, at a particular rate. It is distinct from a fee which the borrower may pay the lender or some third party. It is also distinct from dividend which is paid by a company to its shareholders from its profit or reserve, but not at a particular rate decided beforehand, rather on a pro rata basis as a share in the reward gained by risk taking entrepreneurs when the revenue earned exceeds the total costs.

Exam Probability: **High**

54. *Answer choices:*

(see index for correct answer)

- a. Recourse debt
- b. Interest
- c. Credit
- d. Museum of Foreign Debt

Guidance: level 1

:: Trade associations ::

A _____, also known as an industry trade group, business association, sector association or industry body, is an organization founded and funded by businesses that operate in a specific industry. An industry _____ participates in public relations activities such as advertising, education, political donations, lobbying and publishing, but its focus is collaboration between companies. Associations may offer other services, such as producing conferences, networking or charitable events or offering classes or educational materials. Many associations are non-profit organizations governed by bylaws and directed by officers who are also members.

Exam Probability: **Low**

55. *Answer choices:*

(see index for correct answer)

- a. Property Care Association
- b. HISWA
- c. Open Access Scholarly Publishers Association
- d. CompTIA

Guidance: level 1

:: ::

_____ is the practice of deliberately managing the spread of information between an individual or an organization and the public. _____ may include an organization or individual gaining exposure to their audiences using topics of public interest and news items that do not require direct payment. This differentiates it from advertising as a form of marketing communications. _____ is the idea of creating coverage for clients for free, rather than marketing or advertising. But now, advertising is also a part of greater PR Activities. An example of good _____ would be generating an article featuring a client, rather than paying for the client to be advertised next to the article. The aim of _____ is to inform the public, prospective customers, investors, partners, employees, and other stakeholders and ultimately persuade them to maintain a positive or favorable view about the organization, its leadership, products, or political decisions. _____ professionals typically work for PR and marketing firms, businesses and companies, government, and public officials as PIOs and nongovernmental organizations, and nonprofit organizations. Jobs central to _____ include account coordinator, account executive, account supervisor, and media relations manager.

Exam Probability: **Low**

56. *Answer choices:*

(see index for correct answer)

- a. hierarchical perspective
- b. co-culture
- c. Public relations
- d. functional perspective

Guidance: level 1

A _____ service is an online platform which people use to build social networks or social relationship with other people who share similar personal or career interests, activities, backgrounds or real-life connections.

Exam Probability: **Medium**

57. *Answer choices:*

(see index for correct answer)

- a. Character
- b. empathy
- c. hierarchical
- d. information systems assessment

Guidance: level 1

An _____ is an area of the production, distribution, or trade, and consumption of goods and services by different agents. Understood in its broadest sense, 'The _____ is defined as a social domain that emphasize the practices, discourses, and material expressions associated with the production, use, and management of resources'. Economic agents can be individuals, businesses, organizations, or governments. Economic transactions occur when two parties agree to the value or price of the transacted good or service, commonly expressed in a certain currency. However, monetary transactions only account for a small part of the economic domain.

Exam Probability: **Low**

58. *Answer choices:*

(see index for correct answer)

- a. hierarchical perspective
- b. Sarbanes-Oxley act of 2002
- c. imperative
- d. Economy

Guidance: level 1

:: Cultural appropriation ::

_____ is a social and economic order that encourages the acquisition of goods and services in ever-increasing amounts. With the industrial revolution, but particularly in the 20th century, mass production led to an economic crisis: there was overproduction—the supply of goods would grow beyond consumer demand, and so manufacturers turned to planned obsolescence and advertising to manipulate consumer spending. In 1899, a book on _____ published by Thorstein Veblen, called The Theory of the Leisure Class, examined the widespread values and economic institutions emerging along with the widespread "leisure time" in the beginning of the 20th century. In it Veblen "views the activities and spending habits of this leisure class in terms of conspicuous and vicarious consumption and waste. Both are related to the display of status and not to functionality or usefulness."

Exam Probability: **Low**

59. *Answer choices:*

(see index for correct answer)

- a. Playing Indian
- b. Consumerism
- c. Washington Redskins name controversy
- d. Cool

Guidance: level 1

Manufacturing

Manufacturing is the production of merchandise for use or sale using labor and machines, tools, chemical and biological processing, or formulation. The term may refer to a range of human activity, from handicraft to high tech, but is most commonly applied to industrial design , in which raw materials are transformed into finished goods on a large scale. Such finished goods may be sold to other manufacturers for the production of other, more complex products, such as aircraft, household appliances, furniture, sports equipment or automobiles, or sold to wholesalers, who in turn sell them to retailers, who then sell them to end users and consumers.

:: Product management ::

_____ is the state of being which occurs when an object, service, or practice is no longer wanted even though it may still be in good working order; however, the international standard EN62402 _____ Management - Application Guide defines _____ as being the "transition from availability of products by the original manufacturer or supplier to unavailability". _____ frequently occurs because a replacement has become available that has, in sum, more advantages compared to the disadvantages incurred by maintaining or repairing the original. Obsolete also refers to something that is already disused or discarded, or antiquated. Typically, _____ is preceded by a gradual decline in popularity.

Exam Probability: **Medium**

1. *Answer choices:*

(see index for correct answer)

- a. Technology acceptance model
- b. Brand extension
- c. Obsolescence
- d. Scarcity Development Cycle

Guidance: level 1

:: Information technology management ::

_____ within quality management systems and information technology systems is a process—either formal or informal—used to ensure that changes to a product or system are introduced in a controlled and coordinated manner. It reduces the possibility that unnecessary changes will be introduced to a system without forethought, introducing faults into the system or undoing changes made by other users of software. The goals of a _____ procedure usually include minimal disruption to services, reduction in back-out activities, and cost-effective utilization of resources involved in implementing change.

Exam Probability: **High**

2. *Answer choices:*

(see index for correct answer)

- a. Building lifecycle management
- b. Website promotion
- c. Intelligent workload management
- d. Change control

Guidance: level 1

:: Management ::

_____ is a formal technique useful where many possible courses of action are competing for attention. In essence, the problem-solver estimates the benefit delivered by each action, then selects a number of the most effective actions that deliver a total benefit reasonably close to the maximal possible one.

Exam Probability: **High**

3. *Answer choices:*

(see index for correct answer)

- a. Allegiance
- b. Outrage constraint
- c. Pareto analysis
- d. Continuous-flow manufacturing

Guidance: level 1

:: Management ::

A process is a unique combination of tools, materials, methods, and people engaged in producing a measurable output; for example a manufacturing line for machine parts. All processes have inherent statistical variability which can be evaluated by statistical methods.

Exam Probability: **Medium**

4. *Answer choices:*

(see index for correct answer)

- a. Private defense agency
- b. Process capability
- c. Success trap

- d. Integrative thinking

Guidance: level 1

:: Commercial item transport and distribution ::

_____ in logistics and supply chain management is an organization's use of third-party businesses to outsource elements of its distribution, warehousing, and fulfillment services.

Exam Probability: **High**

5. *Answer choices:*

(see index for correct answer)

- a. LNG carrier
- b. Cargo sampling
- c. Toll Global Logistics
- d. Third-party logistics

Guidance: level 1

:: Industrial engineering ::

The _____ is the design of any task that aims to describe or explain the variation of information under conditions that are hypothesized to reflect the variation. The term is generally associated with experiments in which the design introduces conditions that directly affect the variation, but may also refer to the design of quasi-experiments, in which natural conditions that influence the variation are selected for observation.

Exam Probability: **High**

6. *Answer choices:*

(see index for correct answer)

- a. Industrial ecology
- b. Package testing
- c. Service quality
- d. Design of experiments

Guidance: level 1

:: Chemical processes ::

_____ is the understanding and application of the fundamental principles and laws of nature that allow us to transform raw material and energy into products that are useful to society, at an industrial level. By taking advantage of the driving forces of nature such as pressure, temperature and concentration gradients, as well as the law of conservation of mass, process engineers can develop methods to synthesize and purify large quantities of desired chemical products. _____ focuses on the design, operation, control, optimization and intensification of chemical, physical, and biological processes. _____ encompasses a vast range of industries, such as agriculture, automotive, biotechnical, chemical, food, material development, mining, nuclear, petrochemical, pharmaceutical, and software development. The application of systematic computer-based methods to _____ is "process systems engineering".

Exam Probability: **High**

7. *Answer choices:*

(see index for correct answer)

- a. Process engineering
- b. Vapor-compression evaporation
- c. Anthraquinone process
- d. Petersen matrix

Guidance: level 1

_____ is the process of finding an estimate, or approximation, which is a value that is usable for some purpose even if input data may be incomplete, uncertain, or unstable. The value is nonetheless usable because it is derived from the best information available. Typically, _____ involves "using the value of a statistic derived from a sample to estimate the value of a corresponding population parameter". The sample provides information that can be projected, through various formal or informal processes, to determine a range most likely to describe the missing information. An estimate that turns out to be incorrect will be an overestimate if the estimate exceeded the actual result, and an underestimate if the estimate fell short of the actual result.

Exam Probability: **Low**

8. *Answer choices:*

(see index for correct answer)

- a. co-culture
- b. Estimation
- c. cultural
- d. personal values

Guidance: level 1

:: Help desk ::

A high-explosive anti-tank warhead is a type of shaped charge explosive that uses the Munroe effect to penetrate thick tank armor. The warhead functions by having the explosive charge collapse a metal liner inside the warhead into a high-velocity superplastic jet. This superplastic jet is capable of penetrating armor steel to a depth of seven or more times the diameter of the charge but is usually used to immobilize or destroy tanks. Due to the way they work, they do not have to be fired as fast as an armor piercing shell, allowing less recoil. Contrary to a widespread misconception, the jet does not melt its way through armor, as its effect is purely kinetic in nature. The _____ warhead has become less effective against tanks and other armored vehicles due to the use of composite armor, explosive-reactive armor, and active protection systems which destroy the _____ warhead before it hits the tank. Even though _____ rounds are less effective against the heavy armor found on 2010s main battle tanks, _____ warheads remain a threat against less-armored parts of a main battle tank and against lighter armored vehicles or unarmored vehicles and helicopters.

Exam Probability: **High**

9. *Answer choices:*

(see index for correct answer)

- a. SysAid Technologies
- b. Supportworks
- c. Technical support
- d. Computer-aided maintenance

Guidance: level 1

:: Production and manufacturing ::

_____ is a concept in purchasing and project management for securing the quality and timely delivery of goods and components.

Exam Probability: **Medium**

10. *Answer choices:*

(see index for correct answer)

- a. Expediting
- b. Craft production
- c. Material requirements planning
- d. production control

Guidance: level 1

:: Computer memory companies ::

_____ Corporation is a Japanese multinational conglomerate headquartered in Tokyo, Japan. Its diversified products and services include information technology and communications equipment and systems, electronic components and materials, power systems, industrial and social infrastructure systems, consumer electronics, household appliances, medical equipment, office equipment, as well as lighting and logistics.

Exam Probability: **High**

11. *Answer choices:*

(see index for correct answer)

- a. Toshiba
- b. Qimonda
- c. Grandis
- d. EDGE Tech

Guidance: level 1

:: Commercial item transport and distribution ::

In commerce, supply-chain management, the management of the flow of goods and services, involves the movement and storage of raw materials, of work-in-process inventory, and of finished goods from point of origin to point of consumption. Interconnected or interlinked networks, channels and node businesses combine in the provision of products and services required by end customers in a supply chain. Supply-chain management has been defined as the "design, planning, execution, control, and monitoring of supply-chain activities with the objective of creating net value, building a competitive infrastructure, leveraging worldwide logistics, synchronizing supply with demand and measuring performance globally."SCM practice draws heavily from the areas of industrial engineering, systems engineering, operations management, logistics, procurement, information technology, and marketing and strives for an integrated approach. Marketing channels play an important role in supply-chain management. Current research in supply-chain management is concerned with topics related to sustainability and risk management, among others. Some suggest that the "people dimension" of SCM, ethical issues, internal integration, transparency/visibility, and human capital/talent management are topics that have, so far, been underrepresented on the research agenda.

Exam Probability: **Low**

12. *Answer choices:*

(see index for correct answer)

- a. Supply chain management
- b. Backhaul
- c. Trade facilitation
- d. Tanker

Guidance: level 1

:: Management ::

_____ is the process of thinking about the activities required to achieve a desired goal. It is the first and foremost activity to achieve desired results. It involves the creation and maintenance of a plan, such as psychological aspects that require conceptual skills. There are even a couple of tests to measure someone's capability of _____ well. As such, _____ is a fundamental property of intelligent behavior. An important further meaning, often just called "_____" is the legal context of permitted building developments.

Exam Probability: **High**

13. *Answer choices:*

(see index for correct answer)

- a. Tata Management Training Centre
- b. Evidence-based management

- c. Planning
- d. Change advisory board

Guidance: level 1

:: Water ::

_____ is a transparent, tasteless, odorless, and nearly colorless chemical substance, which is the main constituent of Earth's streams, lakes, and oceans, and the fluids of most living organisms. It is vital for all known forms of life, even though it provides no calories or organic nutrients. Its chemical formula is H2O, meaning that each of its molecules contains one oxygen and two hydrogen atoms, connected by covalent bonds. _____ is the name of the liquid state of H2O at standard ambient temperature and pressure. It forms precipitation in the form of rain and aerosols in the form of fog. Clouds are formed from suspended droplets of _____ and ice, its solid state. When finely divided, crystalline ice may precipitate in the form of snow. The gaseous state of _____ is steam or _____ vapor. _____ moves continually through the _____ cycle of evaporation, transpiration, condensation, precipitation, and runoff, usually reaching the sea.

Exam Probability: **High**

14. *Answer choices:*

(see index for correct answer)

- a. Moat
- b. Super-Dense Water
- c. Water
- d. Delta Blues

Guidance: level 1

:: Metals ::

A _____ is a material that, when freshly prepared, polished, or fractured, shows a lustrous appearance, and conducts electricity and heat relatively well. _____ s are typically malleable or ductile . A _____ may be a chemical element such as iron, or an alloy such as stainless steel.

Exam Probability: **Medium**

15. *Answer choices:*

(see index for correct answer)

- a. Tamahagane
- b. Thulium
- c. Conservation and restoration of silver objects
- d. Metallurgy

Guidance: level 1

:: Project management ::

In economics, _____ is the assignment of available resources to various uses. In the context of an entire economy, resources can be allocated by various means, such as markets or central planning.

Exam Probability: **Medium**

16. *Answer choices:*

(see index for correct answer)

- a. Global Alliance for Project Performance Standards
- b. Soft Costs
- c. Resource allocation
- d. Work package

Guidance: level 1

:: Quality ::

A _____ is an initiating cause of either a condition or a causal chain that leads to an outcome or effect of interest. The term denotes the earliest, most basic, `deepest`, cause for a given behavior; most often a fault. The idea is that you can only see an error by its manifest signs. Those signs can be widespread, multitudinous, and convoluted, whereas the _____ leading to them often is a lot simpler.

Exam Probability: **Low**

17. *Answer choices:*

(see index for correct answer)

- a. Dualistic Petri nets
- b. Sportsmark
- c. Root cause
- d. Cleaning validation

Guidance: level 1

:: Management ::

> _____ is a process by which entities review the quality of all factors involved in production. ISO 9000 defines _____ as "A part of quality management focused on fulfilling quality requirements".

Exam Probability: **Medium**

18. *Answer choices:*

(see index for correct answer)

- a. Intopia
- b. manager's right to manage
- c. Business plan
- d. Quality control

Guidance: level 1

:: Marketing ::

_____ or stock control can be broadly defined as "the activity of checking a shop's stock." However, a more focused definition takes into account the more science-based, methodical practice of not only verifying a business' inventory but also focusing on the many related facets of inventory management "within an organisation to meet the demand placed upon that business economically." Other facets of _____ include supply chain management, production control, financial flexibility, and customer satisfaction. At the root of _____, however, is the _____ problem, which involves determining when to order, how much to order, and the logistics of those decisions.

Exam Probability: **Low**

19. *Answer choices:*
(see index for correct answer)

- a. Inventory control
- b. Customer to customer
- c. Decoy effect
- d. Servicescape

Guidance: level 1

:: Data management ::

_____ is the ability of a physical product to remain functional, without requiring excessive maintenance or repair, when faced with the challenges of normal operation over its design lifetime. There are several measures of _____ in use, including years of life, hours of use, and number of operational cycles. In economics, goods with a long usable life are referred to as durable goods.

Exam Probability: **Medium**

20. *Answer choices:*
(see index for correct answer)

- a. Wiping
- b. Query language
- c. Network transparency
- d. Durability

Guidance: level 1

:: Project management ::

_____ is the right to exercise power, which can be formalized by a state and exercised by way of judges, appointed executives of government, or the ecclesiastical or priestly appointed representatives of a God or other deities.

Exam Probability: **Low**

21. *Answer choices:*

(see index for correct answer)

- a. TimeTac
- b. Duration
- c. Initiative
- d. Project team

Guidance: level 1

:: Industrial organization ::

In economics, specifically general equilibrium theory, a perfect market is defined by several idealizing conditions, collectively called _____ . In theoretical models where conditions of _____ hold, it has been theoretically demonstrated that a market will reach an equilibrium in which the quantity supplied for every product or service, including labor, equals the quantity demanded at the current price. This equilibrium would be a Pareto optimum.

Exam Probability: **Medium**

22. *Answer choices:*

(see index for correct answer)

- a. Perfect competition
- b. Worldwide Responsible Accredited Production
- c. Putting-out system

- d. Minimum efficient scale

Guidance: level 1

:: Accounting source documents ::

A _____ is a commercial document and first official offer issued by a buyer to a seller indicating types, quantities, and agreed prices for products or services. It is used to control the purchasing of products and services from external suppliers. _____ s can be an essential part of enterprise resource planning system orders.

Exam Probability: **Low**

23. *Answer choices:*

(see index for correct answer)

- a. Banknote
- b. Purchase order
- c. Superbill
- d. Remittance advice

Guidance: level 1

:: Supply chain management terms ::

In business and finance, _____ is a system of organizations, people, activities, information, and resources involved in moving a product or service from supplier to customer. _____ activities involve the transformation of natural resources, raw materials, and components into a finished product that is delivered to the end customer. In sophisticated _____ systems, used products may re-enter the _____ at any point where residual value is recyclable. _____ s link value chains.

Exam Probability: **Low**

24. *Answer choices:*

(see index for correct answer)

- a. Capital spare
- b. Consumables
- c. Work in process
- d. Supply chain

Guidance: level 1

:: ::

_____ refers to the confirmation of certain characteristics of an object, person, or organization. This confirmation is often, but not always, provided by some form of external review, education, assessment, or audit. Accreditation is a specific organization's process of _____. According to the National Council on Measurement in Education, a _____ test is a credentialing test used to determine whether individuals are knowledgeable enough in a given occupational area to be labeled "competent to practice" in that area.

Exam Probability: **Low**

25. *Answer choices:*

(see index for correct answer)

- a. interpersonal communication
- b. Sarbanes-Oxley act of 2002
- c. empathy
- d. Certification

Guidance: level 1

:: Process management ::

A _____ is a diagram commonly used in chemical and process engineering to indicate the general flow of plant processes and equipment. The PFD displays the relationship between major equipment of a plant facility and does not show minor details such as piping details and designations. Another commonly used term for a PFD is a flowsheet.

Exam Probability: **High**

26. *Answer choices:*

(see index for correct answer)

- a. Proactive contracting
- b. Contingency allowance
- c. Business process redesign
- d. Process flow diagram

Guidance: level 1

:: Production and manufacturing ::

In industry, _____ is a system of maintaining and improving the integrity of production and quality systems through the machines, equipment, processes, and employees that add business value to an organization.

Exam Probability: **Medium**

27. *Answer choices:*

(see index for correct answer)

- a. Order to cash
- b. Job production
- c. Total quality management
- d. Time to market

Guidance: level 1

:: Planning ::

_____ is a high level plan to achieve one or more goals under conditions of uncertainty. In the sense of the "art of the general," which included several subsets of skills including tactics, siegecraft, logistics etc., the term came into use in the 6th century C.E. in East Roman terminology, and was translated into Western vernacular languages only in the 18th century. From then until the 20th century, the word "_____" came to denote "a comprehensive way to try to pursue political ends, including the threat or actual use of force, in a dialectic of wills" in a military conflict, in which both adversaries interact.

Exam Probability: **Medium**

28. *Answer choices:*

(see index for correct answer)

- a. Strategy
- b. Implementation intention
- c. Plano Trienal
- d. Territorialist School

Guidance: level 1

:: Information technology management ::

_____ is a collective term for all approaches to prepare, support and help individuals, teams, and organizations in making organizational change. The most common change drivers include: technological evolution, process reviews, crisis, and consumer habit changes; pressure from new business entrants, acquisitions, mergers, and organizational restructuring. It includes methods that redirect or redefine the use of resources, business process, budget allocations, or other modes of operation that significantly change a company or organization. Organizational _____ considers the full organization and what needs to change, while _____ may be used solely to refer to how people and teams are affected by such organizational transition. It deals with many different disciplines, from behavioral and social sciences to information technology and business solutions.

Exam Probability: **High**

29. *Answer choices:*

(see index for correct answer)

- a. HP Open Extensibility Platform
- b. Change management
- c. Building lifecycle management
- d. Information model

Guidance: level 1

:: Project management ::

_____ is a marketing activity that does an aggregate plan for the production process, in advance of 6 to 18 months, to give an idea to management as to what quantity of materials and other resources are to be procured and when, so that the total cost of operations of the organization is kept to the minimum over that period.

Exam Probability: **Medium**

30. *Answer choices:*

(see index for correct answer)

- a. Phased implementation
- b. Aggregate planning
- c. ISO 31000
- d. Agile management

Guidance: level 1

:: ::

The _____ is a project plan of how the production budget will be spent over a given timescale, for every phase of a business project.

Exam Probability: **Low**

31. *Answer choices:*

(see index for correct answer)

- a. corporate values
- b. Production schedule
- c. open system
- d. co-culture

Guidance: level 1

:: Management ::

In inventory management, _____ is the order quantity that minimizes the total holding costs and ordering costs. It is one of the oldest classical production scheduling models. The model was developed by Ford W. Harris in 1913, but R. H. Wilson, a consultant who applied it extensively, and K. Andler are given credit for their in-depth analysis.

Exam Probability: **Medium**

32. *Answer choices:*

(see index for correct answer)

- a. Logistics management
- b. Management buyout
- c. Quality control
- d. Economic order quantity

Guidance: level 1

:: Distribution, retailing, and wholesaling ::

The _____ is a distribution channel phenomenon in which forecasts yield supply chain inefficiencies. It refers to increasing swings in inventory in response to shifts in customer demand as one moves further up the supply chain. The concept first appeared in Jay Forrester's Industrial Dynamics and thus it is also known as the Forrester effect. The _____ was named for the way the amplitude of a whip increases down its length. The further from the originating signal, the greater the distortion of the wave pattern. In a similar manner, forecast accuracy decreases as one moves upstream along the supply chain. For example, many consumer goods have fairly consistent consumption at retail but this signal becomes more chaotic and unpredictable as the focus moves away from consumer purchasing behavior.

Exam Probability: **Medium**

33. *Answer choices:*
(see index for correct answer)

- a. Bullwhip effect
- b. Sacrificial leg
- c. Wholesale list
- d. Capital City Distribution

Guidance: level 1

:: ::

In production, research, retail, and accounting, a _____ is the value of money that has been used up to produce something or deliver a service, and hence is not available for use anymore. In business, the _____ may be one of acquisition, in which case the amount of money expended to acquire it is counted as _____. In this case, money is the input that is gone in order to acquire the thing. This acquisition _____ may be the sum of the _____ of production as incurred by the original producer, and further _____s of transaction as incurred by the acquirer over and above the price paid to the producer. Usually, the price also includes a mark-up for profit over the _____ of production.

Exam Probability: **Medium**

34. *Answer choices:*

(see index for correct answer)

- a. personal values
- b. corporate values
- c. Cost
- d. functional perspective

Guidance: level 1

:: Management ::

In organizational studies, _____ is the efficient and effective development of an organization's resources when they are needed. Such resources may include financial resources, inventory, human skills, production resources, or information technology and natural resources.

Exam Probability: **Low**

35. *Answer choices:*

(see index for correct answer)

- a. middle manager
- b. Context analysis
- c. Project management information system
- d. Resource management

Guidance: level 1

:: Finance ::

_____ is a financial estimate intended to help buyers and owners determine the direct and indirect costs of a product or system. It is a management accounting concept that can be used in full cost accounting or even ecological economics where it includes social costs.

Exam Probability: **High**

36. *Answer choices:*

(see index for correct answer)

- a. Stub period
- b. Total cost of ownership
- c. Liquid Tradable Securities

- d. Rule of 78s

Guidance: level 1

:: Monopoly (economics) ::

_____ are "efficiencies formed by variety, not volume". For example, a gas station that sells gasoline can sell soda, milk, baked goods, etc through their customer service representatives and thus achieve gasoline companies _____ .

Exam Probability: **High**

37. *Answer choices:*

(see index for correct answer)

- a. Economies of scope
- b. Network effect
- c. Complementary monopoly
- d. Herfindahl index

Guidance: level 1

:: Management ::

_____ is an iterative four-step management method used in business for the control and continuous improvement of processes and products. It is also known as the Deming circle/cycle/wheel, the Shewhart cycle, the control circle/cycle, or plan–do–study–act . Another version of this _____ cycle is O _____ . The added "O" stands for observation or as some versions say: "Observe the current condition." This emphasis on observation and current condition has currency with the literature on lean manufacturing and the Toyota Production System. The _____ cycle, with Ishikawa's changes, can be traced back to S. Mizuno of the Tokyo Institute of Technology in 1959.

Exam Probability: **Medium**

38. *Answer choices:*

(see index for correct answer)

- a. Focused improvement
- b. Management cockpit
- c. PDCA
- d. Vendor relationship management

Guidance: level 1

:: Outsourcing ::

_____ is an institutional procurement process that continuously improves and re-evaluates the purchasing activities of a company. In the services industry, _____ refers to a service solution, sometimes called a strategic partnership, which is specifically customized to meet the client's individual needs. In a production environment, it is often considered one component of supply chain management. Modern supply chain management professionals have placed emphasis on defining the distinct differences between _____ and procurement. Procurement operations support tactical day-to-day transactions such as issuing Purchase Orders to suppliers, whereas _____ represents to strategic planning, supplier development, contract negotiation, supply chain infrastructure, and outsourcing models.

Exam Probability: **Low**

39. *Answer choices:*

(see index for correct answer)

- a. Virtual CFO
- b. Service level objective
- c. Outsourcing of animation
- d. Minacs

Guidance: level 1

:: Semiconductor companies ::

_____ Corporation is a Japanese multinational conglomerate corporation headquartered in Konan, Minato, Tokyo. Its diversified business includes consumer and professional electronics, gaming, entertainment and financial services. The company owns the largest music entertainment business in the world, the largest video game console business and one of the largest video game publishing businesses, and is one of the leading manufacturers of electronic products for the consumer and professional markets, and a leading player in the film and television entertainment industry. _____ was ranked 97th on the 2018 Fortune Global 500 list.

Exam Probability: **Medium**

40. *Answer choices:*

(see index for correct answer)

- a. Sony
- b. Freescale Semiconductor
- c. GreenPeak Technologies
- d. Fujitsu

Guidance: level 1

:: Manufacturing ::

A _____ is an object used to extend the ability of an individual to modify features of the surrounding environment. Although many animals use simple _____ s, only human beings, whose use of stone _____ s dates back hundreds of millennia, use _____ s to make other _____ s. The set of _____ s needed to perform different tasks that are part of the same activity is called gear or equipment.

Exam Probability: **Medium**

41. *Answer choices:*

(see index for correct answer)

- a. Optical comparator
- b. Tool
- c. Acheson process
- d. ANSI/ISA-95

Guidance: level 1

:: Quality management ::

_____ is a not-for-profit membership foundation in Brussels, established in 1989 to increase the competitiveness of the European economy. The initial impetus for forming _____ was a response to the work of W. Edwards Deming and the development of the concepts of Total Quality Management.

Exam Probability: **Low**

42. *Answer choices:*

(see index for correct answer)

- a. E-TQM College
- b. EFQM
- c. TL 9000
- d. Quality Management Maturity Grid

Guidance: level 1

:: Help desk ::

Data center management is the collection of tasks performed by those responsible for managing ongoing operation of a data center This includes Business service management and planning for the future.

Exam Probability: **Low**

43. *Answer choices:*

(see index for correct answer)

- a. HEAT
- b. KnowledgeBase Manager Pro
- c. Supportworks
- d. SysAid Technologies

Guidance: level 1

:: Production and manufacturing ::

_____ is the process of determining the production capacity needed by an organization to meet changing demands for its products. In the context of _____, design capacity is the maximum amount of work that an organization is capable of completing in a given period. Effective capacity is the maximum amount of work that an organization is capable of completing in a given period due to constraints such as quality problems, delays, material handling, etc.

Exam Probability: **Medium**

44. *Answer choices:*

(see index for correct answer)

- a. Remanufacturing
- b. Capacity planning
- c. Transfer cars
- d. Value engineering

Guidance: level 1

:: ::

Some scenarios associate "this kind of planning" with learning "life skills". Schedules are necessary, or at least useful, in situations where individuals need to know what time they must be at a specific location to receive a specific service, and where people need to accomplish a set of goals within a set time period.

Exam Probability: **Low**

45. *Answer choices:*

(see index for correct answer)

- a. Scheduling
- b. Character
- c. hierarchical perspective
- d. surface-level diversity

Guidance: level 1

:: Management ::

_____ is the discipline of strategically planning for, and managing, all interactions with third party organizations that supply goods and/or services to an organization in order to maximize the value of those interactions. In practice, SRM entails creating closer, more collaborative relationships with key suppliers in order to uncover and realize new value and reduce risk of failure.

Exam Probability: **High**

46. Answer choices:

(see index for correct answer)

- a. Supplier relationship management
- b. U-procedure and Theory U
- c. Organizational space
- d. Planning fallacy

Guidance: level 1

:: Supply chain management ::

A _____ is a type of auction in which the traditional roles of buyer and seller are reversed. Thus, there is one buyer and many potential sellers. In an ordinary auction, buyers compete to obtain goods or services by offering increasingly higher prices. In contrast, in a _____, the sellers compete to obtain business from the buyer and prices will typically decrease as the sellers underbid each other.

Exam Probability: **Medium**

47. Answer choices:

(see index for correct answer)

- a. Disintermediation
- b. Corporate sourcing
- c. Reverse auction
- d. LLamasoft

Guidance: level 1

:: Packaging materials ::

_____ is a thin material produced by pressing together moist fibres of cellulose pulp derived from wood, rags or grasses, and drying them into flexible sheets. It is a versatile material with many uses, including writing, printing, packaging, cleaning, decorating, and a number of industrial and construction processes. _____ s are essential in legal or non-legal documentation.

Exam Probability: **Low**

48. *Answer choices:*

(see index for correct answer)

- a. Greensulate
- b. Paper
- c. Jute
- d. Pullulan

Guidance: level 1

:: ::

_____ is the production of products for use or sale using labour and machines, tools, chemical and biological processing, or formulation. The term may refer to a range of human activity, from handicraft to high tech, but is most commonly applied to industrial design, in which raw materials are transformed into finished goods on a large scale. Such finished goods may be sold to other manufacturers for the production of other, more complex products, such as aircraft, household appliances, furniture, sports equipment or automobiles, or sold to wholesalers, who in turn sell them to retailers, who then sell them to end users and consumers.

Exam Probability: **High**

49. *Answer choices:*

(see index for correct answer)

- a. co-culture
- b. Manufacturing
- c. process perspective
- d. corporate values

Guidance: level 1

:: Production and manufacturing ::

_____ is a systematic method to improve the "value" of goods or products and services by using an examination of function. Value, as defined, is the ratio of function to cost. Value can therefore be manipulated by either improving the function or reducing the cost. It is a primary tenet of _____ that basic functions be preserved and not be reduced as a consequence of pursuing value improvements.

Exam Probability: **Medium**

50. *Answer choices:*

(see index for correct answer)

- a. Wireless DNC
- b. Highly accelerated life test
- c. Product layout
- d. Factory Instrumentation Protocol

Guidance: level 1

:: Management ::

A _____ is an idea of the future or desired result that a person or a group of people envisions, plans and commits to achieve. People endeavor to reach _____ s within a finite time by setting deadlines.

Exam Probability: **High**

51. *Answer choices:*

(see index for correct answer)

- a. Linear scheduling method
- b. Goal
- c. Smiling curve
- d. DMSMS

Guidance: level 1

:: Industries ::

The _____ comprises the companies that produce industrial chemicals. Central to the modern world economy, it converts raw materials into more than 70,000 different products. The plastics industry contains some overlap, as most chemical companies produce plastic as well as other chemicals.

Exam Probability: **Low**

52. *Answer choices:*

(see index for correct answer)

- a. Alcohol industry
- b. New manufacturing economy
- c. Chemical industry
- d. Semiconductor industry

Guidance: level 1

:: Materials ::

A _____, also known as a feedstock, unprocessed material, or primary commodity, is a basic material that is used to produce goods, finished products, energy, or intermediate materials which are feedstock for future finished products. As feedstock, the term connotes these materials are bottleneck assets and are highly important with regard to producing other products. An example of this is crude oil, which is a _____ and a feedstock used in the production of industrial chemicals, fuels, plastics, and pharmaceutical goods; lumber is a _____ used to produce a variety of products including all types of furniture. The term "_____" denotes materials in minimally processed or unprocessed in states; e.g., raw latex, crude oil, cotton, coal, raw biomass, iron ore, air, logs, or water i.e. "...any product of agriculture, forestry, fishing and any other mineral that is in its natural form or which has undergone the transformation required to prepare it for internationally marketing in substantial volumes."

Exam Probability: **Medium**

53. *Answer choices:*
(see index for correct answer)

- a. Nordic Institute of Dental Materials
- b. Bio-based material
- c. Richlite
- d. Raw material

Guidance: level 1

:: Business planning ::

_____ is an organization's process of defining its strategy, or direction, and making decisions on allocating its resources to pursue this strategy. It may also extend to control mechanisms for guiding the implementation of the strategy. _____ became prominent in corporations during the 1960s and remains an important aspect of strategic management. It is executed by strategic planners or strategists, who involve many parties and research sources in their analysis of the organization and its relationship to the environment in which it competes.

Exam Probability: **High**

54. *Answer choices:*

(see index for correct answer)

- a. Strategic planning
- b. Customer Demand Planning
- c. Business war games
- d. Stakeholder management

Guidance: level 1

:: Asset ::

In financial accounting, an _____ is any resource owned by the business. Anything tangible or intangible that can be owned or controlled to produce value and that is held by a company to produce positive economic value is an _____. Simply stated, _____ s represent value of ownership that can be converted into cash. The balance sheet of a firm records the monetary value of the _____ s owned by that firm. It covers money and other valuables belonging to an individual or to a business.

Exam Probability: **Low**

55. *Answer choices:*
(see index for correct answer)

- a. Current asset
- b. Asset

Guidance: level 1

:: Production and manufacturing ::

An _____ is a manufacturing process in which parts are added as the semi-finished assembly moves from workstation to workstation where the parts are added in sequence until the final assembly is produced. By mechanically moving the parts to the assembly work and moving the semi-finished assembly from work station to work station, a finished product can be assembled faster and with less labor than by having workers carry parts to a stationary piece for assembly.

Exam Probability: **High**

56. Answer choices:

(see index for correct answer)

- a. Predetermined motion time system
- b. Assembly line
- c. Scientific management
- d. SynqNet

Guidance: level 1

:: Project management ::

A _____ is a type of bar chart that illustrates a project schedule, named after its inventor, Henry Gantt, who designed such a chart around the years 1910–1915. Modern _____ s also show the dependency relationships between activities and current schedule status.

Exam Probability: **High**

57. Answer choices:

(see index for correct answer)

- a. Gantt chart
- b. Graphical Evaluation and Review Technique
- c. Social project management
- d. Agile management

Guidance: level 1

:: Lean manufacturing ::

_____ is a Japanese term that means "mistake-proofing" or "inadvertent error prevention". A _____ is any mechanism in any process that helps an equipment operator avoid mistakes. Its purpose is to eliminate product defects by preventing, correcting, or drawing attention to human errors as they occur. The concept was formalised, and the term adopted, by Shigeo Shingo as part of the Toyota Production System. It was originally described as baka-yoke, but as this means "fool-proofing" the name was changed to the milder _____ .

Exam Probability: **Low**

58. *Answer choices:*
(see index for correct answer)

- a. takt
- b. Poka-yoke
- c. Production leveling
- d. Kanban

Guidance: level 1

:: Costs ::

In economics, _____ is the total economic cost of production and is made up of variable cost, which varies according to the quantity of a good produced and includes inputs such as labour and raw materials, plus fixed cost, which is independent of the quantity of a good produced and includes inputs that cannot be varied in the short term: fixed costs such as buildings and machinery, including sunk costs if any. Since cost is measured per unit of time, it is a flow variable.

Exam Probability: **High**

59. *Answer choices:*

(see index for correct answer)

- a. Further processing cost
- b. Explicit cost
- c. Total cost
- d. Repugnancy costs

Guidance: level 1

Commerce

Commerce relates to "the exchange of goods and services, especially on a large scale." It includes legal, economic, political, social, cultural and technological systems that operate in any country or internationally.

:: Commercial item transport and distribution ::

In a contract of carriage, the _____ is the entity who is financially responsible for the receipt of a shipment. Generally, but not always, the _____ is the same as the receiver.

Exam Probability: **Medium**

1. *Answer choices:*

(see index for correct answer)

- a. Materiel
- b. Backhaul
- c. Voice-directed warehousing
- d. Toll Global Logistics

Guidance: level 1

:: ::

In law, a _____ is a coming together of parties to a dispute, to present information in a tribunal, a formal setting with the authority to adjudicate claims or disputes. One form of tribunal is a court. The tribunal, which may occur before a judge, jury, or other designated trier of fact, aims to achieve a resolution to their dispute.

Exam Probability: **Low**

2. *Answer choices:*

(see index for correct answer)

- a. process perspective
- b. similarity-attraction theory
- c. Trial
- d. functional perspective

Guidance: level 1

:: Marketing analytics ::

> _____ is a long-term, forward-looking approach to planning with the fundamental goal of achieving a sustainable competitive advantage. Strategic planning involves an analysis of the company's strategic initial situation prior to the formulation, evaluation and selection of market-oriented competitive position that contributes to the company's goals and marketing objectives.

Exam Probability: **High**

3. *Answer choices:*

(see index for correct answer)

- a. Perceptual map
- b. Marketing strategy
- c. Advertising adstock
- d. Marketing performance measurement and management

Guidance: level 1

:: ::

_____ is the exchange of capital, goods, and services across international borders or territories.

Exam Probability: **Medium**

4. *Answer choices:*

(see index for correct answer)

- a. personal values
- b. International trade
- c. levels of analysis
- d. cultural

Guidance: level 1

:: ::

In international relations, _____ is – from the perspective of governments – a voluntary transfer of resources from one country to another.

Exam Probability: **Low**

5. *Answer choices:*

(see index for correct answer)

- a. Aid

- b. hierarchical perspective
- c. information systems assessment
- d. personal values

Guidance: level 1

:: Organizational structure ::

An _____ defines how activities such as task allocation, coordination, and supervision are directed toward the achievement of organizational aims.

Exam Probability: **Low**

6. *Answer choices:*
(see index for correct answer)

- a. Organization of the New York City Police Department
- b. Automated Bureaucracy
- c. Followership
- d. Organizational structure

Guidance: level 1

:: Management ::

Logistics is generally the detailed organization and implementation of a complex operation. In a general business sense, logistics is the management of the flow of things between the point of origin and the point of consumption in order to meet requirements of customers or corporations. The resources managed in logistics may include tangible goods such as materials, equipment, and supplies, as well as food and other consumable items. The logistics of physical items usually involves the integration of information flow, materials handling, production, packaging, inventory, transportation, warehousing, and often security.

Exam Probability: **High**

7. *Answer choices:*

(see index for correct answer)

- a. Logistics Management
- b. Competitive heterogeneity
- c. Action item
- d. Core competency

Guidance: level 1

A _____ is a fund into which a sum of money is added during an employee's employment years, and from which payments are drawn to support the person's retirement from work in the form of periodic payments. A _____ may be a "defined benefit plan" where a fixed sum is paid regularly to a person, or a "defined contribution plan" under which a fixed sum is invested and then becomes available at retirement age. _____s should not be confused with severance pay; the former is usually paid in regular installments for life after retirement, while the latter is typically paid as a fixed amount after involuntary termination of employment prior to retirement.

Exam Probability: **High**

8. *Answer choices:*

(see index for correct answer)

- a. personal values
- b. Pension
- c. Character
- d. co-culture

Guidance: level 1

:: E-commerce ::

A _____ is a financial transaction involving a very small sum of money and usually one that occurs online. A number of _____ systems were proposed and developed in the mid-to-late 1990s, all of which were ultimately unsuccessful. A second generation of _____ systems emerged in the 2010s.

Exam Probability: **High**

9. *Answer choices:*

(see index for correct answer)

- a. Consumer-to-consumer
- b. Micropayment
- c. Online marketplace
- d. Trymedia

Guidance: level 1

:: ::

A _____ is a professional who provides expert advice in a particular area such as security, management, education, accountancy, law, human resources, marketing, finance, engineering, science or any of many other specialized fields.

Exam Probability: **Medium**

10. *Answer choices:*

(see index for correct answer)

- a. levels of analysis
- b. Consultant
- c. surface-level diversity

- d. open system

Guidance: level 1

:: Scientific method ::

In the social sciences and life sciences, a _____ is a research method involving an up-close, in-depth, and detailed examination of a subject of study, as well as its related contextual conditions.

Exam Probability: **Low**

11. *Answer choices:*

(see index for correct answer)

- a. Case study
- b. Preference test
- c. explanatory research
- d. Causal research

Guidance: level 1

:: ::

_____ Corporation is an American multinational technology company with headquarters in Redmond, Washington. It develops, manufactures, licenses, supports and sells computer software, consumer electronics, personal computers, and related services. Its best known software products are the _____ Windows line of operating systems, the _____ Office suite, and the Internet Explorer and Edge Web browsers. Its flagship hardware products are the Xbox video game consoles and the _____ Surface lineup of touchscreen personal computers. As of 2016, it is the world's largest software maker by revenue, and one of the world's most valuable companies. The word "_____" is a portmanteau of "microcomputer" and "software". _____ is ranked No. 30 in the 2018 Fortune 500 rankings of the largest United States corporations by total revenue.

Exam Probability: **High**

12. *Answer choices:*

(see index for correct answer)

- a. cultural
- b. information systems assessment
- c. Microsoft
- d. Sarbanes-Oxley act of 2002

Guidance: level 1

:: Globalization-related theories ::

_____ is the process in which a nation is being improved in the sector of the economic, political, and social well-being of its people. The term has been used frequently by economists, politicians, and others in the 20th and 21st centuries. The concept, however, has been in existence in the West for centuries. "Modernization, "westernization", and especially "industrialization" are other terms often used while discussing _____ . _____ has a direct relationship with the environment and environmental issues. _____ is very often confused with industrial development, even in some academic sources.

Exam Probability: **Low**

13. *Answer choices:*

(see index for correct answer)

- a. Economic development
- b. post-industrial
- c. Capitalism

Guidance: level 1

:: Data interchange standards ::

_____ is the concept of businesses electronically communicating information that was traditionally communicated on paper, such as purchase orders and invoices. Technical standards for EDI exist to facilitate parties transacting such instruments without having to make special arrangements.

Exam Probability: **Medium**

14. *Answer choices:*

(see index for correct answer)

- a. Electronic data interchange
- b. ASC X12
- c. Data Interchange Standards Association
- d. Interaction protocol

Guidance: level 1

:: Industry ::

_____ describes various measures of the efficiency of production. Often , a _____ measure is expressed as the ratio of an aggregate output to a single input or an aggregate input used in a production process, i.e. output per unit of input. Most common example is the labour _____ measure, e.g., such as GDP per worker. There are many different definitions of _____ and the choice among them depends on the purpose of the _____ measurement and/or data availability. The key source of difference between various _____ measures is also usually related to how the outputs and the inputs are aggregated into scalars to obtain such a ratio-type measure of _____ .

Exam Probability: **High**

15. *Answer choices:*

(see index for correct answer)

- a. Industrial sociology
- b. Industrial society
- c. Industrial safety system
- d. Productivity

Guidance: level 1

:: Logistics ::

_____ is generally the detailed organization and implementation of a complex operation. In a general business sense, _____ is the management of the flow of things between the point of origin and the point of consumption in order to meet requirements of customers or corporations. The resources managed in _____ may include tangible goods such as materials, equipment, and supplies, as well as food and other consumable items. The _____ of physical items usually involves the integration of information flow, materials handling, production, packaging, inventory, transportation, warehousing, and often security.

Exam Probability: **Low**

16. *Answer choices:*

(see index for correct answer)

- a. StarShipIt
- b. Logistics
- c. Ground Parachute Extraction System
- d. Design for availability

Guidance: level 1

:: Theories ::

A _____ union is a type of multinational political union where negotiated power is delegated to an authority by governments of member states.

Exam Probability: **High**

17. *Answer choices:*

(see index for correct answer)

- a. Taylorism
- b. incrementalism

Guidance: level 1

:: Management ::

A _____ is an idea of the future or desired result that a person or a group of people envisions, plans and commits to achieve. People endeavor to reach _____ s within a finite time by setting deadlines.

Exam Probability: **Medium**

18. *Answer choices:*

(see index for correct answer)

- a. Authoritarian leadership style
- b. Resource breakdown structure
- c. Goal
- d. middle manager

Guidance: level 1

:: ::

_____ is the principled guide to action taken by the administrative executive branches of the state with regard to a class of issues, in a manner consistent with law and institutional customs.

Exam Probability: **High**

19. *Answer choices:*

(see index for correct answer)

- a. interpersonal communication
- b. Public policy
- c. levels of analysis
- d. process perspective

Guidance: level 1

Competition law is a law that promotes or seeks to maintain market competition by regulating anti-competitive conduct by companies. Competition law is implemented through public and private enforcement. Competition law is known as "_____ law" in the United States for historical reasons, and as "anti-monopoly law" in China and Russia. In previous years it has been known as trade practices law in the United Kingdom and Australia. In the European Union, it is referred to as both _____ and competition law.

Exam Probability: **Low**

20. *Answer choices:*

(see index for correct answer)

- a. Antitrust
- b. deep-level diversity
- c. levels of analysis
- d. corporate values

Guidance: level 1

An _____ in international trade is a good or service produced in one country that is bought by someone in another country. The seller of such goods and services is an _____ er; the foreign buyer is an importer.

Exam Probability: **High**

21. *Answer choices:*

(see index for correct answer)

- a. Export
- b. imperative
- c. cultural
- d. hierarchical

Guidance: level 1

:: Industry ::

A _____ is a set of sequential operations established in a factory where materials are put through a refining process to produce an end-product that is suitable for onward consumption; or components are assembled to make a finished article.

Exam Probability: **Low**

22. *Answer choices:*

(see index for correct answer)

- a. Mass production
- b. Production line
- c. International Standard Industrial Classification
- d. Industrial control system

Guidance: level 1

:: E-commerce ::

_____ is a type of performance-based marketing in which a business rewards one or more affiliates for each visitor or customer brought by the affiliate's own marketing efforts.

Exam Probability: **High**

23. *Answer choices:*

(see index for correct answer)

- a. KonaKart
- b. Eurocheque
- c. Mobile payment
- d. Computer security

Guidance: level 1

:: Hospitality industry ::

_____ refers to the relationship between a guest and a host, wherein the host receives the guest with goodwill, including the reception and entertainment of guests, visitors, or strangers. Louis, chevalier de Jaucourt describes _____ in the Encyclopédie as the virtue of a great soul that cares for the whole universe through the ties of humanity.

Exam Probability: **Low**

24. *Answer choices:*
(see index for correct answer)

- a. Hospitality
- b. Restaurant ware
- c. Hospitality industry
- d. Restaurant rating

Guidance: level 1

:: Asset ::

In financial accounting, an _____ is any resource owned by the business. Anything tangible or intangible that can be owned or controlled to produce value and that is held by a company to produce positive economic value is an _____ . Simply stated, _____ s represent value of ownership that can be converted into cash . The balance sheet of a firm records the monetary value of the _____ s owned by that firm. It covers money and other valuables belonging to an individual or to a business.

Exam Probability: **High**

25. *Answer choices:*

(see index for correct answer)

- a. Asset
- b. Current asset

Guidance: level 1

:: Market research ::

_____ is an organized effort to gather information about target markets or customers. It is a very important component of business strategy. The term is commonly interchanged with marketing research; however, expert practitioners may wish to draw a distinction, in that marketing research is concerned specifically about marketing processes, while _____ is concerned specifically with markets.

Exam Probability: **High**

26. *Answer choices:*

(see index for correct answer)

- a. New economic order
- b. Zyfin
- c. High Mark Credit Information Services
- d. Global environmental analysis

Guidance: level 1

:: ::

A _____ is monetary compensation paid by an employer to an employee in exchange for work done. Payment may be calculated as a fixed amount for each task completed, or at an hourly or daily rate, or based on an easily measured quantity of work done.

Exam Probability: **Medium**

27. *Answer choices:*

(see index for correct answer)

- a. co-culture
- b. imperative
- c. deep-level diversity
- d. Wage

Guidance: level 1

:: Auctioneering ::

_____ are electronic auctions, which can be used by sellers to sell their items to many potential buyers. Sellers and buyers can be individuals, organizations etc.

Exam Probability: **High**

28. *Answer choices:*

(see index for correct answer)

- a. Online auction
- b. Forward auction
- c. Auto auction
- d. Unique bid auction

Guidance: level 1

:: ::

_____ is the practical authority granted to a legal body to administer justice within a defined field of responsibility, e.g., Michigan tax law. In federations like the United States, areas of _____ apply to local, state, and federal levels; e.g. the court has _____ to apply federal law.

Exam Probability: **Low**

29. *Answer choices:*

(see index for correct answer)

- a. information systems assessment
- b. Jurisdiction
- c. functional perspective
- d. empathy

Guidance: level 1

:: ::

_____ is the collaborative effort of a team to achieve a common goal or to complete a task in the most effective and efficient way. This concept is seen within the greater framework of a team, which is a group of interdependent individuals who work together towards a common goal. Basic requirements for effective _____ are an adequate team size, available resources for the team to make use of, and clearly defined roles within the team in order for everyone to have a clear purpose. _____ is present in any context where a group of people are working together to achieve a common goal. These contexts include an industrial organization, athletics, a school, and the healthcare system. In each of these settings, the level of _____ and interdependence can vary from low, to intermediate, to high, depending on the amount of communication, interaction, and collaboration present between team members.

Exam Probability: **High**

30. *Answer choices:*

(see index for correct answer)

- a. cultural
- b. Teamwork
- c. information systems assessment
- d. process perspective

Guidance: level 1

:: E-commerce ::

The phrase _____ was originally coined in 1997 by Kevin Duffey at the launch of the Global _____ Forum, to mean "the delivery of electronic commerce capabilities directly into the consumer's hand, anywhere, via wireless technology." Many choose to think of _____ as meaning "a retail outlet in your customer's pocket."

Exam Probability: **Medium**

31. *Answer choices:*

(see index for correct answer)

- a. Online flower delivery
- b. Cleaning card
- c. MOL AccessPortal
- d. Mobile commerce

Guidance: level 1

:: ::

_____ is an American restaurant chain and international franchise which was founded in 1958 by Dan and Frank Carney. The company is known for its Italian-American cuisine menu, including pizza and pasta, as well as side dishes and desserts. _____ has 18,431 restaurants worldwide as of December 31, 2018, making it the world's largest pizza chain in terms of locations. It is a subsidiary of Yum! Brands, Inc., one of the world's largest restaurant companies.

Exam Probability: **Medium**

32. *Answer choices:*

(see index for correct answer)

- a. Pizza Hut
- b. hierarchical
- c. similarity-attraction theory
- d. deep-level diversity

Guidance: level 1

:: ::

A _____ is an individual or institution that legally owns one or more shares of stock in a public or private corporation. _____ s may be referred to as members of a corporation. Legally, a person is not a _____ in a corporation until their name and other details are entered in the corporation's register of _____ s or members.

Exam Probability: **High**

33. *Answer choices:*

(see index for correct answer)

- a. open system
- b. Shareholder

- c. empathy
- d. hierarchical

Guidance: level 1

:: Dot-com bubble ::

_____ was an online grocery business that filed bankruptcy in 2001 after 3 years of operation and was later folded into Amazon.com. It was headquartered in Foster City, California, United States. It delivered products to customers' homes within a 30-minute window of their choosing. At its peak, it offered service in ten US markets: the San Francisco Bay Area; Dallas; Sacramento; San Diego; Los Angeles; Orange County, California; Chicago; Seattle; Portland, Oregon; and Atlanta, Georgia. The company had hoped to expand to 26 cities by 2001.

Exam Probability: **Medium**

34. *Answer choices:*
(see index for correct answer)

- a. Freei
- b. Dot com party
- c. CyberRebate
- d. Webvan

Guidance: level 1

:: ::

A _____ , or also known as foreman, overseer, facilitator, monitor, area coordinator, or sometimes gaffer, is the job title of a low level management position that is primarily based on authority over a worker or charge of a workplace. A _____ can also be one of the most senior in the staff at the place of work, such as a Professor who oversees a PhD dissertation. Supervision, on the other hand, can be performed by people without this formal title, for example by parents. The term _____ itself can be used to refer to any personnel who have this task as part of their job description.

Exam Probability: **High**

35. *Answer choices:*

(see index for correct answer)

- a. Supervisor
- b. Character
- c. levels of analysis
- d. similarity-attraction theory

Guidance: level 1

:: E-commerce ::

An _____, or automated clearinghouse, is an electronic network for financial transactions, generally domestic low value payments. An ACH is a computer-based clearing house and settlement facility established to process the exchange of electronic transactions between participating financial institutions. It is a form of clearing house that is specifically for payments and may support both credit transfers and direct debits.

Exam Probability: **Medium**

36. *Answer choices:*

(see index for correct answer)

- a. Network Security Services
- b. Paid content
- c. Mobile commerce
- d. Wanelo

Guidance: level 1

:: Generally Accepted Accounting Principles ::

In accounting, _____ is the income that a business have from its normal business activities, usually from the sale of goods and services to customers. _____ is also referred to as sales or turnover. Some companies receive _____ from interest, royalties, or other fees. _____ may refer to business income in general, or it may refer to the amount, in a monetary unit, earned during a period of time, as in "Last year, Company X had _____ of $42 million". Profits or net income generally imply total _____ minus total expenses in a given period. In accounting, in the balance statement it is a subsection of the Equity section and _____ increases equity, it is often referred to as the "top line" due to its position on the income statement at the very top. This is to be contrasted with the "bottom line" which denotes net income.

Exam Probability: **Low**

37. *Answer choices:*

(see index for correct answer)

- a. Paid in capital
- b. Normal balance
- c. Shares outstanding
- d. Revenue

Guidance: level 1

:: ::

In the broadest sense, _____ is any practice which contributes to the sale of products to a retail consumer. At a retail in-store level, _____ refers to the variety of products available for sale and the display of those products in such a way that it stimulates interest and entices customers to make a purchase.

Exam Probability: **Low**

38. *Answer choices:*

(see index for correct answer)

- a. process perspective
- b. personal values
- c. co-culture
- d. empathy

Guidance: level 1

:: Insolvency ::

_____ is the process in accounting by which a company is brought to an end in the United Kingdom, Republic of Ireland and United States. The assets and property of the company are redistributed. _____ is also sometimes referred to as winding-up or dissolution, although dissolution technically refers to the last stage of _____. The process of _____ also arises when customs, an authority or agency in a country responsible for collecting and safeguarding customs duties, determines the final computation or ascertainment of the duties or drawback accruing on an entry.

Exam Probability: **High**

39. *Answer choices:*

(see index for correct answer)

- a. Liquidation
- b. Bankruptcy
- c. Insolvency
- d. Financial distress

Guidance: level 1

:: International trade ::

_____ involves the transfer of goods or services from one person or entity to another, often in exchange for money. A system or network that allows _____ is called a market.

Exam Probability: **Medium**

40. *Answer choices:*

(see index for correct answer)

- a. Intervention stocks
- b. Indian Ocean trade
- c. Trade
- d. Bullionism

Guidance: level 1

:: Game theory ::

To _____ is to make a deal between different parties where each party gives up part of their demand. In arguments, _____ is a concept of finding agreement through communication, through a mutual acceptance of terms—often involving variations from an original goal or desires.

Exam Probability: **High**

41. *Answer choices:*

(see index for correct answer)

- a. Pursuit-evasion
- b. Multiunit auction
- c. Compromise
- d. Lewis signaling game

Guidance: level 1

:: ::

In legal terminology, a _____ is any formal legal document that sets out the facts and legal reasons that the filing party or parties believes are sufficient to support a claim against the party or parties against whom the claim is brought that entitles the plaintiff to a remedy. For example, the Federal Rules of Civil Procedure that govern civil litigation in United States courts provide that a civil action is commenced with the filing or service of a pleading called a _____. Civil court rules in states that have incorporated the Federal Rules of Civil Procedure use the same term for the same pleading.

Exam Probability: **Low**

42. *Answer choices:*

(see index for correct answer)

- a. Complaint
- b. functional perspective
- c. personal values
- d. imperative

Guidance: level 1

:: Accounting source documents ::

A _____ is a commercial document and first official offer issued by a buyer to a seller indicating types, quantities, and agreed prices for products or services. It is used to control the purchasing of products and services from external suppliers. _____ s can be an essential part of enterprise resource planning system orders.

Exam Probability: **High**

43. *Answer choices:*

(see index for correct answer)

- a. Purchase order
- b. Credit memorandum
- c. Superbill
- d. Bank statement

Guidance: level 1

:: ::

The Walt _____ Company, commonly known as Walt _____ or simply _____, is an American diversified multinational mass media and entertainment conglomerate headquartered at the Walt _____ Studios in Burbank, California.

Exam Probability: **Low**

44. *Answer choices:*

(see index for correct answer)

- a. personal values
- b. imperative
- c. levels of analysis

- d. corporate values

Guidance: level 1

:: Production economics ::

In economics and related disciplines, a _____ is a cost in making any economic trade when participating in a market.

Exam Probability: **Low**

45. *Answer choices:*

(see index for correct answer)

- a. Value and Capital
- b. Isocost
- c. Socially optimal firm size
- d. Factor price

Guidance: level 1

:: ::

In logic and philosophy, an _____ is a series of statements, called the premises or premisses, intended to determine the degree of truth of another statement, the conclusion. The logical form of an _____ in a natural language can be represented in a symbolic formal language, and independently of natural language formally defined " _____ s" can be made in math and computer science.

Exam Probability: **High**

46. *Answer choices:*

(see index for correct answer)

- a. Argument
- b. Sarbanes-Oxley act of 2002
- c. open system
- d. information systems assessment

Guidance: level 1

:: Management ::

The term _____ refers to measures designed to increase the degree of autonomy and self-determination in people and in communities in order to enable them to represent their interests in a responsible and self-determined way, acting on their own authority. It is the process of becoming stronger and more confident, especially in controlling one's life and claiming one's rights.

_____ as action refers both to the process of self-_____ and to professional support of people, which enables them to overcome their sense of powerlessness and lack of influence, and to recognize and use their resources. To do work with power.

Exam Probability: **High**

47. *Answer choices:*

(see index for correct answer)

- a. Infrastructure asset management
- b. Hierarchical organization
- c. Empowerment
- d. Maryland StateStat

Guidance: level 1

_____, in general use, is a devotion and faithfulness to a nation, cause, philosophy, country, group, or person. Philosophers disagree on what can be an object of _____, as some argue that _____ is strictly interpersonal and only another human being can be the object of _____. The definition of _____ in law and political science is the fidelity of an individual to a nation, either one's nation of birth, or one's declared home nation by oath.

Exam Probability: **High**

48. *Answer choices:*

(see index for correct answer)

- a. cultural
- b. hierarchical perspective
- c. Loyalty
- d. open system

Guidance: level 1

:: ::

In law, an _____ is the process in which cases are reviewed, where parties request a formal change to an official decision. _____ s function both as a process for error correction as well as a process of clarifying and interpreting law. Although appellate courts have existed for thousands of years, common law countries did not incorporate an affirmative right to _____ into their jurisprudence until the 19th century.

Exam Probability: **Low**

49. *Answer choices:*

(see index for correct answer)

- a. Appeal
- b. open system
- c. hierarchical
- d. deep-level diversity

Guidance: level 1

:: ::

_____s and acquisitions are transactions in which the ownership of companies, other business organizations, or their operating units are transferred or consolidated with other entities. As an aspect of strategic management, M&A can allow enterprises to grow or downsize, and change the nature of their business or competitive position.

Exam Probability: **Medium**

50. *Answer choices:*

(see index for correct answer)

- a. Sarbanes-Oxley act of 2002
- b. Merger

- c. cultural
- d. similarity-attraction theory

Guidance: level 1

:: ::

In marketing jargon, product lining is offering several related products for sale individually. Unlike product bundling, where several products are combined into one group, which is then offered for sale as a units, product lining involves offering the products for sale separately. A line can comprise related products of various sizes, types, colors, qualities, or prices. Line depth refers to the number of subcategories a category has. Line consistency refers to how closely related the products that make up the line are. Line vulnerability refers to the percentage of sales or profits that are derived from only a few products in the line.

Exam Probability: **High**

51. *Answer choices:*

(see index for correct answer)

- a. Sarbanes-Oxley act of 2002
- b. interpersonal communication
- c. hierarchical
- d. information systems assessment

Guidance: level 1

:: Management ::

_____ is the process of thinking about the activities required to achieve a desired goal. It is the first and foremost activity to achieve desired results. It involves the creation and maintenance of a plan, such as psychological aspects that require conceptual skills. There are even a couple of tests to measure someone's capability of _____ well. As such, _____ is a fundamental property of intelligent behavior. An important further meaning, often just called " _____ " is the legal context of permitted building developments.

Exam Probability: **Medium**

52. *Answer choices:*

(see index for correct answer)

- a. Planning
- b. Task-oriented and relationship-oriented leadership
- c. Sensemaking
- d. Value migration

Guidance: level 1

:: Cryptography ::

In cryptography, _____ is the process of encoding a message or information in such a way that only authorized parties can access it and those who are not authorized cannot. _____ does not itself prevent interference, but denies the intelligible content to a would-be interceptor. In an _____ scheme, the intended information or message, referred to as plaintext, is encrypted using an _____ algorithm – a cipher – generating ciphertext that can be read only if decrypted. For technical reasons, an _____ scheme usually uses a pseudo-random _____ key generated by an algorithm. It is in principle possible to decrypt the message without possessing the key, but, for a well-designed _____ scheme, considerable computational resources and skills are required. An authorized recipient can easily decrypt the message with the key provided by the originator to recipients but not to unauthorized users.

Exam Probability: **Medium**

53. *Answer choices:*

(see index for correct answer)

- a. ciphertext
- b. plaintext
- c. Encryption
- d. cryptosystem

Guidance: level 1

:: Credit cards ::

A _____ is a payment card issued to users to enable the cardholder to pay a merchant for goods and services based on the cardholder's promise to the card issuer to pay them for the amounts plus the other agreed charges. The card issuer creates a revolving account and grants a line of credit to the cardholder, from which the cardholder can borrow money for payment to a merchant or as a cash advance.

Exam Probability: **Medium**

54. *Answer choices:*

(see index for correct answer)

- a. Rail travel card
- b. Cashplus
- c. EnRoute
- d. Credit card

Guidance: level 1

:: Income ::

_____ is the application of disciplined analytics that predict consumer behaviour at the micro-market levels and optimize product availability and price to maximize revenue growth. The primary aim of _____ is selling the right product to the right customer at the right time for the right price and with the right pack. The essence of this discipline is in understanding customers' perception of product value and accurately aligning product prices, placement and availability with each customer segment.

Exam Probability: **Medium**

55. *Answer choices:*

(see index for correct answer)

- a. Revenue management
- b. Return on investment
- c. Per capita income
- d. Net national income

Guidance: level 1

:: ::

The _____ is a political and economic union of 28 member states that are located primarily in Europe. It has an area of 4,475,757 km2 and an estimated population of about 513 million. The EU has developed an internal single market through a standardised system of laws that apply in all member states in those matters, and only those matters, where members have agreed to act as one. EU policies aim to ensure the free movement of people, goods, services and capital within the internal market, enact legislation in justice and home affairs and maintain common policies on trade, agriculture, fisheries and regional development. For travel within the Schengen Area, passport controls have been abolished. A monetary union was established in 1999 and came into full force in 2002 and is composed of 19 EU member states which use the euro currency.

Exam Probability: **High**

56. Answer choices:

(see index for correct answer)

- a. corporate values
- b. European Union
- c. Sarbanes-Oxley act of 2002
- d. Character

Guidance: level 1

:: Information technology management ::

_____s or pop-ups are forms of online advertising on the World Wide Web. A pop-up is a graphical user interface display area, usually a small window, that suddenly appears in the foreground of the visual interface. The pop-up window containing an advertisement is usually generated by JavaScript that uses cross-site scripting, sometimes with a secondary payload that uses Adobe Flash. They can also be generated by other vulnerabilities/security holes in browser security.

Exam Probability: **High**

57. Answer choices:

(see index for correct answer)

- a. Building lifecycle management
- b. Mung
- c. Wire data

- d. Pop-up ad

Guidance: level 1

:: ::

Employment is a relationship between two parties, usually based on a contract where work is paid for, where one party, which may be a corporation, for profit, not-for-profit organization, co-operative or other entity is the employer and the other is the employee. Employees work in return for payment, which may be in the form of an hourly wage, by piecework or an annual salary, depending on the type of work an employee does or which sector she or he is working in. Employees in some fields or sectors may receive gratuities, bonus payment or stock options. In some types of employment, employees may receive benefits in addition to payment. Benefits can include health insurance, housing, disability insurance or use of a gym. Employment is typically governed by employment laws, regulations or legal contracts.

Exam Probability: **Medium**

58. *Answer choices:*
(see index for correct answer)

- a. Personnel
- b. levels of analysis
- c. empathy
- d. process perspective

Guidance: level 1

:: ::

_____ is the practice of deliberately managing the spread of information between an individual or an organization and the public. _____ may include an organization or individual gaining exposure to their audiences using topics of public interest and news items that do not require direct payment. This differentiates it from advertising as a form of marketing communications. _____ is the idea of creating coverage for clients for free, rather than marketing or advertising. But now, advertising is also a part of greater PR Activities. An example of good _____ would be generating an article featuring a client, rather than paying for the client to be advertised next to the article. The aim of _____ is to inform the public, prospective customers, investors, partners, employees, and other stakeholders and ultimately persuade them to maintain a positive or favorable view about the organization, its leadership, products, or political decisions. _____ professionals typically work for PR and marketing firms, businesses and companies, government, and public officials as PIOs and nongovernmental organizations, and nonprofit organizations. Jobs central to _____ include account coordinator, account executive, account supervisor, and media relations manager.

Exam Probability: **High**

59. *Answer choices:*

(see index for correct answer)

- a. Public relations
- b. surface-level diversity
- c. corporate values
- d. Sarbanes-Oxley act of 2002

Guidance: level 1

Business ethics

   Business ethics (also known as corporate ethics) is a form of applied ethics or professional ethics, that examines ethical principles and moral or ethical problems that can arise in a business environment. It applies to all aspects of business conduct and is relevant to the conduct of individuals and entire organizations. These ethics originate from individuals, organizational statements or from the legal system. These norms, values, ethical, and unethical practices are what is used to guide business. They help those businesses maintain a better connection with their stakeholders.

The _____ is an agency of the United States Department of Labor. Congress established the agency under the Occupational Safety and Health Act, which President Richard M. Nixon signed into law on December 29, 1970. OSHA's mission is to "assure safe and healthy working conditions for working men and women by setting and enforcing standards and by providing training, outreach, education and assistance". The agency is also charged with enforcing a variety of whistleblower statutes and regulations. OSHA is currently headed by Acting Assistant Secretary of Labor Loren Sweatt. OSHA's workplace safety inspections have been shown to reduce injury rates and injury costs without adverse effects to employment, sales, credit ratings, or firm survival.

Exam Probability: **High**

1. *Answer choices:*

(see index for correct answer)

- a. personal values
- b. Occupational Safety and Health Administration
- c. open system
- d. corporate values

Guidance: level 1

The American Recovery and Reinvestment Act of 2009, nicknamed the _____, was a stimulus package enacted by the 111th U.S. Congress and signed into law by President Barack Obama in February 2009. Developed in response to the Great Recession, the ARRA's primary objective was to save existing jobs and create new ones as soon as possible. Other objectives were to provide temporary relief programs for those most affected by the recession and invest in infrastructure, education, health, and renewable energy.

Exam Probability: **High**

2. *Answer choices:*

(see index for correct answer)

- a. interpersonal communication
- b. Recovery Act
- c. hierarchical
- d. co-culture

Guidance: level 1

Sustainability is the process of people maintaining change in a balanced environment, in which the exploitation of resources, the direction of investments, the orientation of technological development and institutional change are all in harmony and enhance both current and future potential to meet human needs and aspirations. For many in the field, sustainability is defined through the following interconnected domains or pillars: environment, economic and social, which according to Fritjof Capra is based on the principles of Systems Thinking. Sub-domains of _____ development have been considered also: cultural, technological and political. While _____ development may be the organizing principle for sustainability for some, for others, the two terms are paradoxical. _____ development is the development that meets the needs of the present without compromising the ability of future generations to meet their own needs. Brundtland Report for the World Commission on Environment and Development introduced the term of _____ development.

Exam Probability: **High**

3. *Answer choices:*

(see index for correct answer)

- a. Sustainable
- b. interpersonal communication
- c. cultural
- d. hierarchical perspective

Guidance: level 1

:: Renewable energy ::

A _____ is a fuel that is produced through contemporary biological processes, such as agriculture and anaerobic digestion, rather than a fuel produced by geological processes such as those involved in the formation of fossil fuels, such as coal and petroleum, from prehistoric biological matter. If the source biomatter can regrow quickly, the resulting fuel is said to be a form of renewable energy.

Exam Probability: **Low**

4. *Answer choices:*

(see index for correct answer)

- a. Hi-VAWT
- b. Micro combined heat and power
- c. Army Energy Initiatives Task Force
- d. Biofuel

Guidance: level 1

:: ::

The _____ is an institution of the European Union, responsible for proposing legislation, implementing decisions, upholding the EU treaties and managing the day-to-day business of the EU. Commissioners swear an oath at the European Court of Justice in Luxembourg City, pledging to respect the treaties and to be completely independent in carrying out their duties during their mandate. Unlike in the Council of the European Union, where members are directly and indirectly elected, and the European Parliament, where members are directly elected, the Commissioners are proposed by the Council of the European Union, on the basis of suggestions made by the national governments, and then appointed by the European Council after the approval of the European Parliament.

Exam Probability: **High**

5. *Answer choices:*

(see index for correct answer)

- a. surface-level diversity
- b. functional perspective
- c. information systems assessment
- d. European Commission

Guidance: level 1

:: Auditing ::

_____ is a general term that can reflect various types of evaluations intended to identify environmental compliance and management system implementation gaps, along with related corrective actions. In this way they perform an analogous function to financial audits. There are generally two different types of _____ s: compliance audits and management systems audits. Compliance audits tend to be the primary type in the US or within US-based multinationals.

Exam Probability: **Low**

6. *Answer choices:*

(see index for correct answer)

- a. Verified Audit Circulation
- b. Certified Quality Auditor
- c. Utility bill audit
- d. Audit Bureau of Circulations

Guidance: level 1

:: Supply chain management terms ::

In business and finance, _____ is a system of organizations, people, activities, information, and resources involved in moving a product or service from supplier to customer. _____ activities involve the transformation of natural resources, raw materials, and components into a finished product that is delivered to the end customer. In sophisticated _____ systems, used products may re-enter the _____ at any point where residual value is recyclable. _____ s link value chains.

Exam Probability: **Low**

7. *Answer choices:*

(see index for correct answer)

- a. Stockout
- b. Supply Chain
- c. Consumables
- d. Last mile

Guidance: level 1

:: Price fixing convictions ::

_____ AG is a German multinational conglomerate company headquartered in Berlin and Munich and the largest industrial manufacturing company in Europe with branch offices abroad.

Exam Probability: **Medium**

8. *Answer choices:*

(see index for correct answer)

- a. United States v. Archer Daniels Midland Co.
- b. Grolsch Brewery
- c. Christmas tree production in Denmark
- d. YKK Group

Guidance: level 1

:: Cultural appropriation ::

_____ is a social and economic order that encourages the acquisition of goods and services in ever-increasing amounts. With the industrial revolution, but particularly in the 20th century, mass production led to an economic crisis: there was overproduction—the supply of goods would grow beyond consumer demand, and so manufacturers turned to planned obsolescence and advertising to manipulate consumer spending. In 1899, a book on _____ published by Thorstein Veblen, called The Theory of the Leisure Class, examined the widespread values and economic institutions emerging along with the widespread "leisure time" in the beginning of the 20th century. In it Veblen "views the activities and spending habits of this leisure class in terms of conspicuous and vicarious consumption and waste. Both are related to the display of status and not to functionality or usefulness."

Exam Probability: **Medium**

9. *Answer choices:*

(see index for correct answer)

- a. Consumerism
- b. Coon Chicken Inn
- c. Hollywood Indian
- d. Pretty Fly

Guidance: level 1

:: Industrial ecology ::

_____ is a strategy for reducing the amount of waste created and released into the environment, particularly by industrial facilities, agriculture, or consumers. Many large corporations view P2 as a method of improving the efficiency and profitability of production processes by technology advancements. Legislative bodies have enacted P2 measures, such as the _____ Act of 1990 and the Clean Air Act Amendments of 1990 by the United States Congress.

Exam Probability: **Low**

10. *Answer choices:*

(see index for correct answer)

- a. Pollution Prevention
- b. Zero waste
- c. Energetics
- d. Ecological modernization

Guidance: level 1

:: Minimum wage ::

A _____ is the lowest remuneration that employers can legally pay their workers—the price floor below which workers may not sell their labor. Most countries had introduced _____ legislation by the end of the 20th century.

Exam Probability: **Medium**

11. *Answer choices:*

(see index for correct answer)

- a. Minimum Wage Fairness Act
- b. Minimum wage in the United States
- c. Guaranteed minimum income
- d. Minimum wage

Guidance: level 1

:: ::

Competition law is a law that promotes or seeks to maintain market competition by regulating anti-competitive conduct by companies. Competition law is implemented through public and private enforcement. Competition law is known as "_____ law" in the United States for historical reasons, and as "anti-monopoly law" in China and Russia. In previous years it has been known as trade practices law in the United Kingdom and Australia. In the European Union, it is referred to as both _____ and competition law.

Exam Probability: **High**

12. *Answer choices:*

(see index for correct answer)

- a. Character

- b. open system
- c. personal values
- d. cultural

Guidance: level 1

:: ::

A _____ is a problem offering two possibilities, neither of which is unambiguously acceptable or preferable. The possibilities are termed the horns of the _____, a clichéd usage, but distinguishing the _____ from other kinds of predicament as a matter of usage.

Exam Probability: **High**

13. *Answer choices:*

(see index for correct answer)

- a. imperative
- b. Dilemma
- c. process perspective
- d. corporate values

Guidance: level 1

:: Types of marketing ::

_____ is an advertisement strategy in which a company uses surprise and/or unconventional interactions in order to promote a product or service. It is a type of publicity. The term was popularized by Jay Conrad Levinson's 1984 book _____ .

Exam Probability: **Medium**

14. *Answer choices:*

(see index for correct answer)

- a. Close Range Marketing
- b. Relationship marketing
- c. Social pull marketing
- d. Influencer marketing

Guidance: level 1

:: Business ::

_____ , or built-in obsolescence, in industrial design and economics is a policy of planning or designing a product with an artificially limited useful life, so that it becomes obsolete after a certain period of time. The rationale behind this strategy is to generate long-term sales volume by reducing the time between repeat purchases .

Exam Probability: **Medium**

15. *Answer choices:*

(see index for correct answer)

- a. Business interaction networks
- b. Planned obsolescence
- c. Business mileage reimbursement rate
- d. Service recovery

Guidance: level 1

:: Parental leave ::

_____ , or family leave, is an employee benefit available in almost all countries. The term " _____ " may include maternity, paternity, and adoption leave; or may be used distinctively from "maternity leave" and "paternity leave" to describe separate family leave available to either parent to care for small children. In some countries and jurisdictions, "family leave" also includes leave provided to care for ill family members. Often, the minimum benefits and eligibility requirements are stipulated by law.

Exam Probability: **Medium**

16. *Answer choices:*

(see index for correct answer)

- a. Parental leave
- b. Pregnancy discrimination
- c. Sara Hlupekile Longwe

- d. Motherhood penalty

Guidance: level 1

:: ::

_____ is a non-governmental environmental organization with offices in over 39 countries and an international coordinating body in Amsterdam, the Netherlands. _____ was founded in 1971 by Irving Stowe, and Dorothy Stowe, Canadian and US ex-pat environmental activists. _____ states its goal is to "ensure the ability of the Earth to nurture life in all its diversity" and focuses its campaigning on worldwide issues such as climate change, deforestation, overfishing, commercial whaling, genetic engineering, and anti-nuclear issues. It uses direct action, lobbying, research, and ecotage to achieve its goals. The global organization does not accept funding from governments, corporations, or political parties, relying on three million individual supporters and foundation grants. _____ has a general consultative status with the United Nations Economic and Social Council and is a founding member of the INGO Accountability Charter, an international non-governmental organization that intends to foster accountability and transparency of non-governmental organizations.

Exam Probability: **High**

17. *Answer choices:*

(see index for correct answer)

- a. empathy
- b. hierarchical perspective
- c. information systems assessment

- d. Greenpeace

Guidance: level 1

:: Carbon finance ::

The _____ is an international treaty which extends the 1992 United Nations Framework Convention on Climate Change that commits state parties to reduce greenhouse gas emissions, based on the scientific consensus that global warming is occurring and it is extremely likely that human-made CO2 emissions have predominantly caused it. The _____ was adopted in Kyoto, Japan on 11 December 1997 and entered into force on 16 February 2005. There are currently 192 parties to the Protocol.

Exam Probability: **Low**

18. *Answer choices:*

(see index for correct answer)

- a. Chinese national carbon trading scheme
- b. CEB VER
- c. Carbon finance
- d. Kyoto Protocol

Guidance: level 1

:: Agricultural labor ::

The _____ of America, or more commonly just _____, is a labor union for farmworkers in the United States. It originated from the merger of two workers' rights organizations, the Agricultural Workers Organizing Committee led by organizer Larry Itliong, and the National Farm Workers Association led by César Chávez and Dolores Huerta. They became allied and transformed from workers' rights organizations into a union as a result of a series of strikes in 1965, when the mostly Filipino farmworkers of the AWOC in Delano, California initiated a grape strike, and the NFWA went on strike in support. As a result of the commonality in goals and methods, the NFWA and the AWOC formed the _____ Organizing Committee on August 22, 1966. This organization was accepted into the AFL-CIO in 1972 and changed its name to the _____ Union.

Exam Probability: **Low**

19. *Answer choices:*

(see index for correct answer)

- a. Bailleur
- b. United Farm Workers
- c. Kibbutz
- d. Bracero program

Guidance: level 1

:: Social enterprise ::

Corporate social responsibility is a type of international private business self-regulation. While once it was possible to describe CSR as an internal organisational policy or a corporate ethic strategy, that time has passed as various international laws have been developed and various organisations have used their authority to push it beyond individual or even industry-wide initiatives. While it has been considered a form of corporate self-regulation for some time, over the last decade or so it has moved considerably from voluntary decisions at the level of individual organisations, to mandatory schemes at regional, national and even transnational levels.

Exam Probability: **Low**

20. *Answer choices:*

(see index for correct answer)

- a. Social enterprise
- b. Corporate citizenship

Guidance: level 1

:: International trade ::

_____ involves the transfer of goods or services from one person or entity to another, often in exchange for money. A system or network that allows _____ is called a market.

Exam Probability: **High**

21. *Answer choices:*

(see index for correct answer)

- a. Directive on services in the internal market
- b. Gains from trade
- c. Trade
- d. Producer support estimate

Guidance: level 1

:: Management ::

_____ is the identification, evaluation, and prioritization of risks followed by coordinated and economical application of resources to minimize, monitor, and control the probability or impact of unfortunate events or to maximize the realization of opportunities.

Exam Probability: **High**

22. *Answer choices:*

(see index for correct answer)

- a. Security management
- b. Risk management
- c. Industrial democracy
- d. Core competency

Guidance: level 1

:: Business ethics ::

_____ is a type of international private business self-regulation. While once it was possible to describe CSR as an internal organisational policy or a corporate ethic strategy, that time has passed as various international laws have been developed and various organisations have used their authority to push it beyond individual or even industry-wide initiatives. While it has been considered a form of corporate self-regulation for some time, over the last decade or so it has moved considerably from voluntary decisions at the level of individual organisations, to mandatory schemes at regional, national and even transnational levels.

Exam Probability: **High**

23. *Answer choices:*

(see index for correct answer)

- a. Enron Code of Ethics
- b. Corporate social responsibility
- c. United Nations Global Compact
- d. Equator Principles

Guidance: level 1

:: Utilitarianism ::

_____ is a school of thought that argues that the pursuit of pleasure and intrinsic goods are the primary or most important goals of human life. A hedonist strives to maximize net pleasure. However upon finally gaining said pleasure, happiness may remain stationary.

Exam Probability: **Low**

24. *Answer choices:*

(see index for correct answer)

- a. Utilitarianism
- b. Hedonism
- c. The Theory of Good and Evil
- d. Act utilitarianism

Guidance: level 1

:: Business ethics ::

The _____ are the names of two corporate codes of conduct, developed by the African-American preacher Rev. Leon Sullivan, promoting corporate social responsibility.

Exam Probability: **Low**

25. *Answer choices:*

(see index for correct answer)

- a. Anatomy of Greed
- b. Sullivan principles
- c. The Crooked E: The Unshredded Truth About Enron
- d. Equator Principles

Guidance: level 1

:: ::

A _____ is an astronomical body orbiting a star or stellar remnant that is massive enough to be rounded by its own gravity, is not massive enough to cause thermonuclear fusion, and has cleared its neighbouring region of _____ esimals.

Exam Probability: **Medium**

26. *Answer choices:*

(see index for correct answer)

- a. Character
- b. similarity-attraction theory
- c. Planet
- d. hierarchical

Guidance: level 1

:: Human resource management ::

_____ is the ethics of an organization, and it is how an organization responds to an internal or external stimulus. _____ is interdependent with the organizational culture. Although it is akin to both organizational behavior and industrial and organizational psychology as well as business ethics on the micro and macro levels, _____ is neither OB or I/O psychology, nor is it solely business ethics. _____ express the values of an organization to its employees and/or other entities irrespective of governmental and/or regulatory laws.

Exam Probability: **Medium**

27. *Answer choices:*

(see index for correct answer)

- a. Emotional labor
- b. Organizational ethics
- c. Job enlargement
- d. Management by objectives

Guidance: level 1

:: United States federal labor legislation ::

The _____ of 1988 is a United States federal law that generally prevents employers from using polygraph tests, either for pre-employment screening or during the course of employment, with certain exemptions.

Exam Probability: **Low**

28. *Answer choices:*

(see index for correct answer)

- a. Anti-Pinkerton Act
- b. Civil Rights Act of 1964
- c. Employee Polygraph Protection Act
- d. Federal Employers Liability Act

Guidance: level 1

:: Anti-competitive behaviour ::

_____ is a secret cooperation or deceitful agreement in order to deceive others, although not necessarily illegal, as a conspiracy. A secret agreement between two or more parties to limit open competition by deceiving, misleading, or defrauding others of their legal rights, or to obtain an objective forbidden by law typically by defrauding or gaining an unfair market advantage is an example of _____. It is an agreement among firms or individuals to divide a market, set prices, limit production or limit opportunities. It can involve "unions, wage fixing, kickbacks, or misrepresenting the independence of the relationship between the colluding parties". In legal terms, all acts effected by _____ are considered void.

Exam Probability: **Low**

29. *Answer choices:*

(see index for correct answer)

- a. Collusion
- b. Field-of-use limitation
- c. Barriers to entry
- d. Unilateral policy

Guidance: level 1

:: Social responsibility ::

The United Nations Global Compact is a non-binding United Nations pact to encourage businesses worldwide to adopt sustainable and socially responsible policies, and to report on their implementation. The _____ is a principle-based framework for businesses, stating ten principles in the areas of human rights, labor, the environment and anti-corruption. Under the Global Compact, companies are brought together with UN agencies, labor groups and civil society. Cities can join the Global Compact through the Cities Programme.

Exam Probability: **High**

30. *Answer choices:*

(see index for correct answer)

- a. Stakeholder engagement
- b. UN Global Compact
- c. Collective impact
- d. Footprints network

Guidance: level 1

:: ::

_____ is an eight-block-long street running roughly northwest to southeast from Broadway to South Street, at the East River, in the Financial District of Lower Manhattan in New York City. Over time, the term has become a metonym for the financial markets of the United States as a whole, the American financial services industry, or New York–based financial interests.

Exam Probability: **High**

31. *Answer choices:*

(see index for correct answer)

- a. Wall Street
- b. process perspective
- c. similarity-attraction theory
- d. hierarchical

Guidance: level 1

:: ::

The _____ of 1906 was the first of a series of significant consumer protection laws which was enacted by Congress in the 20th century and led to the creation of the Food and Drug Administration. Its main purpose was to ban foreign and interstate traffic in adulterated or mislabeled food and drug products, and it directed the U.S. Bureau of Chemistry to inspect products and refer offenders to prosecutors. It required that active ingredients be placed on the label of a drug's packaging and that drugs could not fall below purity levels established by the United States Pharmacopeia or the National Formulary. The Jungle by Upton Sinclair with its graphic and revolting descriptions of unsanitary conditions and unscrupulous practices rampant in the meatpacking industry, was an inspirational piece that kept the public's attention on the important issue of unhygienic meat processing plants that later led to food inspection legislation. Sinclair quipped, "I aimed at the public's heart and by accident I hit it in the stomach," as outraged readers demanded and got the pure food law.

Exam Probability: **Low**

32. *Answer choices:*

(see index for correct answer)

- a. personal values
- b. hierarchical perspective
- c. information systems assessment
- d. Pure Food and Drug Act

Guidance: level 1

A _____ is a set of rules, often written, with regards to clothing. _____s are created out of social perceptions and norms, and vary based on purpose, circumstances and occasions. Different societies and cultures are likely to have different _____s.

Exam Probability: **High**

33. *Answer choices:*

(see index for correct answer)

- a. Sarbanes-Oxley act of 2002
- b. information systems assessment
- c. Dress code
- d. process perspective

Guidance: level 1

:: Corporate governance ::

_____ refers to the practice of members of a corporate board of directors serving on the boards of multiple corporations. A person that sits on multiple boards is known as a multiple director. Two firms have a direct interlock if a director or executive of one firm is also a director of the other, and an indirect interlock if a director of each sits on the board of a third firm. This practice, although widespread and lawful, raises questions about the quality and independence of board decisions.

Exam Probability: **Medium**

34. Answer choices:

(see index for correct answer)

- a. Yasser Akkaoui
- b. Interlocking directorate
- c. Director of communications
- d. Financial mismanagement

Guidance: level 1

:: ::

The _____ to Fight AIDS, Tuberculosis and Malaria is an international financing organization that aims to "attract, leverage and invest additional resources to end the epidemics of HIV/AIDS, tuberculosis and malaria to support attainment of the Sustainable Development Goals established by the United Nations." A public-private partnership, the organization maintains its secretariat in Geneva, Switzerland. The organization began operations in January 2002. Microsoft founder Bill Gates was one of the first private foundations among many bilateral donors to provide seed money for the partnership.

Exam Probability: **Low**

35. Answer choices:

(see index for correct answer)

- a. hierarchical
- b. Global Fund

- c. deep-level diversity
- d. levels of analysis

Guidance: level 1

:: ::

Bernard Lawrence _____ is an American former market maker, investment advisor, financier, fraudster, and convicted felon, who is currently serving a federal prison sentence for offenses related to a massive Ponzi scheme. He is the former non-executive chairman of the NASDAQ stock market, the confessed operator of the largest Ponzi scheme in world history, and the largest financial fraud in U.S. history. Prosecutors estimated the fraud to be worth $64.8 billion based on the amounts in the accounts of _____ 's 4,800 clients as of November 30, 2008.

Exam Probability: **Medium**

36. *Answer choices:*

(see index for correct answer)

- a. open system
- b. process perspective
- c. interpersonal communication
- d. Madoff

Guidance: level 1

:: ::

_____ is the means to see, hear, or become aware of something or someone through our fundamental senses. The term _____ derives from the Latin word perceptio, and is the organization, identification, and interpretation of sensory information in order to represent and understand the presented information, or the environment.

Exam Probability: **High**

37. *Answer choices:*

(see index for correct answer)

- a. information systems assessment
- b. open system
- c. Perception
- d. Sarbanes-Oxley act of 2002

Guidance: level 1

:: Monopoly (economics) ::

A _____ is a form of intellectual property that gives its owner the legal right to exclude others from making, using, selling, and importing an invention for a limited period of years, in exchange for publishing an enabling public disclosure of the invention. In most countries _____ rights fall under civil law and the _____ holder needs to sue someone infringing the _____ in order to enforce his or her rights. In some industries _____s are an essential form of competitive advantage; in others they are irrelevant.

Exam Probability: **Low**

38. *Answer choices:*

(see index for correct answer)

- a. Regulatory economics
- b. Patent
- c. Copyright law of the European Union
- d. Cost per procedure

Guidance: level 1

:: ::

An _____ is the release of a liquid petroleum hydrocarbon into the environment, especially the marine ecosystem, due to human activity, and is a form of pollution. The term is usually given to marine _____ s, where oil is released into the ocean or coastal waters, but spills may also occur on land. _____ s may be due to releases of crude oil from tankers, offshore platforms, drilling rigs and wells, as well as spills of refined petroleum products and their by-products, heavier fuels used by large ships such as bunker fuel, or the spill of any oily refuse or waste oil.

Exam Probability: **High**

39. *Answer choices:*

(see index for correct answer)

- a. Character
- b. open system
- c. Oil spill
- d. personal values

Guidance: level 1

:: Competition regulators ::

The _____ is an independent agency of the United States government, established in 1914 by the _____ Act. Its principal mission is the promotion of consumer protection and the elimination and prevention of anticompetitive business practices, such as coercive monopoly. It is headquartered in the _____ Building in Washington, D.C.

Exam Probability: **Medium**

40. *Answer choices:*

(see index for correct answer)

- a. Queensland Competition Authority
- b. Directorate-General for Competition
- c. Superintendency of Industry and Commerce
- d. Federal Trade Commission

Guidance: level 1

:: ::

_____ or accountancy is the measurement, processing, and communication of financial information about economic entities such as businesses and corporations. The modern field was established by the Italian mathematician Luca Pacioli in 1494. _____ , which has been called the "language of business", measures the results of an organization's economic activities and conveys this information to a variety of users, including investors, creditors, management, and regulators. Practitioners of _____ are known as accountants. The terms " _____ " and "financial reporting" are often used as synonyms.

Exam Probability: **Low**

41. *Answer choices:*

(see index for correct answer)

- a. deep-level diversity
- b. functional perspective
- c. empathy
- d. interpersonal communication

Guidance: level 1

:: ::

A _____ is an organization, usually a group of people or a company, authorized to act as a single entity and recognized as such in law. Early incorporated entities were established by charter. Most jurisdictions now allow the creation of new _____ s through registration.

Exam Probability: **High**

42. *Answer choices:*

(see index for correct answer)

- a. information systems assessment
- b. hierarchical perspective
- c. Character
- d. process perspective

Guidance: level 1

:: Private equity ::

In finance, a high-yield bond is a bond that is rated below investment grade. These bonds have a higher risk of default or other adverse credit events, but typically pay higher yields than better quality bonds in order to make them attractive to investors.

Exam Probability: **Low**

43. *Answer choices:*

(see index for correct answer)

- a. Tembusu Partners Private Limited
- b. Junk bond
- c. Publicly traded private equity
- d. Vintage year

Guidance: level 1

:: Leadership ::

_____ is a theory of leadership where a leader works with teams to identify needed change, creating a vision to guide the change through inspiration, and executing the change in tandem with committed members of a group; it is an integral part of the Full Range Leadership Model. _____ serves to enhance the motivation, morale, and job performance of followers through a variety of mechanisms; these include connecting the follower's sense of identity and self to a project and to the collective identity of the organization; being a role model for followers in order to inspire them and to raise their interest in the project; challenging followers to take greater ownership for their work, and understanding the strengths and weaknesses of followers, allowing the leader to align followers with tasks that enhance their performance.

Exam Probability: **Medium**

44. *Answer choices:*

(see index for correct answer)

- a. Agentic leadership
- b. Transformational leadership
- c. Superleadership
- d. The Leadership Council

Guidance: level 1

:: Globalization-related theories ::

_____ is an economic system based on the private ownership of the means of production and their operation for profit. Characteristics central to _____ include private property, capital accumulation, wage labor, voluntary exchange, a price system, and competitive markets. In a capitalist market economy, decision-making and investment are determined by every owner of wealth, property or production ability in financial and capital markets, whereas prices and the distribution of goods and services are mainly determined by competition in goods and services markets.

Exam Probability: **Low**

45. *Answer choices:*

(see index for correct answer)

- a. post-industrial
- b. postmodernism
- c. Capitalism

Guidance: level 1

:: Product certification ::

_____ is food produced by methods that comply with the standards of organic farming. Standards vary worldwide, but organic farming features practices that cycle resources, promote ecological balance, and conserve biodiversity. Organizations regulating organic products may restrict the use of certain pesticides and fertilizers in the farming methods used to produce such products. _____s typically are not processed using irradiation, industrial solvents, or synthetic food additives.

Exam Probability: **High**

46. *Answer choices:*

(see index for correct answer)

- a. Listing and approval use and compliance
- b. Organic certification
- c. Organic food
- d. UTZ Certified

Guidance: level 1

:: Natural gas ::

_____ is a naturally occurring hydrocarbon gas mixture consisting primarily of methane, but commonly including varying amounts of other higher alkanes, and sometimes a small percentage of carbon dioxide, nitrogen, hydrogen sulfide, or helium. It is formed when layers of decomposing plant and animal matter are exposed to intense heat and pressure under the surface of the Earth over millions of years. The energy that the plants originally obtained from the sun is stored in the form of chemical bonds in the gas.

Exam Probability: **High**

47. *Answer choices:*

(see index for correct answer)

- a. Natural gas

- b. Petrochemistry
- c. Associated petroleum gas
- d. True vapor pressure

Guidance: level 1

:: Market-based policy instruments ::

> Cause marketing is defined as a type of corporate social responsibility, in which a company's promotional campaign has the dual purpose of increasing profitability while bettering society.

Exam Probability: **Low**

48. *Answer choices:*

(see index for correct answer)

- a. Cause-related marketing
- b. Tax choice
- c. Tax on trees
- d. Public choice

Guidance: level 1

:: ::

_____ Corporation was an American energy, commodities, and services company based in Houston, Texas. It was founded in 1985 as a merger between Houston Natural Gas and InterNorth, both relatively small regional companies. Before its bankruptcy on December 3, 2001, _____ employed approximately 29,000 staff and was a major electricity, natural gas, communications and pulp and paper company, with claimed revenues of nearly $101 billion during 2000. Fortune named _____ "America's Most Innovative Company" for six consecutive years.

Exam Probability: **Medium**

49. *Answer choices:*

(see index for correct answer)

- a. hierarchical perspective
- b. open system
- c. personal values
- d. Sarbanes-Oxley act of 2002

Guidance: level 1

:: ::

The _____ , founded in 1912, is a private, nonprofit organization whose self-described mission is to focus on advancing marketplace trust, consisting of 106 independently incorporated local BBB organizations in the United States and Canada, coordinated under the Council of _____ s in Arlington, Virginia.

Exam Probability: **High**

50. *Answer choices:*

(see index for correct answer)

- a. empathy
- b. cultural
- c. surface-level diversity
- d. Better Business Bureau

Guidance: level 1

:: Social philosophy ::

The _____ describes the unintended social benefits of an individual's self-interested actions. Adam Smith first introduced the concept in The Theory of Moral Sentiments, written in 1759, invoking it in reference to income distribution. In this work, however, the idea of the market is not discussed, and the word "capitalism" is never used.

Exam Probability: **Low**

51. *Answer choices:*

(see index for correct answer)

- a. Societal attitudes towards abortion
- b. Veil of Ignorance

- c. Freedom to contract
- d. Invisible hand

Guidance: level 1

:: ::

_____ is "property consisting of land and the buildings on it, along with its natural resources such as crops, minerals or water; immovable property of this nature; an interest vested in this an item of real property, buildings or housing in general. Also: the business of _____ ; the profession of buying, selling, or renting land, buildings, or housing." It is a legal term used in jurisdictions whose legal system is derived from English common law, such as India, England, Wales, Northern Ireland, United States, Canada, Pakistan, Australia, and New Zealand.

Exam Probability: **Medium**

52. *Answer choices:*

(see index for correct answer)

- a. levels of analysis
- b. Real estate
- c. deep-level diversity
- d. open system

Guidance: level 1

A _____ is a form of business network, for example, a local organization of businesses whose goal is to further the interests of businesses. Business owners in towns and cities form these local societies to advocate on behalf of the business community. Local businesses are members, and they elect a board of directors or executive council to set policy for the chamber. The board or council then hires a President, CEO or Executive Director, plus staffing appropriate to size, to run the organization.

Exam Probability: **High**

53. *Answer choices:*

(see index for correct answer)

- a. co-culture
- b. similarity-attraction theory
- c. Chamber of Commerce
- d. interpersonal communication

Guidance: level 1

:: United States federal defense and national security legislation ::

The USA _____ is an Act of the U.S. Congress that was signed into law by President George W. Bush on October 26, 2001. The title of the Act is a contrived three letter initialism preceding a seven letter acronym, which in combination stand for Uniting and Strengthening America by Providing Appropriate Tools Required to Intercept and Obstruct Terrorism Act of 2001. The acronym was created by a 23 year old Congressional staffer, Chris Kyle.

Exam Probability: **Medium**

54. *Answer choices:*

(see index for correct answer)

- a. USA PATRIOT Act
- b. Patriot Act

Guidance: level 1

:: Labor rights ::

The _____ is the concept that people have a human _____, or engage in productive employment, and may not be prevented from doing so. The _____ is enshrined in the Universal Declaration of Human Rights and recognized in international human rights law through its inclusion in the International Covenant on Economic, Social and Cultural Rights, where the _____ emphasizes economic, social and cultural development.

Exam Probability: **Low**

55. *Answer choices:*

(see index for correct answer)

- a. Right to work
- b. Swift raids
- c. Grievance
- d. The Hyatt 100

Guidance: level 1

:: ::

The _____ is an 1848 political pamphlet by the German philosophers Karl Marx and Friedrich Engels. Commissioned by the Communist League and originally published in London just as the Revolutions of 1848 began to erupt, the Manifesto was later recognised as one of the world's most influential political documents. It presents an analytical approach to the class struggle and the conflicts of capitalism and the capitalist mode of production, rather than a prediction of communism's potential future forms.

Exam Probability: **Low**

56. *Answer choices:*

(see index for correct answer)

- a. similarity-attraction theory
- b. interpersonal communication
- c. Communist Manifesto

- d. hierarchical perspective

Guidance: level 1

:: ::

_____ is a cognitive process that elicits emotion and rational associations based on an individual's moral philosophy or value system. _____ stands in contrast to elicited emotion or thought due to associations based on immediate sensory perceptions and reflexive responses, as in sympathetic central nervous system responses. In common terms, _____ is often described as leading to feelings of remorse when a person commits an act that conflicts with their moral values. An individual's moral values and their dissonance with familial, social, cultural and historical interpretations of moral philosophy are considered in the examination of cultural relativity in both the practice and study of psychology. The extent to which _____ informs moral judgment before an action and whether such moral judgments are or should be based on reason has occasioned debate through much of modern history between theories of modern western philosophy in juxtaposition to the theories of romanticism and other reactionary movements after the end of the Middle Ages.

Exam Probability: **Low**

57. *Answer choices:*

(see index for correct answer)

- a. hierarchical perspective
- b. process perspective
- c. personal values

- d. similarity-attraction theory

Guidance: level 1

:: ::

A _____ service is an online platform which people use to build social networks or social relationship with other people who share similar personal or career interests, activities, backgrounds or real-life connections.

Exam Probability: **Medium**

58. *Answer choices:*

(see index for correct answer)

- a. Social networking
- b. hierarchical perspective
- c. cultural
- d. open system

Guidance: level 1

:: Toxicology ::

_____ or lead-based paint is paint containing lead. As pigment, lead chromate, Lead oxide, and lead carbonate are the most common forms. Lead is added to paint to accelerate drying, increase durability, maintain a fresh appearance, and resist moisture that causes corrosion. It is one of the main health and environmental hazards associated with paint. In some countries, lead continues to be added to paint intended for domestic use, whereas countries such as the U.S. and the UK have regulations prohibiting this, although _____ may still be found in older properties painted prior to the introduction of such regulations. Although lead has been banned from household paints in the United States since 1978, paint used in road markings may still contain it. Alternatives such as water-based, lead-free traffic paint are readily available, and many states and federal agencies have changed their purchasing contracts to buy these instead.

Exam Probability: **Low**

59. *Answer choices:*

(see index for correct answer)

- a. Toxidrome
- b. Toxicogenomics
- c. Lead paint
- d. Persistent, bioaccumulative and toxic substances

Guidance: level 1

Accounting

Accounting or accountancy is the measurement, processing, and communication of financial information about economic entities such as businesses and corporations. The modern field was established by the Italian mathematician Luca Pacioli in 1494. Accounting, which has been called the "language of business", measures the results of an organization's economic activities and conveys this information to a variety of users, including investors, creditors, management, and regulators.

:: Accounting in the United States ::

The _____ is located in Norwalk, Connecticut, United States. It was organized in 1972 as a non-stock, Delaware Corporation. It is an independent organization in the private sector, operating with the goal of ensuring objectivity and integrity in financial reporting standards.

Exam Probability: **Medium**

1. *Answer choices:*
(see index for correct answer)

- a. Accounting Research Bulletins
- b. Trueblood Committee
- c. National Association of State Boards of Accountancy
- d. Financial Accounting Foundation

Guidance: level 1

:: Valuation (finance) ::

The _____ is one of three major groups of methodologies, called valuation approaches, used by appraisers. It is particularly common in commercial real estate appraisal and in business appraisal. The fundamental math is similar to the methods used for financial valuation, securities analysis, or bond pricing. However, there are some significant and important modifications when used in real estate or business valuation.

Exam Probability: **Low**

2. *Answer choices:*

(see index for correct answer)

- a. Member of the Appraisal Institute
- b. Post-money valuation
- c. Residual income valuation
- d. Quantitative analyst

Guidance: level 1

:: Accounting source documents ::

A _____ or account statement is a summary of financial transactions which have occurred over a given period on a bank account held by a person or business with a financial institution.

Exam Probability: **Low**

3. *Answer choices:*

(see index for correct answer)

- a. Invoice
- b. Purchase order
- c. Air waybill
- d. Banknote

Guidance: level 1

:: Accounting terminology ::

Double-entry bookkeeping, in accounting, is a system of bookkeeping so named because every entry to an account requires a corresponding and opposite entry to a different account. The double entry has two equal and corresponding sides known as debit and credit. The left-hand side is debit and right-hand side is credit. For instance, recording a sale of $100 might require two entries: a debit of $100 to an account named "Stock" and a credit of $100 to an account named "Revenue."

Exam Probability: **High**

4. *Answer choices:*

(see index for correct answer)

- a. Accrued liabilities
- b. outstanding balance
- c. Share premium
- d. Double-entry accounting

Guidance: level 1

:: Management accounting ::

A _____ is a cost that differs between alternatives being considered. In order for a cost to be a _____ it must be.

Exam Probability: **Medium**

5. *Answer choices:*

(see index for correct answer)

- a. Resource consumption accounting
- b. Direct material price variance
- c. Relevant cost
- d. Cash and cash equivalents

Guidance: level 1

:: Payment systems ::

An _____ is an electronic telecommunications device that enables customers of financial institutions to perform financial transactions, such as cash withdrawals, deposits, transfer funds, or obtaining account information, at any time and without the need for direct interaction with bank staff.

Exam Probability: **High**

6. *Answer choices:*

(see index for correct answer)

- a. Military payment certificate
- b. Cashless catering
- c. BASE24

- d. Automated teller machine

Guidance: level 1

:: Management accounting ::

_____ is the profit the firm makes from serving a customer or customer group over a specified period of time, specifically the difference between the revenues earned from and the costs associated with the customer relationship in a specified period. According to Philip Kotler,"a profitable customer is a person, household or a company that overtime, yields a revenue stream that exceeds by an acceptable amount the company's cost stream of attracting, selling and servicing the customer."

Exam Probability: **Low**

7. *Answer choices:*

(see index for correct answer)

- a. Corporate travel management
- b. Process costing
- c. Cost accounting
- d. Customer profitability

Guidance: level 1

:: Financial markets ::

_____ s are monetary contracts between parties. They can be created, traded, modified and settled. They can be cash, evidence of an ownership interest in an entity, or a contractual right to receive or deliver cash.

Exam Probability: **High**

8. *Answer choices:*

(see index for correct answer)

- a. Global Industry Classification Standard
- b. Financial instrument
- c. Alternative trading system
- d. Latino Community Foundation

Guidance: level 1

:: Accounting terminology ::

A _____ contains all the accounts for recording transactions relating to a company's assets, liabilities, owners' equity, revenue, and expenses. In modern accounting software or ERP, the _____ works as a central repository for accounting data transferred from all subledgers or modules like accounts payable, accounts receivable, cash management, fixed assets, purchasing and projects. The _____ is the backbone of any accounting system which holds financial and non-financial data for an organization. The collection of all accounts is known as the _____ . Each account is known as a ledger account. In a manual or non-computerized system this may be a large book. The statement of financial position and the statement of income and comprehensive income are both derived from the _____ . Each account in the _____ consists of one or more pages. The _____ is where posting to the accounts occurs. Posting is the process of recording amounts as credits, and amounts as debits, in the pages of the _____ . Additional columns to the right hold a running activity total .

Exam Probability: **Low**

9. *Answer choices:*

(see index for correct answer)

- a. Account
- b. Record to report
- c. General ledger
- d. Absorption costing

Guidance: level 1

:: Finance ::

_____ is the ability of a bank customer in the United States and Canada to deposit a check into a bank account from a remote location, such as an office or home, without having to physically deliver the check to the bank. This is typically accomplished by scanning a digital image of a check into a computer, then transmitting that image to the bank. The practice became legal in the United States in 2004 when the Check Clearing for the 21st Century Act took effect, though not all banks have implemented the system.

Exam Probability: **Low**

10. *Answer choices:*

(see index for correct answer)

- a. Remote deposit
- b. Financial Education Instructor of the Year
- c. Standard budget
- d. Property income

Guidance: level 1

:: Management accounting ::

_____ is a managerial accounting cost concept. Under this method, manufacturing overhead is incurred in the period that a product is produced. This addresses the issue of absorption costing that allows income to rise as production rises. Under an absorption cost method, management can push forward costs to the next period when products are sold. This artificially inflates profits in the period of production by incurring less cost than would be incurred under a _____ system. _____ is generally not used for external reporting purposes. Under the Tax Reform Act of 1986, income statements must use absorption costing to comply with GAAP.

Exam Probability: **Low**

11. *Answer choices:*

(see index for correct answer)

- a. Pre-determined overhead rate
- b. Process costing
- c. Backflush accounting
- d. Variable Costing

Guidance: level 1

:: Accounting in the United States ::

The _____ is the source of generally accepted accounting principles used by state and local governments in the United States. As with most of the entities involved in creating GAAP in the United States, it is a private, non-governmental organization.

Exam Probability: **Medium**

12. *Answer choices:*

(see index for correct answer)

- a. Accounting Principles Board
- b. Governmental Accounting Standards Board
- c. Accounting Today
- d. Certified Government Financial Manager

Guidance: level 1

:: Business law ::

The expression " _____ " is somewhat confusing as it has a different meaning based on the context that is under consideration. From a product characteristic stand point, this type of a lease, as distinguished from a finance lease, is one where the lessor takes residual risk. As such, the lease is non full payout. From an accounting stand point, this type of lease results in off balance sheet financing.

Exam Probability: **Low**

13. *Answer choices:*

(see index for correct answer)

- a. Unfair Commercial Practices Directive
- b. Operating lease

- c. Starting a Business Index
- d. Financial Security Law of France

Guidance: level 1

:: Project management ::

_____ is the widespread practice of collecting information and attempting to spot a pattern. In some fields of study, the term "_____" has more formally defined meanings.

Exam Probability: **Medium**

14. *Answer choices:*
(see index for correct answer)

- a. Karol Adamiecki
- b. Project planning
- c. Trend analysis
- d. Logical framework approach

Guidance: level 1

:: Inventory ::

_____ is the maximum amount of goods, or inventory, that a company can possibly sell during this fiscal year. It has the formula.

Exam Probability: **High**

15. *Answer choices:*

(see index for correct answer)

- a. Stock keeping unit
- b. Consignment stock
- c. Stock control
- d. Cost of goods available for sale

Guidance: level 1

:: Budgets ::

A _____ is a financial plan for a defined period, often one year. It may also include planned sales volumes and revenues, resource quantities, costs and expenses, assets, liabilities and cash flows. Companies, governments, families and other organizations use it to express strategic plans of activities or events in measurable terms.

Exam Probability: **High**

16. *Answer choices:*

(see index for correct answer)

- a. Zero budget
- b. Black budget
- c. Film budgeting
- d. Budget

Guidance: level 1

:: Auditing ::

An _____ is a security-relevant chronological record, set of records, and/or destination and source of records that provide documentary evidence of the sequence of activities that have affected at any time a specific operation, procedure, or event. Audit records typically result from activities such as financial transactions, scientific research and health care data transactions, or communications by individual people, systems, accounts, or other entities.

Exam Probability: **Medium**

17. *Answer choices:*

(see index for correct answer)

- a. Audit trail
- b. Audit Bureau of Circulations
- c. Audit regime
- d. SOFT audit

Guidance: level 1

:: Management accounting ::

_____ are costs that are not directly accountable to a cost object. _____ may be either fixed or variable. _____ include administration, personnel and security costs. These are those costs which are not directly related to production. Some _____ may be overhead. But some overhead costs can be directly attributed to a project and are direct costs.

Exam Probability: **Medium**

18. *Answer choices:*

(see index for correct answer)

- a. Target costing
- b. Contribution margin
- c. Indirect costs
- d. Certified Management Accountant

Guidance: level 1

:: ::

The _____ is an American stock exchange located at 11 Wall Street, Lower Manhattan, New York City, New York. It is by far the world's largest stock exchange by market capitalization of its listed companies at US$30.1 trillion as of February 2018. The average daily trading value was approximately US$169 billion in 2013. The NYSE trading floor is located at 11 Wall Street and is composed of 21 rooms used for the facilitation of trading. A fifth trading room, located at 30 Broad Street, was closed in February 2007. The main building and the 11 Wall Street building were designated National Historic Landmarks in 1978.

Exam Probability: **High**

19. *Answer choices:*

(see index for correct answer)

- a. hierarchical perspective
- b. imperative
- c. New York Stock Exchange
- d. similarity-attraction theory

Guidance: level 1

:: E-commerce ::

_____ is an e-commerce payment system used in the Netherlands, based on online banking. Introduced in 2005, this payment method allows customers to buy on the Internet using direct online transfers from their bank account.

Exam Probability: **Medium**

20. *Answer choices:*

(see index for correct answer)

- a. FabMart
- b. Interface Technologies
- c. Rising Tide Studios
- d. IDEAL

Guidance: level 1

:: Generally Accepted Accounting Principles ::

The term _____ is most often used to describe a practice or document that is provided as a courtesy or satisfies minimum requirements, conforms to a norm or doctrine, tends to be performed perfunctorily or is considered a formality.

Exam Probability: **Medium**

21. *Answer choices:*

(see index for correct answer)

- a. Consolidation
- b. Gross income
- c. Pro forma

- d. Earnings before interest and taxes

Guidance: level 1

:: Bank regulation ::

_____ is a measure implemented in many countries to protect bank depositors, in full or in part, from losses caused by a bank's inability to pay its debts when due. _____ systems are one component of a financial system safety net that promotes financial stability.

Exam Probability: **High**

22. *Answer choices:*

(see index for correct answer)

- a. United Kingdom banking law
- b. Politically exposed person
- c. Deposit insurance
- d. Office of Fair Trading v Abbey National plc

Guidance: level 1

:: Quality control tools ::

A _____ is a type of diagram that represents an algorithm, workflow or process. _____ can also be defined as a diagramatic representation of an algorithm.

Exam Probability: **High**

23. *Answer choices:*

(see index for correct answer)

- a. X-bar chart
- b. Nelson rules
- c. Scatter plot
- d. Flowchart

Guidance: level 1

:: Accounting journals and ledgers ::

_____ is a daybook or journal which is used to record transactions relating to adjustment entries, opening stock, accounting errors etc. The source documents of this prime entry book are journal voucher, copy of management reports and invoices.

Exam Probability: **Medium**

24. *Answer choices:*

(see index for correct answer)

- a. Journal entry
- b. Subsidiary ledger
- c. Subledger
- d. General journal

Guidance: level 1

:: Finance ::

In accounting, _____ is the portion of a subsidiary corporation's stock that is not owned by the parent corporation. The magnitude of the _____ in the subsidiary company is generally less than 50% of outstanding shares, or the corporation would generally cease to be a subsidiary of the parent.

Exam Probability: **Medium**

25. *Answer choices:*
(see index for correct answer)

- a. Minority interest
- b. Wrap account
- c. Earnings growth
- d. T-model

Guidance: level 1

:: ::

Accounts _____ is a legally enforceable claim for payment held by a business for goods supplied and/or services rendered that customers/clients have ordered but not paid for. These are generally in the form of invoices raised by a business and delivered to the customer for payment within an agreed time frame. Accounts _____ is shown in a balance sheet as an asset. It is one of a series of accounting transactions dealing with the billing of a customer for goods and services that the customer has ordered. These may be distinguished from notes _____ , which are debts created through formal legal instruments called promissory notes.

Exam Probability: **Medium**

26. *Answer choices:*

(see index for correct answer)

- a. functional perspective
- b. Sarbanes-Oxley act of 2002
- c. empathy
- d. surface-level diversity

Guidance: level 1

:: Business ::

The seller, or the provider of the goods or services, completes a sale in response to an acquisition, appropriation, requisition or a direct interaction with the buyer at the point of sale. There is a passing of title of the item, and the settlement of a price, in which agreement is reached on a price for which transfer of ownership of the item will occur. The seller, not the purchaser typically executes the sale and it may be completed prior to the obligation of payment. In the case of indirect interaction, a person who sells goods or service on behalf of the owner is known as a _____ man or _____ woman or _____ person, but this often refers to someone selling goods in a store/shop, in which case other terms are also common, including _____ clerk, shop assistant, and retail clerk.

Exam Probability: **Medium**

27. *Answer choices:*

(see index for correct answer)

- a. Distribution
- b. Planned obsolescence
- c. Business strategy mapping
- d. Open-book contract

Guidance: level 1

:: Valuation (finance) ::

_____ refers to an assessment of the viability, stability, and profitability of a business, sub-business or project.

Exam Probability: **High**

28. *Answer choices:*

(see index for correct answer)

- a. Investment value
- b. Dividend discount model
- c. Financial analysis
- d. Valuation using multiples

Guidance: level 1

:: Tax credits ::

A _____ is a tax incentive which allows certain taxpayers to subtract the amount of the credit they have accrued from the total they owe the state. It may also be a credit granted in recognition of taxes already paid or, as in the United Kingdom, a form of state support.

Exam Probability: **Low**

29. *Answer choices:*

(see index for correct answer)

- a. Landfill Tax Credit Scheme
- b. Nonbusiness Energy Property Tax Credit
- c. Railroad Track Maintenance Tax Credit

- d. Tax credit

Guidance: level 1

:: Management accounting ::

_____ is an accounting methodology that traces and accumulates direct costs, and allocates indirect costs of a manufacturing process. Costs are assigned to products, usually in a large batch, which might include an entire month's production. Eventually, costs have to be allocated to individual units of product. It assigns average costs to each unit, and is the opposite extreme of Job costing which attempts to measure individual costs of production of each unit. _____ is usually a significant chapter. It is a method of assigning costs to units of production in companies producing large quantities of homogeneous products..

Exam Probability: **Low**

30. *Answer choices:*

(see index for correct answer)

- a. Variable cost
- b. Process costing
- c. Inventory valuation
- d. Institute of Management Accountants

Guidance: level 1

:: Types of business entity ::

A _____ is a partnership in which some or all partners have limited liabilities. It therefore can exhibit elements of partnerships and corporations. In a LLP, each partner is not responsible or liable for another partner's misconduct or negligence. This is an important difference from the traditional partnership under the UK Partnership Act 1890, in which each partner has joint and several liability. In a LLP, some or all partners have a form of limited liability similar to that of the shareholders of a corporation. Unlike corporate shareholders, the partners have the right to manage the business directly. In contrast, corporate shareholders must elect a board of directors under the laws of various state charters. The board organizes itself and hires corporate officers who then have as "corporate" individuals the legal responsibility to manage the corporation in the corporation's best interest. A LLP also contains a different level of tax liability from that of a corporation.

Exam Probability: **Low**

31. *Answer choices:*
(see index for correct answer)

- a. Limited liability partnership
- b. Non-profit distributing organisation
- c. Government-owned corporation
- d. Privately held

Guidance: level 1

:: Asset ::

_____ s, also known as tangible assets or property, plant and equipment , is a term used in accounting for assets and property that cannot easily be converted into cash. This can be compared with current assets such as cash or bank accounts, described as liquid assets. In most cases, only tangible assets are referred to as fixed. IAS 16 defines _____ s as assets whose future economic benefit is probable to flow into the entity, whose cost can be measured reliably. _____ s belong to one of 2 types:"Freehold Assets" – assets which are purchased with legal right of ownership and used,and "Leasehold Assets" – assets used by owner without legal right for a particular period of time.

Exam Probability: **Low**

32. *Answer choices:*
(see index for correct answer)

- a. Asset
- b. Fixed asset

Guidance: level 1

:: Financial accounting ::

_____ in accounting is the process of treating investments in associate companies. Equity accounting is usually applied where an investor entity holds 20–50% of the voting stock of the associate company. The investor records such investments as an asset on its balance sheet. The investor's proportional share of the associate company's net income increases the investment , and proportional payments of dividends decrease it. In the investor's income statement, the proportional share of the investor's net income or net loss is reported as a single-line item.

Exam Probability: **Medium**

33. *Answer choices:*

(see index for correct answer)

- a. Intangibles
- b. Equity method
- c. Asset swap
- d. Book value

Guidance: level 1

:: Ethically disputed business practices ::

_____ , in accounting, is the act of intentionally influencing the process of financial reporting to obtain some private gain. _____ involves the alteration of financial reports to mislead stakeholders about the organization's underlying performance, or to "influence contractual outcomes that depend on reported accounting numbers."

Exam Probability: **Medium**

34. *Answer choices:*

(see index for correct answer)

- a. Earnings management
- b. Hollywood accounting
- c. Spiv
- d. Wage slavery

Guidance: level 1

:: Basic financial concepts ::

In finance, maturity or _____ refers to the final payment date of a loan or other financial instrument, at which point the principal is due to be paid.

Exam Probability: **Medium**

35. *Answer choices:*

(see index for correct answer)

- a. Short interest
- b. Lodgement
- c. Maturity date
- d. Forward guidance

Guidance: level 1

:: Value theory ::

Within philosophy, it can be known as ethics or axiology. Early philosophical investigations sought to understand good and evil and the concept of "the good". Today, much of _____ aspires to the scientifically empirical, recording what people do value and attempting to understand why they value it in the context of psychology, sociology, and economics.

Exam Probability: **Low**

36. *Answer choices:*

(see index for correct answer)

- a. Subjective theory of value
- b. Theory of imputation
- c. Marginalism
- d. Paradox of value

Guidance: level 1

:: Investment ::

_____, and investment appraisal, is the planning process used to determine whether an organization's long term investments such as new machinery, replacement of machinery, new plants, new products, and research development projects are worth the funding of cash through the firm's capitalization structure. It is the process of allocating resources for major capital, or investment, expenditures. One of the primary goals of _____ investments is to increase the value of the firm to the shareholders.

Exam Probability: **High**

37. *Answer choices:*

(see index for correct answer)

- a. Investment decisions
- b. Buy-write
- c. Vietnam Asset Management
- d. Lehman scale

Guidance: level 1

:: Banking terms ::

An _____ occurs when money is withdrawn from a bank account and the available balance goes below zero. In this situation the account is said to be "overdrawn". If there is a prior agreement with the account provider for an _____, and the amount overdrawn is within the authorized _____ limit, then interest is normally charged at the agreed rate. If the negative balance exceeds the agreed terms, then additional fees may be charged and higher interest rates may apply.

Exam Probability: **Medium**

38. *Answer choices:*

(see index for correct answer)

- a. Big Five
- b. Overdraft
- c. Call report
- d. Unavailable funds fee

Guidance: level 1

:: Accounting in the United States ::

Founded in 1887, the _____ is the national professional organization of Certified Public Accountants in the United States, with more than 418,000 members in 143 countries in business and industry, public practice, government, education, student affiliates and international associates. It sets ethical standards for the profession and U.S. auditing standards for audits of private companies, non-profit organizations, federal, state and local governments. It also develops and grades the Uniform CPA Examination. The AICPA maintains offices in New York City; Washington, DC; Durham, NC; and Ewing, NJ. The AICPA celebrated the 125th anniversary of its founding in 2012.

Exam Probability: **Low**

39. *Answer choices:*

(see index for correct answer)

- a. Accounting Research Bulletins
- b. American Institute of Certified Public Accountants
- c. Financial Accounting Foundation
- d. International Qualification Examination

Guidance: level 1

:: Finance ::

The _____ of a corporation is the accumulated net income of the corporation that is retained by the corporation at a particular point of time, such as at the end of the reporting period. At the end of that period, the net income at that point is transferred from the Profit and Loss Account to the _____ account. If the balance of the _____ account is negative it may be called accumulated losses, retained losses or accumulated deficit, or similar terminology.

Exam Probability: **Medium**

40. *Answer choices:*

(see index for correct answer)

- a. Offset loan
- b. Retained earnings
- c. Netting
- d. Liquid Tradable Securities

Guidance: level 1

:: Accounting source documents ::

_____ is a letter sent by a customer to a supplier to inform the supplier that their invoice has been paid. If the customer is paying by cheque, the _____ often accompanies the cheque. The advice may consist of a literal letter or of a voucher attached to the side or top of the cheque.

Exam Probability: **Medium**

41. *Answer choices:*

(see index for correct answer)

- a. Invoice
- b. Air waybill
- c. Bank statement
- d. Remittance advice

Guidance: level 1

:: Financial ratios ::

Earnings per share is the monetary value of earnings per outstanding share of common stock for a company.

Exam Probability: **Low**

42. Answer choices:

(see index for correct answer)

- a. Social return on investment
- b. PB ratio
- c. Net income per employee
- d. Net interest spread

Guidance: level 1

:: Accounting ::

_____ are designed to facilitate the process of journalizing and posting transactions. They are used for the most frequent transactions in a business. For example, in merchandising businesses, companies acquire merchandise from vendors, and then in turn sell the merchandise to individuals or other businesses. Sales and purchases are the most common transactions for the merchandising businesses. A business such as a retail store will record the following transactions many times a day for sales on account and cash sales.

Exam Probability: **Low**

43. Answer choices:

(see index for correct answer)

- a. Bookkeeping
- b. Cash sweep

- c. Part exchange
- d. Accounting records

Guidance: level 1

:: Financial ratios ::

_____ is a financial ratio that indicates the percentage of a company's assets that are provided via debt. It is the ratio of total debt and total assets.

Exam Probability: **High**

44. *Answer choices:*

(see index for correct answer)

- a. EV/EBITDA
- b. Implied multiple
- c. Debt ratio
- d. Operating margin

Guidance: level 1

:: ::

A _____ is a fund into which a sum of money is added during an employee's employment years, and from which payments are drawn to support the person's retirement from work in the form of periodic payments. A _____ may be a "defined benefit plan" where a fixed sum is paid regularly to a person, or a "defined contribution plan" under which a fixed sum is invested and then becomes available at retirement age. _____s should not be confused with severance pay; the former is usually paid in regular installments for life after retirement, while the latter is typically paid as a fixed amount after involuntary termination of employment prior to retirement.

Exam Probability: **Low**

45. *Answer choices:*

(see index for correct answer)

- a. similarity-attraction theory
- b. information systems assessment
- c. Pension
- d. levels of analysis

Guidance: level 1

:: Accounting in the United States ::

The _____ is a private-sector, nonprofit corporation created by the Sarbanes–Oxley Act of 2002 to oversee the audits of public companies and other issuers in order to protect the interests of investors and further the public interest in the preparation of informative, accurate and independent audit reports. The PCAOB also oversees the audits of broker-dealers, including compliance reports filed pursuant to federal securities laws, to promote investor protection. All PCAOB rules and standards must be approved by the U.S. Securities and Exchange Commission.

Exam Probability: **Medium**

46. *Answer choices:*

(see index for correct answer)

- a. Governmental Accounting Standards Board
- b. Beta Alpha Psi
- c. Variable interest entity
- d. Public Company Accounting Oversight Board

Guidance: level 1

:: Insolvency ::

_____ is the process in accounting by which a company is brought to an end in the United Kingdom, Republic of Ireland and United States. The assets and property of the company are redistributed. _____ is also sometimes referred to as winding-up or dissolution, although dissolution technically refers to the last stage of _____ . The process of _____ also arises when customs, an authority or agency in a country responsible for collecting and safeguarding customs duties, determines the final computation or ascertainment of the duties or drawback accruing on an entry.

Exam Probability: **High**

47. *Answer choices:*

(see index for correct answer)

- a. Financial distress
- b. Personal Insolvency Arrangement
- c. George Samuel Ford
- d. Liquidation

Guidance: level 1

:: Costs ::

The _____ is computed by dividing the total cost of goods available for sale by the total units available for sale. This gives a weighted-average unit cost that is applied to the units in the ending inventory.

Exam Probability: **Low**

48. Answer choices:

(see index for correct answer)

- a. Direct labor cost
- b. Opportunity cost
- c. Average cost
- d. Average variable cost

Guidance: level 1

:: Management accounting ::

"_____ s are the structural determinants of the cost of an activity, reflecting any linkages or interrelationships that affect it". Therefore we could assume that the _____ s determine the cost behavior within the activities, reflecting the links that these have with other activities and relationships that affect them.

Exam Probability: **Low**

49. Answer choices:

(see index for correct answer)

- a. Operating profit margin
- b. Revenue center
- c. Net present value
- d. Cost driver

Guidance: level 1

:: E-commerce ::

A _____ is a plastic payment card that can be used instead of cash when making purchases. It is similar to a credit card, but unlike a credit card, the money is immediately transferred directly from the cardholder's bank account when performing a transaction.

Exam Probability: **Low**

50. *Answer choices:*

(see index for correct answer)

- a. Confinity
- b. Over-the-top content
- c. Demandware
- d. Alternative currency

Guidance: level 1

:: Organizational structure ::

An _____ defines how activities such as task allocation, coordination, and supervision are directed toward the achievement of organizational aims.

Exam Probability: **Medium**

51. *Answer choices:*

(see index for correct answer)

- a. The Starfish and the Spider
- b. Followership
- c. Unorganisation
- d. Organizational structure

Guidance: level 1

:: Payment systems ::

A _____ or cheque, also called an image cash letter, clearing replacement document, or image replacement document, is a negotiable instrument used in electronic banking systems to represent a physical paper cheque. It may be wholly digital from payment initiation to clearing and settlement or it may be a digital reproduction of an original paper check.

Exam Probability: **High**

52. *Answer choices:*

(see index for correct answer)

- a. Postal Order
- b. BACHO record format

- c. Boleto
- d. EFTPOS

Guidance: level 1

:: Generally Accepted Accounting Principles ::

A _____ or reacquired stock is stock which is bought back by the issuing company, reducing the amount of outstanding stock on the open market.

Exam Probability: **Low**

53. *Answer choices:*

(see index for correct answer)

- a. Treasury stock
- b. Cash method of accounting
- c. Generally Accepted Accounting Practice
- d. Financial position of the United States

Guidance: level 1

:: ::

_____ is the process of making predictions of the future based on past and present data and most commonly by analysis of trends. A commonplace example might be estimation of some variable of interest at some specified future date. Prediction is a similar, but more general term. Both might refer to formal statistical methods employing time series, cross-sectional or longitudinal data, or alternatively to less formal judgmental methods. Usage can differ between areas of application: for example, in hydrology the terms "forecast" and "_____" are sometimes reserved for estimates of values at certain specific future times, while the term "prediction" is used for more general estimates, such as the number of times floods will occur over a long period.

Exam Probability: **High**

54. *Answer choices:*

(see index for correct answer)

- a. deep-level diversity
- b. Forecasting
- c. cultural
- d. empathy

Guidance: level 1

:: Debt ::

A _____ is a party that has a claim on the services of a second party. It is a person or institution to whom money is owed. The first party, in general, has provided some property or service to the second party under the assumption that the second party will return an equivalent property and service. The second party is frequently called a debtor or borrower. The first party is called the _____, which is the lender of property, service, or money.

Exam Probability: **High**

55. *Answer choices:*

(see index for correct answer)

- a. External financing
- b. Creditor
- c. Cohort default rate
- d. Exchangeable bond

Guidance: level 1

:: Corporations law ::

_____, also referred to as the certificate of incorporation or the corporate charter, are a document or charter that establishes the existence of a corporation in the United States and Canada. They generally are filed with the Secretary of State or other company registrar.

Exam Probability: **Medium**

56. Answer choices:

(see index for correct answer)

- a. Corporate opportunity doctrine
- b. Corporate haven
- c. Drag-along right
- d. Articles of incorporation

Guidance: level 1

:: Pricing ::

_____ is the difference between a lower selling price and a higher purchase price, resulting in a financial loss for the seller.

Exam Probability: **High**

57. Answer choices:

(see index for correct answer)

- a. Average usage billing
- b. Value meal
- c. Capital loss
- d. Base point pricing

Guidance: level 1

:: Corporate crime ::

_____ LLP, based in Chicago, was an American holding company. Formerly one of the "Big Five" accounting firms, the firm had provided auditing, tax, and consulting services to large corporations. By 2001, it had become one of the world's largest multinational companies.

Exam Probability: **Low**

58. *Answer choices:*

(see index for correct answer)

- a. Corporate manslaughter
- b. Langbar International
- c. Arthur Andersen
- d. Corporate Manslaughter and Corporate Homicide Act 2007

Guidance: level 1

:: Generally Accepted Accounting Principles ::

In accounting, _____, gross margin, sales profit, or credit sales is the difference between revenue and the cost of making a product or providing a service, before deducting overheads, payroll, taxation, and interest payments. This is different from operating profit. Gross margin is the term normally used in the U.S., while _____ is the more common usage in the UK and Australia.

Exam Probability: **Medium**

59. *Answer choices:*

(see index for correct answer)

- a. Deferral
- b. Operating statement
- c. Expense
- d. Gross profit

Guidance: level 1

INDEX: Correct Answers

Foundations of Business

1. d: Policy

2. d: Frequency

3. : Management system

4. b: Foreign direct investment

5. b: Competition

6. b: ASEAN

7. : Trade agreement

8. d: Benchmarking

9. c: Organizational culture

10. c: Utility

11. c: Corporate governance

12. a: Goal

13. : Strategic alliance

14. d: Six Sigma

15. c: Publicity

16. c: Opportunity cost

17. c: Diagram

18. a: Purchasing

19. : Interest

20. b: Dividend

21. a: Authority

22. a: Balanced scorecard

23. c: Financial crisis

24. b: Social responsibility

25. a: Economic Development

26. c: Industrial Revolution

27. b: Budget

28. c: Return on investment

29. b: Decision-making

30. c: Supply chain

31. c: Variable cost

32. d: Information systems

33. a: Entrepreneurship

34. a: Debt

35. c: Commerce

36. b: Resource

37. c: Manufacturing

38. c: Preference

39. b: Business process

40. d: Free trade

41. d: Cooperation

42. : Payment

43. c: Fraud

44. a: Joint venture

45. b: Planning

46. b: Question

47. a: Small business

48. d: Gross domestic product

49. a: Internal control

50. c: Schedule

51. b: Empowerment

52. d: Meeting

53. d: Explanation

54. a: Credit

55. d: Energies

56. b: Target market

57. : Marketing research

58. d: Scheduling

59. b: Error

Management

1. a: Planning

2. c: Affirmative action

3. b: Span of control

4. d: Problem solving

5. d: Socialization

6. : Leadership style

7. c: Collaboration

8. : Proactive

9. a: Cost

10. c: Compromise

11. a: Organizational performance

12. c: Hotel

13. c: Competitive advantage

14. a: Subsidiary

15. b: Trade agreement

16. b: Entrepreneurship

17. a: Board of directors

18. b: Benchmarking

19. b: Argument

20. a: Good

21. c: Delegation

22. a: Bureaucracy

23. b: Committee

24. d: Cooperation

25. b: Reason

26. d: Workforce

27. b: Business plan

28. b: Industrial Revolution

29. d: Control chart

30. d: Frequency

31. a: Resource management

32. : Contingency theory

33. : Offshoring

34. a: Utility

35. : Bargaining

36. a: Organizational structure

37. d: Brainstorming

38. a: Certification

39. a: Asset

40. d: Inventory control

41. d: Skill

42. d: Overtime

43. c: Description

44. d: Facilitator

45. c: Autonomy

46. c: Problem

47. d: Centralization

48. c: Transactional leadership

49. d: Trade

50. d: Warehouse

51. d: Bottom line

52. c: Knowledge management

53. d: Management process

54. b: Scheduling

55. d: Recruitment

56. c: Collective bargaining

57. d: Franchising

58. a: Vendor

59. d: Authority

Business law

1. a: Cause of action

2. b: Commerce

3. b: Acceleration clause

4. b: Expense

5. a: Bailee

6. b: Social responsibility

7. b: Jury

8. a: Antitrust

9. b: Subsidiary

10. b: Duress

11. a: Delegation

12. d: Standing

13. b: Commerce Clause

14. c: Financial privacy

15. a: Operating agreement

16. a: Property

17. a: Warehouse

18. b: Merger

19. a: Garnishment

20. c: Security interest

21. c: Firm

22. : Commercial speech

23. a: Scienter

24. : Cyberspace

25. c: Consideration

26. c: Warranty

27. d: Insolvency

28. : Surety

29. a: Precedent

30. a: Amendment

31. : Opening statement

32. : Respondeat superior

33. d: Cooperative

34. d: Contract law

35. a: Fraud

36. d: Assumption of risk

37. c: Committee

38. a: Punitive

39. d: Real property

40. c: Anticipatory repudiation

41. a: Corruption

42. : Argument

43. a: Utilitarianism

44. d: Negotiable instrument

45. : Merchant

46. d: Preference

47. c: Res ipsa

48. d: Inventory

49. c: Operation of law

50. : Petition

51. c: Commercial Paper

52. : Guarantee

53. : Apparent authority

54. c: Procedural law

55. b: Shareholder

56. c: Fair use

57. d: Duty

58. a: Misrepresentation

59. c: Misappropriation

Finance

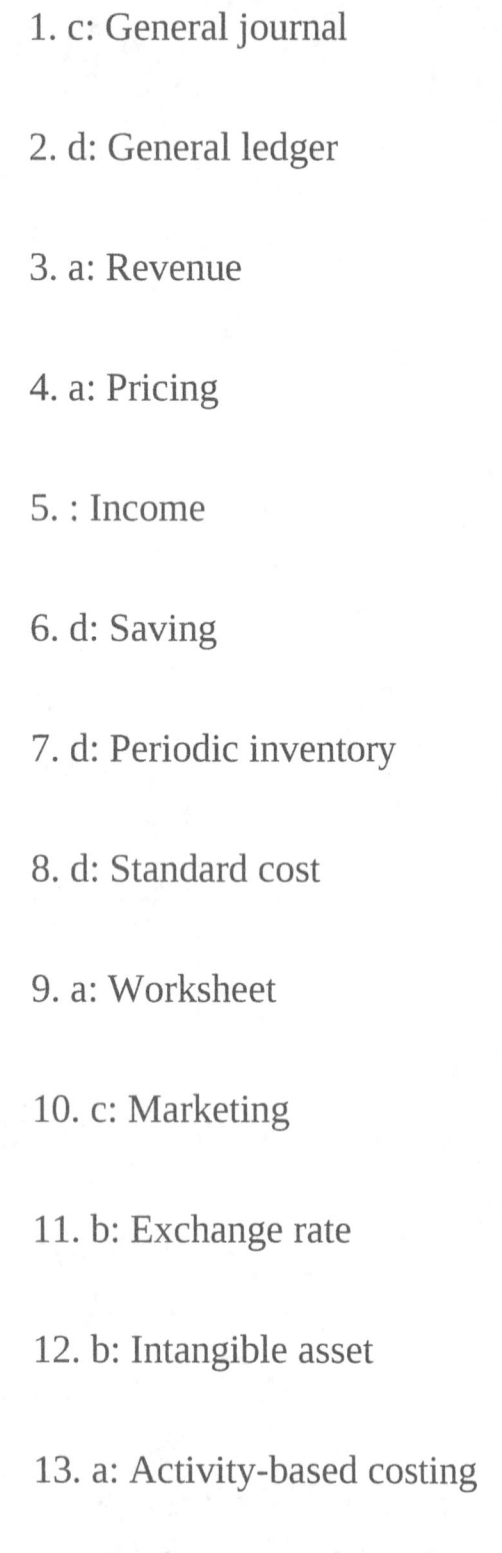

1. c: General journal

2. d: General ledger

3. a: Revenue

4. a: Pricing

5. : Income

6. d: Saving

7. d: Periodic inventory

8. d: Standard cost

9. a: Worksheet

10. c: Marketing

11. b: Exchange rate

12. b: Intangible asset

13. a: Activity-based costing

14. a: Copyright

15. a: Financial management

16. d: Stockholder

17. b: Interest

18. d: S corporation

19. d: Bad debt

20. a: Inflation

21. d: Debt

22. a: Pro forma

23. b: Monte Carlo

24. b: Limited liability

25. a: Presentation

26. : Promissory note

27. a: Consideration

28. d: Cash flow

29. b: Dividend yield

30. : Debt ratio

31. a: Goldman Sachs

32. d: Financial ratio

33. b: Manufacturing cost

34. : Compounding

35. b: Accounts payable

36. : Good

37. d: Public Company Accounting Oversight Board

38. c: Accounting period

39. a: Tax expense

40. : Budget

41. c: Current asset

42. c: Historical cost

43. d: Pension fund

44. a: Current ratio

45. b: Yield to maturity

46. c: Policy

47. d: Financial analysis

48. a: Issuer

49. : Firm

50. : Amortization

51. b: Industry

52. d: Sinking fund

53. c: Balanced scorecard

54. a: Operating leverage

55. a: Return on investment

56. b: Interest rate

57. a: Arbitrage

58. a: Citigroup

59. a: Forward contract

Human resource management

1. : Interactional justice

2. d: Management by objectives

3. c: Sick leave

4. a: Expert power

5. : Employee surveys

6. c: Business model

7. d: Partnership

8. : Bargaining unit

9. d: Performance improvement

10. a: Ricci v. DeStefano

11. c: Employee assistance program

12. d: Expatriate

13. a: Total Quality Management

14. d: Living wage

15. : Persuasion

16. d: Action learning

17. a: Faragher v. City of Boca Raton

18. a: Virtual team

19. : Sexual orientation

20. b: Assessment center

21. : Body language

22. d: Skill

23. b: Workforce management

24. a: Impression management

25. : Cover letter

26. d: Professional association

27. b: Age Discrimination in Employment Act

28. a: Kaizen

29. a: Organizational structure

30. : Free Trade

31. b: Career management

32. : Telecommuting

33. d: Salary

34. c: Locus of control

35. a: Overlearning

36. c: Cross-functional team

37. a: Piece rate

38. b: Person Analysis

39. : Supply chain

40. a: Physician

41. a: Employee stock

42. b: Free agent

43. b: Externship

44. a: Concurrent validity

45. c: Mission statement

46. c: Trainee

47. c: Global workforce

48. b: Onboarding

49. a: Employment

50. a: Executive officer

51. b: Recruitment advertising

52. a: Labor relations

53. : Six Sigma

54. b: Criterion validity

55. d: Price Waterhouse v. Hopkins

56. b: Cross-training

57. a: E-learning

58. : Fair Labor Standards Act

59. d: Online assessment

Information systems

1. d: Keystroke dynamics

2. a: Digital rights management

3. b: Mobile commerce

4. : Information security

5. : Competitive intelligence

6. a: Infrastructure

7. a: Porter five forces analysis

8. a: Entity-relationship

9. : Service level

10. a: Information ethics

11. c: Galileo

12. d: Search engine

13. : Blog

14. b: Critical success factor

15. a: Pop-up ad

16. : Blogger

17. d: Social shopping

18. a: Downtime

19. : Credit card

20. a: Online analytical processing

21. a: Clickstream

22. d: ITunes

23. a: Cybersquatting

24. d: Total cost

25. d: Government-to-business

26. a: Mozy

27. c: Mouse

28. d: Data aggregator

29. c: Mobile computing

30. d: Interaction

31. c: Content management system

32. : Manifesto

33. c: Google Docs

34. c: Non-repudiation

35. : Online advertising

36. d: Network management

37. d: Input device

38. d: Smart card

39. : Craigslist

40. c: Computer-integrated manufacturing

41. d: Password

42. d: Business-to-business

43. a: Intranet

44. : Information silo

45. b: Payment card

46. c: Throughput

47. d: Gmail

48. d: Utility computing

49. a: Payment system

50. d: Benchmarking

51. : Text mining

52. b: Analytics

53. d: Worm

54. a: Business rule

55. a: Competitive advantage

56. c: Commercial off-the-shelf

57. a: PeopleSoft

58. a: Common Criteria

59. c: Virtual team

Marketing

1. c: Complexity

2. d: Monopoly

3. d: Consumer behavior

4. d: Product development

5. c: Brand equity

6. b: Perception

7. d: Security

8. : Logo

9. d: Reinforcement

10. a: Green marketing

11. d: Variable cost

12. a: Corporation

13. : Appeal

14. c: Household

15. c: Personnel

16. b: Database marketing

17. a: Reseller

18. : Information system

19. : Marketing management

20. c: Distribution channel

21. : Competition

22. c: Creative brief

23. b: Electronic data interchange

24. b: Return on investment

25. c: Policy

26. d: Project

27. c: Consumer Protection

28. d: American Express

29. c: Good

30. b: Selling

31. a: Life

32. b: Mass customization

33. c: Mission statement

34. : Market segments

35. : Product manager

36. c: Dimension

37. c: Supply chain management

38. a: Code

39. c: Asset

40. : Marketing channel

41. b: Hearing

42. c: Competitive advantage

43. d: Choice

44. c: Product placement

45. a: Economies of scale

46. a: Negotiation

47. a: Investment

48. b: Product concept

49. a: Loyalty program

50. b: Direct marketing

51. a: Organizational culture

52. b: Expense

53. b: Price war

54. b: Interest

55. : Trade association

56. c: Public relations

57. : Social networking

58. d: Economy

59. b: Consumerism

Manufacturing

1. c: Obsolescence

2. d: Change control

3. c: Pareto analysis

4. b: Process capability

5. d: Third-party logistics

6. d: Design of experiments

7. a: Process engineering

8. b: Estimation

9. : HEAT

10. a: Expediting

11. a: Toshiba

12. a: Supply chain management

13. c: Planning

14. c: Water

15. : Metal

16. c: Resource allocation

17. c: Root cause

18. d: Quality control

19. a: Inventory control

20. d: Durability

21. : Authority

22. a: Perfect competition

23. b: Purchase order

24. d: Supply chain

25. d: Certification

26. d: Process flow diagram

27. : Total productive maintenance

28. a: Strategy

29. b: Change management

30. b: Aggregate planning

31. b: Production schedule

32. d: Economic order quantity

33. a: Bullwhip effect

34. c: Cost

35. d: Resource management

36. b: Total cost of ownership

37. a: Economies of scope

38. c: PDCA

39. : Strategic sourcing

40. a: Sony

41. b: Tool

42. b: EFQM

43. : Technical support

44. b: Capacity planning

45. a: Scheduling

46. a: Supplier relationship management

47. c: Reverse auction

48. b: Paper

49. b: Manufacturing

50. : Value engineering

51. b: Goal

52. c: Chemical industry

53. d: Raw material

54. a: Strategic planning

55. b: Asset

56. b: Assembly line

57. a: Gantt chart

58. b: Poka-yoke

59. c: Total cost

Commerce

1. : Consignee

2. c: Trial

3. b: Marketing strategy

4. b: International trade

5. a: Aid

6. d: Organizational structure

7. a: Logistics Management

8. b: Pension

9. b: Micropayment

10. b: Consultant

11. a: Case study

12. c: Microsoft

13. a: Economic development

14. a: Electronic data interchange

15. d: Productivity

16. b: Logistics

17. c: Supranational

18. c: Goal

19. b: Public policy

20. a: Antitrust

21. a: Export

22. b: Production line

23. : Affiliate marketing

24. a: Hospitality

25. a: Asset

26. : Market research

27. d: Wage

28. b: Forward auction

29. b: Jurisdiction

30. b: Teamwork

31. d: Mobile commerce

32. a: Pizza Hut

33. b: Shareholder

34. d: Webvan

35. a: Supervisor

36. : Automated Clearing House

37. d: Revenue

38. : Merchandising

39. a: Liquidation

40. c: Trade

41. c: Compromise

42. a: Complaint

43. a: Purchase order

44. : Disney

45. : Transaction cost

46. a: Argument

47. c: Empowerment

48. c: Loyalty

49. a: Appeal

50. b: Merger

51. : Product line

52. a: Planning

53. c: Encryption

54. d: Credit card

55. a: Revenue management

56. b: European Union

57. d: Pop-up ad

58. a: Personnel

59. a: Public relations

Business ethics

1. b: Occupational Safety and Health Administration

2. b: Recovery Act

3. a: Sustainable

4. d: Biofuel

5. d: European Commission

6. : Environmental audit

7. b: Supply Chain

8. : Siemens

9. a: Consumerism

10. a: Pollution Prevention

11. d: Minimum wage

12. : Antitrust

13. b: Dilemma

14. : Guerrilla Marketing

15. b: Planned obsolescence

16. a: Parental leave

17. d: Greenpeace

18. d: Kyoto Protocol

19. b: United Farm Workers

20. b: Corporate citizenship

21. c: Trade

22. b: Risk management

23. b: Corporate social responsibility

24. b: Hedonism

25. b: Sullivan principles

26. c: Planet

27. b: Organizational ethics

28. c: Employee Polygraph Protection Act

29. a: Collusion

30. b: UN Global Compact

31. a: Wall Street

32. d: Pure Food and Drug Act

33. c: Dress code

34. b: Interlocking directorate

35. b: Global Fund

36. d: Madoff

37. c: Perception

38. b: Patent

39. c: Oil spill

40. d: Federal Trade Commission

41. : Accounting

42. : Corporation

43. b: Junk bond

44. b: Transformational leadership

45. c: Capitalism

46. c: Organic food

47. a: Natural gas

48. a: Cause-related marketing

49. : Enron

50. d: Better Business Bureau

51. d: Invisible hand

52. b: Real estate

53. c: Chamber of Commerce

54. b: Patriot Act

55. a: Right to work

56. c: Communist Manifesto

57. : Conscience

58. a: Social networking

59. c: Lead paint

Accounting

1. d: Financial Accounting Foundation

2. : Income approach

3. : Bank statement

4. d: Double-entry accounting

5. c: Relevant cost

6. d: Automated teller machine

7. d: Customer profitability

8. b: Financial instrument

9. c: General ledger

10. a: Remote deposit

11. d: Variable Costing

12. b: Governmental Accounting Standards Board

13. b: Operating lease

14. c: Trend analysis

15. d: Cost of goods available for sale

16. d: Budget

17. a: Audit trail

18. c: Indirect costs

19. c: New York Stock Exchange

20. d: IDEAL

21. c: Pro forma

22. c: Deposit insurance

23. d: Flowchart

24. d: General journal

25. a: Minority interest

26. : Receivable

27. : Sales

28. c: Financial analysis

29. d: Tax credit

30. b: Process costing

31. a: Limited liability partnership

32. b: Fixed asset

33. b: Equity method

34. a: Earnings management

35. c: Maturity date

36. : Value theory

37. : Capital budgeting

38. b: Overdraft

39. b: American Institute of Certified Public Accountants

40. b: Retained earnings

41. d: Remittance advice

42. : Diluted earnings per share

43. : Special journals

44. c: Debt ratio

45. c: Pension

46. d: Public Company Accounting Oversight Board

47. d: Liquidation

48. c: Average cost

49. d: Cost driver

50. : Debit card

51. d: Organizational structure

52. : Substitute check

53. a: Treasury stock

54. b: Forecasting

55. b: Creditor

56. d: Articles of incorporation

57. c: Capital loss

58. c: Arthur Andersen

59. d: Gross profit

CPSIA information can be obtained
at www.ICGtesting.com
Printed in the USA
LVHW031108301019
635717LV00004B/343/P